THE WORKS OF WILLIAM ROBERTSON

Volume VI

Printed and bound by
Antony Rowe Ltd., Chippenham, Wiltshire

THE HISTORY OF THE REIGN OF THE EMPEROR CHARLES V

Volume IV

William Robertson

ROUTLEDGE/THOEMMES PRESS

This edition published by Routledge/Thoemmes Press, 1996

Routledge/Thoemmes Press
11 New Fetter Lane
London EC4P 4EE

The Works of William Robertson
12 Volumes : ISBN 0 415 13743 8

This is a reprint of the 1792 edition

Routledge / Thoemmes Press is a joint imprint
of Routledge and Thoemmes Antiquarian Books Ltd.

British Library Cataloguing-in-Publication Data
A CIP record of this set is available from the British Library

Publisher's Note

The publisher has gone to great lengths to ensure the quality of this reprint but points out that some imperfections in the original book may be apparent.

THE HISTORY

OF THE

REIGN

OF THE

EMPEROR CHARLES V.

VOL. IV.

Frontispiece to Vol. 4.

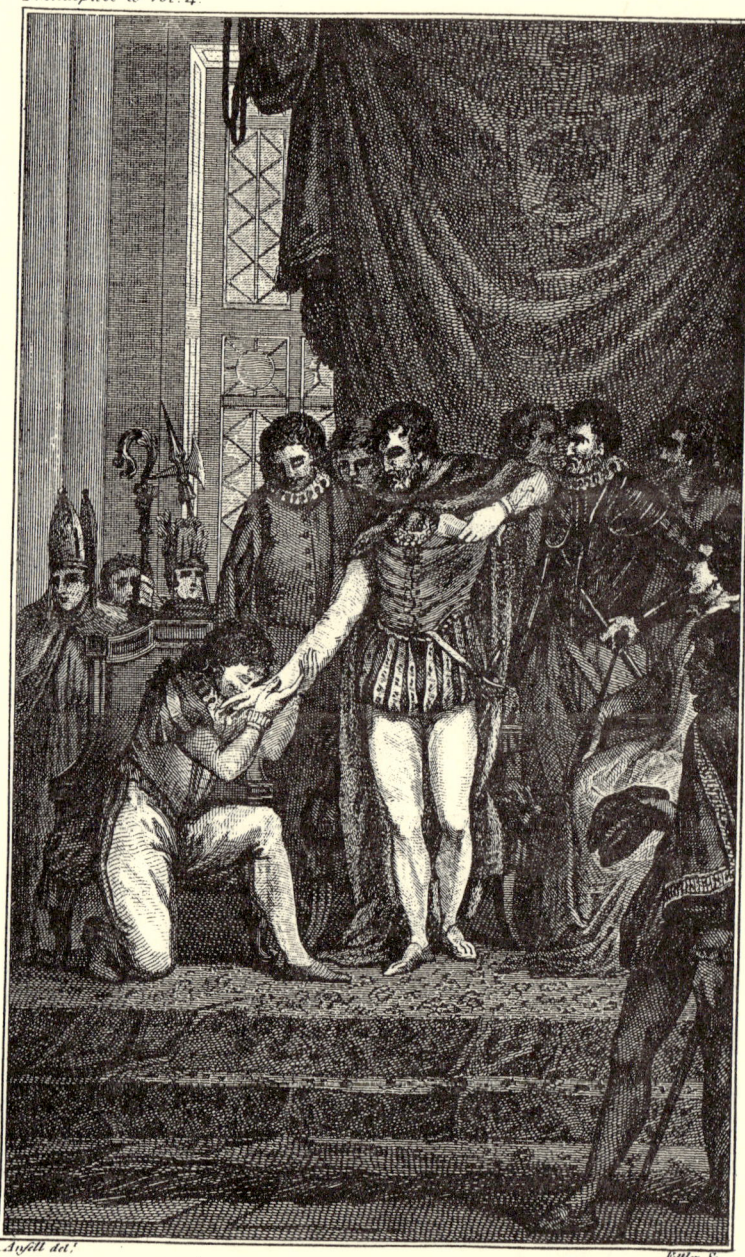

Ansell del. Fittler Sc.

Published as the Act directs, by T. Cadell, Strand, Feb. 1. 1792.

THE
HISTORY
OF THE
REIGN
OF THE
EMPEROR CHARLES V.

By WILLIAM ROBERTSON, D.D.
PRINCIPAL OF THE UNIVERSITY OF EDINBURGH, AND
HISTORIOGRAPHER TO HIS MAJESTY FOR SCOTLAND.

VOLUME IV.

The SEVENTH EDITION, Corrected.

LONDON:
Printed for A. STRAHAN; T. CADELL, in the Strand;
and J. BALFOUR, at Edinburgh.
M DCC XCII.

THE
HISTORY
OF THE
REIGN
OF THE
EMPEROR CHARLES V.

BOOK X.

WHILE Charles laboured, with such unwearied industry, to persuade or to force the Protestants to adopt his regulations with respect to religion, the effects of his steadiness in the execution of his plan were rendered less considerable by his rupture with the Pope, which daily increased. The firm resolution which the Emperor seemed to have taken against restoring Placentia, together with his repeated encroachments on the ecclesiastical jurisdiction, not only by the regulations contained in the Interim, but by his attempt to re-assemble the council at Trent, exasperated Paul to the utmost, who, with the weakness incident to old age, grew more attached to his family, and more jealous of his authority, as he advanced in years. Pushed on by these passions, he made new efforts to draw the French King into

BOOK X.
1549.
The Pope's schemes against the Emperor.

an alliance againſt the Emperor[a]: But finding that Monarch, notwithſtanding the hereditary enmity between him and Charles, and the jealouſy with which he viewed the ſucceſsful progreſs of the Imperial arms, as unwilling as formerly to involve himſelf in immediate hoſtilities, he was obliged to contract his views, and to think of preventing future encroachments, ſince it was not in his power to inflict vengeance on account of thoſe which were paſt. For this purpoſe, he determined to recal his grant of Parma and Placentia, and after declaring them to be re-annexed to the Holy See, to indemnify his grandſon Octavio by a new eſtabliſhment in the eccleſiaſtical ſtate. By this expedient he hoped to gain two points of no ſmall conſequence. He, firſt of all, rendered his poſſeſſion of Parma more ſecure; as the Emperor would be cautious of invading the patrimony of the church, though he might ſeize without ſcruple a town belonging to the houſe of Farneſe. In the next place, he would acquire a better chance of recovering Placentia, as his ſolicitations to that effect might decently be urged with greater importunity, and would infallibly be attended with greater effect, when he was conſidered not as pleading the cauſe of his own family, but as an advocate for the intereſt of the Holy See. But while Paul was priding himſelf on this device, as a happy refinement in policy, Octavio, an ambitious and highſpirited young man, who could not bear with patience to be ſpoiled of one half of his terri-

[a] Mem. de Ribier, ii. 230.

tories by the rapacioufnefs of his father-in-law, and to be deprived of the other by the artifices of his grandfather, took meafures in order to prevent the execution of a plan fatal to his intereft. He fet out fecretly from Rome, and having firft endeavoured to furprize Parma, which attempt was fruftrated by the fidelity of the governor to whom the Pope had entrufted the defence of the town, he made overtures to the Emperor, of renouncing all connexion with the Pope, and of depending entirely on him for his future fortune. This unexpected defection of one of the Pope's own family to an enemy whom he hated, irritated, almoft to madnefs, a mind peevifh with old age; and there was no degree of feverity to which Paul might not have proceeded againft a grandfon whom he reproached as an unnatural apoftate. But, happily for Octavio, death prevented his carrying into execution the harfh refolutions which he had taken with refpect to him, and put an end to his pontificate in the fixteenth year of his adminiftration, and the eighty-fecond of his age *.

As

* Among many inftances of the credulity or weaknefs of hiftorians in attributing the death of illuftrious perfonages to extraordinary caufes, this is one. Almoft all the hiftorians of the fixteenth century affirm, that the death of Paul III. was occafioned by the violent paffions which the behaviour of his grandfon excited ; that being informed, while he was refrefhing himfelf in one of his gardens near Rome, of Octavio's attempt on Parma, as well as of his negociations with the Emperor by means of Gonzaga, he fainted away, continued

fome

As this event had been long expected, there was an extraordinary concourse of Cardinals at Rome; some hours in a swoon, then became feverish, and died within three days. This is the account given of it by Thuanus, lib. vi. 211. Adriani Istor. di suoi Tempi, lib. vii. 480. and by Father Paul, 280. Even cardinal Pallavicini, better informed than any writer with regard to the events which happened in the papal court, and, when not warped by prejudice or system, more accurate in relating them, agrees with their narrative in its chief circumstances. Pallav. b. ii. 74. Paruta, who wrote his history by command of the senate of Venice, relates it in the same manner. Historici Venez. vol. iv. 212. But there was no occasion to search for any extraordinary cause to account for the death of an old man of eighty-two. There remains an authentic account of this event, in which we find none of those marvellous circumstances of which the historians are so fond. The cardinal of Ferrara, who was entrusted with the affairs of France at the court of Rome, and M. D'Urfé, Henry's ambassador in ordinary there, wrote an account to that Monarch of the affair of Parma, and of the Pope's death. By these it appears, that Octavio's attempt to surprize Parma, was made on the twentieth of October; that next day in the evening, and not while he was airing himself in the gardens of Monte-Cavallo, the Pope received intelligence of what he had done; that he was seized with such a transport of passion, and cried so bitterly, that his voice was heard in several apartments of the palace; that next day, however, he was so well as to give an audience to the cardinal of Ferrara, and to go through business of different kinds; that Octavio wrote a letter to the Pope, not to cardinal Farnese his brother, intimating his resolution of throwing himself into the arms of the Emperor: that the Pope received this on the twenty-first without any new symptoms of emotion, and returned an answer to it; that on the twenty-second of October, the day on which the cardinal of Ferrara's letter is dated, the Pope was in his usual state of health. Mem. de Ribier, ii. 247. By a letter of M. D'Urfé, Nov. 5. it appears that the Pope was in such good health,

Rome; and the various competitors having had time to form their parties, and to concert their measures, their ambition and intrigues protracted the conclave to a great length. The Imperial and French factions strove, with emulation, to promote one of their own number, and had, by turns, the prospect of success. But as Paul during a long Pontificate had raised many to the purple, and those chiefly persons of eminent abilities, as well as zealously devoted to his family, Cardinal Farnese had the command of a powerful and united squadron, by whose address and firmness he exalted to the papal throne the Cardinal di Monte, whom Paul had employed as his principal legate in the council of Trent, and trusted with his most secret intentions. He assumed the name of Julius III. and, in order to express his gratitude towards his benefactor, the first act of his administration was to put Octavio Farnese in possession of Parma. When the injury which he did to the Holy See, by alienating a

BOOK X.
1550.

Feb. 7th. The election of Julius III.

that on the third of that month he had celebrated the anniversary of his coronation with the usual solemnities. Ibidem, 251. By another letter from the same person, we learn, that on the sixth of November a catarrh or defluxion fell down on the Pope's lungs, with such dangerous symptoms, that his life was immediately despaired of. Ibid. 252. And by a third letter we are informed, that he died November the tenth. In none of these letters is his death imputed to any extraordinary cause. It appears, that more than twenty days elapsed between Octavio's attempt on Parma, and the death of his grandfather, and that the disease was the natural effect of old age, not one of those occasioned by violence of passion.

territory of such value, was mentioned by some of the Cardinals, he briskly replied, " That he would rather be a poor Pope, with the reputation of a gentleman, than a rich one, with the infamy of having forgotten the obligations conferred upon him, and the promises which he had made [b]." But all the lustre of this candour or generosity he quickly effaced by an action most shockingly indecent. According to an ancient and established practice, every Pope upon his election considers it as his privilege to bestow, on whom he pleases, the Cardinal's hat, which falls to be disposed of by his being invested with the triple crown. Julius, to the astonishment of the sacred college, conferred this mark of distinction, together with ample ecclesiastical revenues, and the right of bearing his name and arms, upon one Innocent, a youth of sixteen, born of obscure parents, and known by the name of the Ape, from his having been trusted with the care of an animal of that species, in the Cardinal di Monte's family. Such a prostitution of the highest dignity in the church would have given offence, even in those dark periods, when the credulous superstition of the people emboldened ecclesiastics to venture on the most flagrant violations of decorum. But in an enlightened age, when, by the progress of knowledge and philosophy, the obligations of duty and decency were better understood, when a blind veneration for the Pontifical character was every

[b] Mem. de Ribier.

where abated, and one half of Christendom in open rebellion against the Papal See, this action was viewed with horror. Rome was immediately filled with libels and pasquinades, which imputed the Pope's extravagant regard for such an unworthy object to the most criminal passions. The Protestants exclaimed against the absurdity of supposing that the infallible spirit of divine truth could dwell in a breast so impure, and called more loudly than ever, and with greater appearance of justice, for the immediate and thorough reformation of a church, the Head of which was a disgrace to the Christian name [c]. The rest of the Pope's conduct was of a piece with this first specimen of his dispositions. Having now reached the summit of ecclesiastical ambition, he seemed eager to indemnify himself, by an unrestrained indulgence of his desires, for the self-denial or dissimulation which he had thought it prudent to practise while in a subordinate station. He became careless, to so great a degree, of all serious business, that he could seldom be brought to attend to it, but in cases of extreme necessity; and giving up himself to amusements and dissipation of every kind, he imitated the luxurious elegance of Leo rather than the severe virtue of Adrian, the latter of which it was necessary to display, in contending with a sect which derived great credit from the rigid and austere manners of its teachers [d].

[c] Sleid. 492. F. Paul, 281. Pallav. ii. 76. Thuan. lib. vi. 215. [d] F. Paul, ibid.

BOOK X.

1550.
His views and proceedings with respect to the general council.

The Pope, however ready to fulfil his engagements to the family of Farnese, discovered no inclination to observe the oath, which each Cardinal had taken when he entered the conclave, that if the choice should fall on him, he would immediately call the council to re-assume its deliberations. Julius knew, by experience, how difficult it was to confine such a body of men within the narrow limits which it was the interest of the see of Rome to prescribe; and how easily the zeal of some members, the rashness of others, or the suggestions of the Princes on whom they depended, might precipitate a popular and ungovernable assembly into forbidden inquiries, as well as dangerous decisions. He wished, for these reasons, to have eluded the obligation of his oath, and gave an ambiguous answer to the first proposals which were made to him by the Emperor, with regard to that matter. But Charles, either from his natural obstinacy in adhering to the measures which he had once adopted, or from the mere pride of accomplishing what was held to be almost impossible, persisted in his resolution of forcing the Protestants to return into the bosom of the church. Having persuaded himself, that the authoritative decisions of the council might be employed with efficacy in combating their prejudices, he, in consequence of that persuasion, continued to solicit earnestly that a new bull of convocation might be issued; and the Pope could not, with decency, reject that request. When Julius found that

that he could not prevent the calling of a council, he endeavoured to take to himself all the merit of having procured the meeting of an assembly, which was the object of such general desire and expectation. A congregation of Cardinals, to whom he referred the consideration of what was necessary for restoring peace to the church, recommended, by his direction, the speedy convocation of a council, as the most effectual expedient for that purpose; and as the new heresies raged with the greatest violence in Germany, they proposed Trent as the place of its meeting, that, by a near inspection of the evil, the remedy might be applied with greater discernment and certainty of success. The Pope warmly approved of this advice, which he himself had dictated, and sent nuncios to the Imperial and French courts, in order to make known his intentions [e].

About this time, the Emperor had summoned a new diet to meet at Augsburg, in order to enforce the observation of the Interim, and to procure a more authentic act of the supreme court in the Empire, acknowledging the jurisdiction of the council, as well as an explicit promise of conforming to its decrees. He appeared there in person, together with his son the Prince of Spain. Few Electors were present, but all sent deputies in their name. Charles, notwithstanding the despotic authority with which he had given law in

[e] F. Paul, 281. Pallav. ii. 77.

the Empire during two years, knew that the spirit of independence among the Germans was not entirely subdued, and for that reason took care to over-awe the diet by a considerable body of Spanish troops which escorted him thither. The first point submitted to the consideration of the diet, was the necessity of holding a council. All the Popish members agreed, without difficulty, that the meeting of that assembly should be renewed at Trent, and promised an implicit acquiescence in its decrees. The Protestants, intimidated and disunited, must have followed their example, and the resolution of the diet would have proved unanimous, if Maurice of Saxony had not begun at this time to disclose new intentions, and to act a part very different from that which he had so long assumed.

Maurice begins to form designs against the Emperor.

By an artful dissimulation of his own sentiments; by address in paying court to the Emperor; and by the seeming zeal with which he forwarded all his ambitious schemes, Maurice had raised himself to the Electoral dignity; and having added the dominions of the elder branch of the Saxon family to his own, he was become the most powerful Prince in Germany. But his long and intimate union with the Emperor had afforded him many opportunities of observing narrowly the dangerous tendency of that Monarch's schemes. He saw the yoke that was preparing for his country; and from the rapid as well as formidable progress of the Imperial power, was convinced that but a few

few steps more remained to be taken, in order to render Charles as absolute a Monarch in Germany as he had become in Spain. The more eminent the condition was to which he himself had been exalted, the more solicitous did Maurice naturally become to maintain all its rights and privileges, and the more did he dread the thoughts of descending from the rank of a Prince almost independent, to that of a vassal subject to the commands of a master. At the same time, he perceived that Charles was bent on exacting a rigid conformity to the doctrines and rites of the Romish church, instead of allowing liberty of conscience, the promise of which had allured several Protestant Princes to assist him in the war against the confederates of Smalkalde. As he himself, notwithstanding all the compliances which he had made from motives of interest, or an excess of confidence in the Emperor, was sincerely attached to the Lutheran tenets, he determined not to be a tame spectator of the overthrow of a system which he believed to be founded in truth.

The political motives which influenced him.

This resolution, flowing from the love of liberty, or zeal for religion, was strengthened by political and interested considerations. In that elevated station in which Maurice was now placed, new and more extensive prospects opened to his view. His rank and power entitled him to be the head of the Protestants in the Empire. His predecessor, the degraded Elector, with inferior

ferior abilities, and territories less considerable, had acquired such an ascendant over the councils of the party; and Maurice neither wanted discernment to see the advantage of this pre-eminence, nor ambition to aim at attaining it. But he found himself in a situation which rendered the attempt no less difficult, than the object of it was important. On the one hand, the connexion which he had formed with the Emperor was so intimate, that he could scarcely hope to take any step which tended to dissolve it, without alarming his jealousy, and drawing on himself the whole weight of that power, which had crushed the greatest confederacy ever formed in Germany. On the other hand, the calamities which he had brought on the Protestant party were so recent, as well as great, that it seemed almost impossible to regain their confidence, or to rally and reanimate a body, after he himself had been the chief instrument in breaking its union and vigour. These considerations were sufficient to have discouraged any person of a spirit less adventurous than Maurice's. But to him the grandeur and difficulty of the enterprise were allurements; and he boldly resolved on measures, the idea of which a genius of an inferior order could not have conceived, or would have trembled at the thoughts of the danger that attended the execution of them.

The passions which co-operated with these.

His passions concurred with his interest in confirming this resolution; and the resentment excited

cited by an injury, which he fenfibly felt, added new force to the motives for oppofing the Emperor, which found policy fuggefted. Maurice, by his authority, had prevailed on the Landgrave of Heffe to put his perfon in the Emperor's power, and had obtained a promife from the Imperial minifters that he fhould not be detained a prifoner. This had been violated in the manner already related. The unhappy Landgrave exclaimed as loudly againft his fon-in-law as againft Charles. The Princes of Heffe required Maurice to fulfil his engagements to their father, who had loft his liberty by trufting to him; and all Germany fufpected him of having betrayed, to an implacable enemy, the friend whom he was moft bound to protect. Roufed by thefe folicitations or reproaches, as well as prompted by duty and affection to his father-in-law, Maurice had employed not only entreaties but remonftrances in order to procure his releafe. All thefe Charles had difregarded; and the fhame of having been firft deceived, and then flighted, by a Prince whom he had ferved with zeal as well as fuccefs, which merited a very different return, made fuch a deep impreffion on Maurice, that he waited with impatience for an opportunity of being revenged.

The utmoft caution as well as the moft delicate addrefs were requifite in taking every ftep towards this end; as he had to guard, on the one hand, againft giving a premature alarm to the Emperor; while

The caution and addrefs with which he carries on his fchemes.

while, on the other, something considerable and explicit was necessary to be done, in order to regain the confidence of the Protestant party. Maurice had accordingly applied all his powers of art and dissimulation to attain both these points. As he knew Charles to be inflexible with regard to the submission which he required to the Interim, he did not hesitate one moment whether he should establish that form of doctrine and worship in his dominions: But being sensible how odious it was to his subjects, instead of violently imposing it on them by the mere terror of authority, as had been done in other parts of Germany, he endeavoured to render their obedience a voluntary deed of their own. For this purpose, he had assembled the clergy of his country at Leipsick, and had laid the Interim before them, together with the reasons which made it necessary to conform to it. He had gained some of them by promises, others he had wrought upon by threats, and all were intimidated by the rigour with which obedience to the Interim was extorted in the neighbouring provinces. Even Melancthon, whose merit of every kind entitled him to the first place among the Protestant divines, being now deprived of the manly counsels of Luther, which were wont to inspire him with fortitude, and to preserve him steady amidst the storms and dangers that threatened the church, was seduced into unwarrantable concessions, by the timidity of his temper, his fond desire of peace, and his excessive complaisance towards persons of high rank.

He enforces the Interim in Saxony.

rank. By his arguments and authority, no less than by Maurice's address, the assembly was prevailed on to declare, "that, in points which were purely indifferent, obedience was due to the commands of a lawful superior." Founding upon this maxim, no less uncontrovertible in theory, than dangerous when carried into practice, especially in religious matters, many of the Protestant Ecclesiastics whom Maurice consulted, proceeded to class, among the number of things indifferent, several doctrines, which Luther had pointed out as gross and pernicious errors in the Romish creed; and placing in the same rank many of those rites which distinguished the Reformed from the Popish worship, they exhorted their people to comply with the Emperor's injunctions concerning these particulars [f].

By this dextrous conduct, the introduction of the Interim excited none of those violent convulsions in Saxony which it occasioned in other provinces. But though the Saxons submitted, the more zealous Lutherans exclaimed against Melancthon and his associates, as false brethren, who were either so wicked as to apostatize from the truth altogether; or so crafty as to betray it by subtle distinctions; or so feeble-spirited as to give it up from pusillanimity and criminal complaisance to a prince, capable of sacrificing to his political interest that which he himself regarded

Makes professions of zeal for the Protestant religion.

[f] Sleid. 481. 485. Jo. Laur. Moshemii Institutionum Hist. Ecclesiasticæ, lib. iv. Helmst. 1755, 4to. p. 748. J° And. Schmidii Historia Interimistica, p. 70, &c. Helmst. 1730.

as most sacred. Maurice, being conscious what a colour of probability his past conduct gave to those accusations, as well as afraid of losing entirely the confidence of the Protestants, issued a declaration containing professions of his zealous attachment to the Reformed religion, and of his resolution to guard against all the errors or encroachments of the Papal see [g].

At the same time courts the Emperor.

HAVING gone so far in order to remove the fears and jealousies of the Protestants, he found it necessary to efface the impression which such a declaration might make upon the Emperor. For that purpose, he not only renewed his professions of an inviolable adherence to his alliance with him, but as the city of Magdeburg still persisted in rejecting the Interim, he undertook to reduce it to obedience, and instantly set about levying troops to be employed in that service. This damped all the hopes which the Protestants begun to conceive of Maurice, in consequence of his declaration, and left them more than ever at a loss to guess at his real intentions. Their former suspicion and distrust of him revived, and the divines of Magdeburg filled Germany with writings in which they represented him as the most formidable enemy of the Protestant religion, who treacherously assumed an appearance of zeal for its interest, that he might more effectually execute his schemes for its destruction.

[g] Sleid. 485.

EMPEROR CHARLES V.

This charge, supported by the evidence of recent facts, as well as by his present dubious conduct, gained such universal credit, that Maurice was obliged to take a vigorous step in his own vindication. As soon as the re-assembling of the council at Trent was proposed in the diet, his ambassadors protested that their master would not acknowledge its authority, unless all the points which had been already decided there, were reviewed, and considered as still undetermined; unless the Protestant divines had a full hearing granted them, and were allowed a decisive voice in the council; and unless the Pope renounced his pretensions to preside in the council, engaged to submit to its decrees, and to absolve the bishops from their oath of obedience, that they might deliver their sentiments with greater freedom. These demands, which were higher than any that the Reformers had ventured to make, even when the zeal of their party was warmest, or their affairs most prosperous, counterbalanced, in some degree, the impression which Maurice's preparations against Magdeburg had made upon the minds of the Protestants, and kept them in suspense with regard to his designs. At the same time, he had dexterity enough to represent this part of his conduct in such a light to the Emperor, that it gave him no offence, and occasioned no interruption of the strict confidence which subsisted between them. What the pretexts were which he employed, in order to give such a bold declaration an innocent appearance, the contem-

Book X. 1550. Protests against the mode of proceeding in the council.

porary historians have not explained; that they imposed upon Charles is certain, for he still continued not only to prosecute his plan, as well concerning the Interim as the council, with the same ardour, but to place the same confidence in Maurice, with regard to the execution of both.

The diet resolve to make war on the city of Magdeburg.

THE Pope's resolution concerning the council not being yet known at Augsburg, the chief business of the diet was to enforce the observation of the Interim. As the senate of Magdeburg, notwithstanding various endeavours to frighten or to sooth them into compliance, not only persevered obstinately in their opposition to the Interim, but began to strengthen the fortifications of their city, and to levy troops in their own defence, Charles required the diet to assist him in quelling this audacious rebellion against a decree of the Empire. Had the members of the diet been left to act agreeably to their own inclination, this demand would have been rejected without hesitation. All the Germans who favoured, in any degree, the new opinions in religion, and many who were influenced by no other consideration than jealousy of the Emperor's growing power, regarded this effort of the citizens of Magdeburg, as a noble stand for the liberties of their country. Even such as had not resolution to exert the same spirit, admired the gallantry of their enterprise, and wished it success. But the presence of the Spanish troops, together with the dread of the Emperor's displeasure,

pleasure, overawed the members of the diet to such a degree, that, without venturing to utter their own sentiments, they tamely ratified, by their votes, whatever the Emperor was pleased to prescribe. The rigorous decrees, which Charles had issued by his own authority against the Magdeburgers, were confirmed; a resolution was taken to raise troops in order to besiege the city in form; and persons were named to fix the contingent in men or money to be furnished by each state. At the same time, the diet petitioned that Maurice might be entrusted with the command of that army; to which Charles gave his consent with great alacrity, and with high encomiums upon the wisdom of the choice which they had made [h]. As Maurice conducted all his schemes with profound and impenetrable secrecy, it is probable that he took no step avowedly in order to obtain this charge. The recommendation of his countrymen was either purely accidental, or flowed from the opinion generally entertained of his great abilities; and neither the diet had any foresight, nor the Emperor any dread, of the consequences which followed upon this nomination. Maurice accepted, without hesitation, the command to which he was recommended, instantly discerning the important advantages which he might derive from having it committed to him.

MEANWHILE, Julius, in preparing the bull for the convocation of the council, observed all those tedious

[h] Sleid. 503. 512.

tedious forms which the court of Rome can artfully employ to retard any difagreeable meafure. At laft however it was publifhed, and the council was fummoned to meet at Trent on the firft day of the enfuing month of May. As he knew that many of the Germans rejected or difputed the authority and jurifdiction which the Papal See claims with refpect to general councils, he took care, in the preamble of the bull, to affert, in the ftrongeft terms, his own right, not only to call and prefide in that affembly, but to direct its proceedings; nor would he foften thefe expreffions, in any degree, in compliance with the repeated folicitations of the Emperor, who forefaw what offence they would give, and what conftruction might be put on them. They were cenfured accordingly with great feverity by feveral members of the diet; but whatever difguft or fufpicion they excited, fuch complete influence over all their deliberations had the Emperor acquired, that he procured a recefs, in which the authority of the council was recognifed, and declared to be the proper remedy for the evils which at that time afflicted the church; all the Princes and ftates of the Empire, fuch as had made innovations in religion, as well as thofe who adhered to the fyftem of their forefathers, were required to fend their reprefentatives to the council; the Emperor engaged to grant a fafe-conduct to fuch as demanded it, and to fecure them an impartial hearing in the council; he promifed to fix his refidence in fome city of the Empire, in the

the neighbourhood of Trent, that he might protect the members of the council by his presence, and take care that, by conducting their deliberations agreeably to scripture and the doctrine of the fathers, they might bring them to a desirable issue. In this recess, the observation of the Interim was more strictly enjoined than ever; and the Emperor threatened all who had hitherto neglected or refused to conform to it, with the severest effects of his vengeance, if they persisted in their disobedience[i].

During the meeting of this diet, a new attempt was made, in order to procure liberty to the Landgrave. That Prince, nowise reconciled to his situation by time, grew every day more impatient of restraint. Having often applied to Maurice and the Elector of Brandenburg, who took every occasion of soliciting the Emperor in his behalf, though without any effect, he now commanded his sons to summon them, with legal formality, to perform what was contained in the bond which they had granted him, by surrendering themselves into their hands to be treated with the same rigour as the Emperor had used him. This furnished them with a fresh pretext for renewing their application to the Emperor, together with an additional argument to enforce it. Charles firmly resolved not to grant their request; though, at the same time, being extremely desirous to be

Another fruitless attempt to procure the Landgrave liberty.

[i] Sleid. 512. Thuan. lib. vi. 233. Goldasti Constit. Imperiales, vol. ii. 340.

delivered

delivered from their inceffant importunity, he endeavoured to prevail on the Landgrave to give up the bond which he had received from the two Electors. But that Prince refufing to part with a fecurity which he deemed effential to his fafety, the Emperor boldly cut the knot which he could not untie; and by a public deed annulled the bond which Maurice and the Elector of Brandenburg had granted, abfolving them from all their engagements to the Landgrave. No pretenfion to a power fo pernicious to fociety as that of abrogating at pleafure the moft facred laws of honour, and moft formal obligations of public faith, had hitherto been formed by any but the Roman Pontiffs, who, in confequence of their claim of fupreme power on earth, arrogate the right of difpenfing with precepts and duties of every kind. All Germany was filled with aftonifhment, when Charles affumed the fame prerogative. The ftate of fubjection, to which the Empire was reduced, appeared to be more rigorous, as well as intolerable, than that of the moft wretched and enflaved nations, if the Emperor, by an arbitrary decree, might cancel thofe folemn contracts, which are the foundation of that mutual confidence whereby men are held together in focial union. The Landgrave himfelf now gave up all hopes of recovering his liberty by the Emperor's confent, and endeavoured to procure it by his own addrefs. But the plan which he had formed to deceive his guards being difcovered, fuch of his attendants as he had gained to favour his efcape, escape, were put to death, and he was confined in the citadel of Mechlin more closely than ever [k].

Another transaction was carried on during this diet, with respect to an affair more nearly interesting to the Emperor, and which occasioned likewise a general alarm among the Princes of the Empire. Charles, though formed with talents which fitted him for conceiving and conducting great designs, was not capable, as has been often observed, of bearing extraordinary success. Its operation on his mind was so violent and intoxicating, that it elevated him beyond what was moderate or attainable, and turned his whole attention to the pursuit of vast but chimerical objects. Such had been the effect of his victory over the confederates of Smalkalde. He did not long rest satisfied with the substantial and certain advantages which were the result of that event, but, despising these, as poor or inconsiderable fruits of such great success, he aimed at nothing less than at bringing all Germany to an uniformity in religion, and at rendering the Imperial power despotic. These were objects extremely splendid indeed, and alluring to an ambitious mind; the pursuit of them, however, was attended with manifest danger, and the hope of attaining them very uncertain. But the steps which he had already taken towards them, having been accompanied with such success, his imagination, warmed with

Charles's plan of procuring the Imperial crown for his son Philip.

[k] Sleid. 504. Thuan. l. vi. 234, 235.

contemplating this alluring object, overlooked or despised all remaining difficulties. As he conceived the execution of his plan to be certain, he began to be solicitous how he might render the possession of such an important acquisition perpetual in his family, by transmitting the German Empire, together with the kingdoms of Spain, and his dominions in Italy and the Low-Countries, to his son. Having long revolved this flattering idea in his mind, without communicating it, even to those ministers whom he most trusted, he had called Philip out of Spain, in hopes that his presence would facilitate the carrying forward the scheme.

The obstacles that stood in its way.

GREAT obstacles, however, and such as would have deterred any ambition less accustomed to overcome difficulties, were to be surmounted. He had, in the year one thousand five hundred and thirty, imprudently assisted in procuring his brother Ferdinand the dignity of King of the Romans, and there was no probability that this Prince, who was still in the prime of life, and had a son grown up to the years of manhood, would relinquish, in favour of his nephew, the near prospect of the Imperial throne, which Charles's infirmities and declining state of health opened to himself. This did not deter the Emperor from venturing to make the proposition; and when Ferdinand, notwithstanding his profound reverence for his brother, and obsequious submission to his will in other instances, rejected it it in a peremptory tone, he was not discouraged by one repulse. He renewed his applications to him by his sister, Mary Queen of Hungary, to whom Ferdinand stood indebted for the crowns both of Hungary and Bohemia, and who, by her great abilities, tempered with extreme gentleness of disposition, had acquired an extraordinary influence over both the brothers. She entered warmly into a measure, which tended so manifestly to aggrandize the house of Austria; and, flattering herself that she could tempt Ferdinand to renounce the reversionary possession of the Imperial dignity for an immediate establishment, she assured him that the Emperor, by way of compensation for his giving up his chance of succession, would instantly bestow upon him territories of very considerable value, and pointed out in particular those of the Duke of Wurtemburg, which might be confiscated upon different pretexts. But neither by her address nor intreaties, could she induce Ferdinand to approve of a plan, which would not only have degraded him from the highest rank among the Monarchs of Europe to that of a subordinate and dependent Prince, but would have involved both him and his posterity in perpetual contests. He was, at the same time, more attached to his children, than by a rash concession to frustrate all the high hopes, in prospect of which they had been educated.

BOOK X.
1551.

Notwithstanding the immoveable firmness which Ferdinand discovered, the Emperor did not abandon his scheme. He flattered himself that

His endeavours to surmount these.

BOOK X.
1551.

that he might attain the object in view by another channel, and that it was not impossible to prevail on the Electors to cancel their former choice of Ferdinand, or at least to elect Philip a second King of the Romans, substituting him as next in succession to his uncle. With this view, he took Philip along with him to the diet, that the Germans might have an opportunity to observe and become acquainted with the Prince, in behalf of whom he courted their interest; and he himself employed all the arts of address or insinuation to gain the Electors, and to prepare them for listening with a favourable ear to the proposal. But no sooner did he venture upon mentioning it to them, than they, at once, saw and trembled at the consequences with which it would be attended. They had long felt all the inconveniencies of having placed at the head of the Empire a Prince whose power and dominions were so extensive; if they should now repeat the folly, and continue the Imperial crown, like an hereditary dignity, in the same family, they foresaw that they would give the son an opportunity of carrying on that system of oppression which the father had begun; and would put it in his power to overturn whatever was yet left entire in the ancient and venerable fabrick of the German constitution.

Philip's character disagreeable to the Germans.

THE character of the Prince, in whose favour this extraordinary proposition was made, rendered it still less agreeable. Philip, though possessed

with

with an insatiable desire of power, was a stranger to all the arts of conciliating good-will. Haughty, reserved, and severe, he, instead of gaining new friends, disgusted the ancient and most devoted partizans of the Austrian interest. He scorned to take the trouble of acquiring the language of the country to the government of which he aspired; nor would he condescend to pay the Germans the compliment of accommodating himself, during his residence among them, to their manners and customs. He allowed the Electors and most illustrious Princes in Germany, to remain in his presence uncovered, affecting a stately and distant demeanour, which the greatest of the German Emperors, and even Charles himself, amidst the pride of power and victory, had never assumed[1]. On the other hand, Ferdinand, from the time of his arrival in Germany, had studied to render himself acceptable to the people, by a conformity to their manners, which seemed to flow from choice; and his son Maximilian, who was born in Germany, possessed, in an eminent degree, such amiable qualities as rendered him the darling of his countrymen, and induced them to look forward to his election as a most desirable event. Their esteem and affection for him, fortified the resolution which sound policy had suggested; and determined the Germans to prefer the popular virtues of Ferdinand and his son, to

[1] Frediman Andreæ Zulich Dissertatio politico-historica de Nævis politicis Caroli V. Lipf. 1706. 4to. p. 21.

the stubborn austerity of Philip, which interest could not soften, nor ambition teach him to disguise. All the electors, the ecclesiastical as well as secular, concurred in expressing such strong disapprobation of the measure, that Charles, notwithstanding the reluctance with which he gave up any point, was obliged to drop the scheme as impracticable. By his unseasonable perseverance in pushing it, he had not only filled the Germans with new jealousy of his ambitious designs, but laid the foundation of rivalship and discord in the Austrian family, and forced his brother Ferdinand, in self-defence, to court the Electors, particularly Maurice of Saxony, and to form such connexions with them, as cut off all prospect of renewing the proposal with success. Philip, soured by his disappointment, was sent back to Spain, to be called thence when any new scheme of ambition should render his presence necessary [m].

HAVING relinquished this plan of domestic ambition, which had long occupied and engrossed him, Charles imagined that he would now have leisure to turn all his attention towards his grand scheme of establishing uniformity of religion in the Empire, by forcing all the contending parties to acquiesce in the decisions of the council of Trent. But such was the extent of his dominions, the variety of connections in which this

[m] Sleid. 505. Thuan. 180. 238. Memoir. de Ribier, ii. 219. 281. 314. Adriani Istor. lib. viii. 507. 520.

entangled

entangled him, and the multiplicity of events to which thefe gave rife, as feldom allowed him to apply his whole force to any one object. The machine which he had to conduct was fo great and complicated, that an unforefeen irregularity or obftruction in one of the inferior wheels, often difconcerted the motion of the whole, and prevented his deriving from them, all the beneficial effects which he expected. Such an unlooked-for occurrence happened at this juncture, and created new obftacles to the execution of his fchemes with regard to religion. Julius III. though he had confirmed Octavio Farnefe in the poffeffion of the dutchy of Parma, during the firft effufions of his joy and gratitude on his promotion to the papal throne, foon began to repent of his own generofity, and to be apprehenfive of confequences which either he did not forefee, or had difregarded, while the fenfe of his obligations to the family of Farnefe was recent. The Emperor ftill retained Placentia in his hands, and had not relinquifhed his pretenfions to Parma as a fief of the Empire. Gonzaga, the governor of Milan, having, by the part which he took in the murder of the late Duke Peter Ludovico, offered an infult to the family of Farnefe, which he knew could never be forgiven, had, for that reafon, vowed its deftruction; and employed all the influence which his great abilities, as well as long fervices, gave him with the Emperor, in perfuading him to feize Parma by force of arms. Charles, in compliance with his folicitations, and that he might gratify

his

his own desire of annexing Parma to the Milanese, listened to the proposal; and Gonzaga, ready to take encouragement from the slightest appearance of approbation, began to assemble troops, and to make other preparations for the execution of his scheme.

Octavio Farnese courts the assistance of France.

OCTAVIO, who saw the impending danger, found it necessary, for his own safety, to encrease the garrison of his capital, and to levy soldiers for defending the rest of the country. But as the expence of such an effort far exceeded his scanty revenues, he represented his situation to the Pope, and implored that protection and assistance which was due to him as a vassal of the church. The Imperial minister, however, had already pre-occupied the Pope's ear; and by discoursing continually concerning the danger of giving offence to the Emperor, as well as the imprudence of supporting Octavio in an usurpation so detrimental to the Holy See, had totally alienated him from the family of Farnese. Octavio's remonstrance and petition met, of consequence, with a cold reception; and he, despairing of any assistance from Julius, began to look round for protection from some other quarter. Henry II. of France was the only Prince powerful enough to afford him this protection, and fortunately he was now in a situation which allowed him to grant it. He had brought his transactions with the two British kingdoms, which had hitherto diverted his attention from the affairs of the Continent,

tinent, to such an issue as he desired. This he had effected partly by the vigour of his arms, partly by his dexterity in taking advantage of the political factions which raged in both kingdoms to such a degree, as rendered the councils of the Scots violent and precipitate, and the operations of the English feeble and unsteady. He had procured from the English favourable conditions of peace for his allies the Scots; he had prevailed on the nobles of Scotland not only to affiance their young Queen to his son the Dauphin, but even to send her into France, that she might be educated under his eye; and had recovered Boulogne, together with its dependencies, which had been conquered by Henry VIII.

THE French king having gained points of so much consequence to his crown, and disengaged himself with such honour from the burden of supporting the Scots, and maintaining a war against England, was now at full leisure to pursue the measures which his hereditary jealousy of the Emperor's power naturally suggested. He listened, accordingly, to the first overtures which Octavio Farnese made him; and embracing eagerly an opportunity of recovering footing in Italy, he instantly concluded a treaty, in which he bound himself to espouse his cause, and to furnish him all the assistance which he desired. This transaction could not be long kept secret from the Pope, who, foreseeing the calamities which must follow if war were rekindled so near the ecclesiastical state, immediately

His league with Henry II.

mediately issued monitory letters, requiring Octavio to relinquish his new alliance. Upon his refusal to comply with the requisition, he soon after pronounced his fief to be forfeited, and declared war against him as a disobedient and rebellious vassal. But as, with his own forces alone, he could not hope to subdue Octavio while supported by such a powerful ally as the King of France, he had recourse to the Emperor, who being extremely solicitous to prevent the establishment of the French in Parma, ordered Gonzaga to second Julius with all his troops. Thus the French took the field as the allies of Octavio; the Imperialists as the protectors of the Holy See; and hostilities commenced between them, while Charles and Henry themselves still affected to give out that they would adhere inviolably to the peace of Crespy. The war of Parma was not distinguished by any memorable event. Many small rencountres happened with alternate success; the French ravaged part of the ecclesiastical territories; the Imperialists laid waste the Parmesan; and the latter, after having begun to besiege Parma in form, were obliged to abandon the enterprise with disgrace [n].

But the motions and alarm which this war, or the preparations for it, occasioned in Italy, prevented most of the Italian prelates from repairing

[n] Adriani Istor. lib. viii. 505. 514. 524. Sleid. 513. Paruta, p. 220. Lettere del Caro scritte al nome del Card. Farnese, tom. ii. p. 11, &c.

to Trent on the first of May, the day appointed for re-assembling the council; and though the papal legate and nuncios reforted thither, they were obliged to adjourn the council to the first of September, hoping such a number of prelates might then assemble, that they might with decency begin their deliberations. At that time about sixty prelates, mostly from the ecclesiastical state, or from Spain, together with a few Germans, convened[o]. The session was opened with the accustomed formalities, and the fathers were about to proceed to business, when the abbot of Bellozane appeared, and presenting letters of credence as ambassador from the King of France, demanded audience. Having obtained it, he protested in Henry's name, against an assembly called at such an improper juncture, when a war, wantonly kindled by the Pope, made it impossible for the deputies from the Gallican church to resort to Trent in safety, or to deliberate concerning articles of faith and discipline with the requisite tranquillity; he declared, that his master did not acknowledge this to be a general or oecumenic council, but must consider, and would treat it, as a particular and partial convention[p]. The legate affected to despise this protest; and the prelates proceeded, notwithstanding, to examine and decide the great points in controversy concerning the sacrament of the Lord's Supper, penance, and extreme unction. This measure of the French Monarch,

Henry protests against the council.

[o] F. Paul, 268.
[p] Sleid. 518. Thuan. 282. F. Paul, 301.

however,

however, gave a deep wound to the credit of the council, at the very commencement of its deliberations. The Germans could not pay much regard to an assembly, the authority of which the second Prince in Christendom had formally disclaimed, or feel any great reverence for the decisions of a few men, who arrogated to themselves all the rights belonging to the representatives of the church universal, a title to which they had such poor pretensions.

Violence of the Emperor's proceedings against the Protestants.

The Emperor, nevertheless, was straining his authority to the utmost, in order to establish the reputation and jurisdiction of the council. He had prevailed on the three ecclesiastical Electors, the prelates of greatest power and dignity in the church next to the Pope, to repair thither in person. He had obliged several German bishops of inferior rank, to go to Trent themselves, or to send their proxies. He granted an Imperial safe-conduct to the ambassadors nominated by the Elector of Brandenburg, the duke of Wurtemberg, and other Protestants, to attend the council; and exhorted them to send their divines thither, in order to propound, explain, and defend their doctrine. At the same time, his zeal anticipated the decrees of the council; and as if the opinions of the Protestants had already been condemned, he took large steps towards exterminating them. With this intention, he called together the ministers of Augsburg; and after interrogating them concerning several controverted

verted points, enjoined them to teach nothing with respect to these, contrary to the tenets of the Romish church. Upon their declining to comply with a requisition so contrary to the dictates of their consciences, he commanded them to leave the town in three days, without revealing to any person the cause of their banishment; he prohibited them to preach for the future in any province of the Empire; and obliged them to take an oath that they would punctually obey these injunctions. They were not the only victims to his zeal. The Protestant clergy, in most of the cities in the circle of Swabia, were ejected with the same violence; and in many places, such magistrates as had distinguished themselves by their attachment to the new opinions, were dismissed with the most abrupt irregularity, and their offices filled, in consequence of the Emperor's arbitrary appointment, with the most bigoted of their adversaries. The Reformed worship was almost entirely suppressed throughout that extensive province. The ancient and fundamental privileges of the free cities were violated. The people were compelled to attend the ministration of priests, whom they regarded with horror as idolaters; and to submit to the jurisdiction of magistrates, whom they detested as usurpers [q].

The Emperor, after this discovery, which was more explicit than any that he had hitherto made,

His endeavours to support the council.

[q] Sleid. 516. 528. Thuan. 276.

of his intention to subvert the German constitution, as well as to extirpate the Protestant religion, set out for Inspruck in the Tyrol. He fixed his residence in that city, as, by its situation in the neighbourhood of Trent, and on the confines of Italy, it appeared a commodious station, whence he might inspect the operations of the council, and observe the progress of the war in the Parmesan, without losing sight of such occurrences as might happen in Germany [r].

The siege of Magdeburg.

During these transactions, the siege of Magdeburg was carried on with various success. At the time when Charles proscribed the citizens of Magdeburg, and put them under the ban of the Empire, he had exhorted and even enjoined all the neighbouring states to take arms against them, as rebels and common enemies. Encouraged by his exhortations as well as promises, George of Mecklenburg, a younger brother of the reigning Duke, an active and ambitious Prince, collected a considerable number of those soldiers of fortune who had accompanied Henry of Brunswick in all his wild enterprises; and though a zealous Lutheran himself, invaded the territories of the Magdeburgers, hoping that, by the merit of this service, he might procure some part of their domains to be allotted to him as an establishment. The citizens, unaccustomed as yet to endure patiently the calamities of war, could not be restrained from sallying out in order to save their

[r] Sleid. 329.

lands

lands from being laid waste. They attacked the Duke of Mecklenburg with more resolution than conduct, and were repulsed with great slaughter. But as they were animated with that unconquerable spirit, which flows from zeal for religion co-operating with the love of civil liberty, far from being disheartened by their misfortune, they prepared to defend themselves with vigour. Many of the veteran soldiers who had served in the long wars between the Emperor and King of France, crowding to their standards under able and experienced officers, the citizens acquired military skill by degrees, and added all the advantages of that to the efforts of undaunted courage. The Duke of Mecklenburg, notwithstanding the severe blow which he had given the Magdeburgers, not daring to invest a town strongly fortified, and defended by such a garrison, continued to ravage the open country.

As the hopes of booty drew many adventurers to the camp of this young Prince, Maurice of Saxony began to be jealous of the power which he possessed by being at the head of such a numerous body, and marching towards Magdeburg with his own troops, assumed the supreme command of the whole army, an honour to which his high rank and great abilities, as well as the nomination of the diet, gave him an indisputable title. With this united force, he invested the town, and began the siege in form; claiming great merit with the Emperor on that account,

Maurice takes the command of the army which carried on the siege.

as from his zeal to execute the Imperial decree, he was exposing himself once more to the censures and maledictions of the party with which he agreed in religious sentiments. But the approaches to the town went on slowly; the garrison interrupted the besiegers by frequent sallies, in one of which George of Mecklenburg was taken prisoner, levelled part of their works, and cut off the soldiers in their advanced posts. While the citizens of Magdeburg, animated by the discourses of their pastors, and the soldiers, encouraged by the example of their officers, endured all the hardships of a siege without murmuring, and defended themselves with the same ardour which they had at first discovered; the troops of the besiegers acted with extreme remissness, repining at every thing that they suffered in a service which they disliked. They broke out, more than once, into open mutiny, demanding the arrears of their pay, which, as the members of the Germanic body sent in their contributions towards defraying the expences of the war sparingly and with great reluctance, amounted to a considerable sum[s]. Maurice, too, had particular motives, though such as he durst not avow at that juncture, which induced him not to push the siege with vigour, and made him chuse rather to continue at the head of an army exposed to all the imputations which his dilatory proceedings drew upon him, than to precipitate a conquest that might

[s] Thuan. 277. Sleid. 514.

have

have brought him some accession of reputation, but would have rendered it necessary to disband his forces.

The city surrenders to Maurice.

AT last, the inhabitants of the town beginning to suffer distress from want of provisions, and Maurice, finding it impossible to protract matters any longer without filling the Emperor with such suspicions as might have disconcerted all his measures, he concluded a treaty of capitulation with the city upon the following conditions; that the Magdeburgers should humbly implore pardon of the Emperor; that they should not for the future take arms, or enter into any alliance against the house of Austria; that they should submit to the authority of the Imperial chamber; that they should conform to the decree of the diet at Augsburg with respect to religion; that the new fortifications added to the town should be demolished; that they should pay a fine of fifty thousand crowns, deliver up twelve pieces of ordnance to the Emperor, and set the Duke of Mecklenburg, together with their other prisoners, at liberty, without ransom. Next day their garrison marched out, and Maurice took possession of the town with great military pomp.

Novemb. 3.

BEFORE the terms of capitulation were settled, Maurice had held many conferences with Albert count Mansfeldt, who had the chief command in Magdeburg. He consulted likewise with count Heideck, an officer who had served with great reputation

Maurice's views at this juncture.

reputation in the army of the league of Smalkalde, whom the Emperor had profcribed on account of his zeal for that caufe, but whom Maurice had, notwithftanding, fecretly engaged in his fervice, and admitted into the moft intimate confidence. To them he communicated a fcheme, which he had long revolved in his mind, for procuring liberty to his father-in-law the Landgrave, for vindicating the privileges of the Germanic body, and fetting bounds to the dangerous encroachments of the Imperial power. Having deliberated with them concerning the meafures which might be neceffary for fecuring the fuccefs of fuch an arduous enterprife, he gave Mansfeldt fecret affurances that the fortifications of Magdeburg fhould not be deftroyed, and that the inhabitants fhould neither be difturbed in the exercife of their religion, nor be deprived of any of their ancient immunities. In order to engage Maurice more thoroughly from confiderations of intereft to fulfil thefe engagements, the fenate of Magdeburg elected him their Burgrave, a dignity which had formerly belonged to the electoral houfe of Saxony, and which entitled him to a very ample jurifdiction not only in the city but in its dependencies [t].

The advantages he derived from his negociations with the Magdeburgers.

THUS the citizens of Magdeburg, after enduring a fiege of twelve months, and ftruggling

[t] Sleid. 528. Thuan. 276. Obfidionis Magdeburgici Defcriptio per Sebaft. Beffelmeierum, ap. Scard. ii. 518.

for their liberties, religious and civil, with an invincible fortitude, worthy of the cause in which it was exerted, had at last the good fortune to conclude a treaty, which left them in a better condition than the rest of their countrymen, whom their timidity or want of public spirit had betrayed into such mean submissions to the Emperor. But while a great part of Germany applauded the gallant conduct of the Magdeburgers, and rejoiced in their having escaped the destruction with which they had been threatened, all admired Maurice's address in the conduct of his negociation with them, as well as the dexterity with which he converted every event to his own advantage. They saw, with amazement, that after having afflicted the Magdeburgers during many months with all the calamities of war, he was at last, by their voluntary election, advanced to the station of highest authority in that city which he had so lately besieged; that after having been so long the object of their satirical invectives as an apostate, and an enemy to the religion which he professed, they seemed now to place unbounded confidence in his zeal and good-will [u]. At the same time, the public articles in the treaty of capitulation were so perfectly conformable to those which the Emperor had granted to the other Protestant cities, and Maurice took such care to magnify his merit in having reduced a place which had defended itself with so much obstinacy, that

[u] Arnoldi vita Maurit. apud Menken, ii. 1227.

Charles,

Charles, far from suspecting any thing fraudulent or collusive in the terms of accommodation, ratified them without hesitation, and absolved the Magdeburgers from the sentence of ban which had been denounced against them.

<small>His expedient for keeping an army on foot.</small>

The only point that now remained to embarrass Maurice was how to keep together the veteran troops which had served under him, as well as those which had been employed in the defence of the town. For this, too, he found an expedient with singular art and felicity. His schemes against the Emperor were not yet so fully ripened, that he durst venture to disclose them, and proceed openly to carry them into execution. The winter was approaching, which made it impossible to take the field immediately. He was afraid that it would give a premature alarm to the Emperor, if he should retain such a considerable body in his pay until the season of action returned in the spring. As soon then as Magdedurg opened its gates, he sent home his Saxon subjects, whom he could command to take arms and re-assemble on the shortest warning; and at the same time, paying part of the arrears due to the mercenary troops, who had followed his standard, as well as to the soldiers who had served in the garrison, he absolved them from their respective oaths of fidelity, and disbanded them. But the moment he gave them their discharge, George of Mecklenburg, who was now set at liberty, offered to take them into his service, and to become surety furety for the payment of what was still owing to them. As such adventurers were accustomed often to change masters, they instantly accepted the offer. Thus these troops were kept united, and ready to march wherever Maurice should call them, while the Emperor, deceived by this artifice, and imagining that George of Mecklenburg had hired them with an intention to assert his claim to a part of his brother's territories by force of arms, suffered this transaction to pass without observation, as if it had been a matter of no consequence [x].

His address in concealing his intentions from the Emperor.

HAVING ventured to take these steps, which were of so much consequence towards the execution of his schemes, Maurice, that he might divert the Emperor from observing their tendency too narrowly, and prevent the suspicions which that must have excited, saw the necessity of employing some new artifice in order to engage his attention, and to confirm him in his present security. As he knew that the chief object of the Emperor's solicitude at this juncture, was how he might prevail with the Protestant States of Germany to recognize the authority of the council of Trent, and to send thither ambassadors in their own name, as well as deputies from their respective churches, he took hold of this predominating passion in order to amuse and to deceive

---

[x] Thuan. 278. Struv. corp. hist. Germ. 1064. Arnoldi vita Mauritii, apud Menken, ii. 1227.

him. He affected a wonderful zeal to gratify Charles in what he defired with regard to this matter; he nominated ambaffadors, whom he empowered to attend the council; he made choice of Melancthon and fome of the moft eminent among his brethren to prepare a confeffion of faith, and to lay it before that affembly. After his example, and probably in confequence of his folicitations, the Duke of Wurtemberg, the city of Strafburg, and other Proteftant States, appointed ambaffadors and divines to attend the council. They all applied to the Emperor for his fafe-conduct, which they obtained in the moft ample form. This was deemed fufficient for the fecurity of the ambaffadors, and they proceeded accordingly on their journey; but a feparate fafe-conduct from the council itfelf was demanded for the Proteftant divines. The fate of John Hufs and Jerome of Prague, whom the council of Conftance, in the preceding century, had condemned to the flames without regarding the Imperial fafe-conduct which had been granted them, rendered this precaution prudent and neceffary. But as the Pope was no lefs unwilling that the Proteftants fhould be admitted to an hearing in the council, than the Emperor had been eager in bringing them to demand it, the legate by promifes and threats prevailed on the fathers of the council to decline iffuing a fafe-conduct in the fame form with that which the council of Bafil had granted to the followers of Hufs. The Proteftants, on their part, infifted upon the council's copying

copying the precise words of that instrument. The Imperial ambassadors interposed, in order to obtain what would satisfy them. Alterations in the form of the writ were proposed; expedients were suggested; protests and counter-protests were taken: the legate, together with his associates, laboured to gain their point by artifice and chicane; the Protestants adhered to theirs with firmness and obstinacy. An account of every thing that passed in Trent was transmitted to the Emperor at Inspruck, who, attempting, from an excess of zeal, or of confidence in his own address, to reconcile the contending parties, was involved in a labyrinth of inextricable negociations. By means of this, however, Maurice gained all that he had in view; the Emperor's time was wholly engrossed, and his attention diverted; while he himself had leisure to mature his schemes, to carry on his intrigues, and to finish his preparations, before he threw off the mask, and struck the blow which he had so long meditated [y].

But previous to entering into any farther detail concerning Maurice's operations, some account must be given of a new revolution in Hungary, which contributed not a little towards their producing such extraordinary effects. When Solyman, in the year 1541, by a stratagem, which suited the base and insidious policy of a petty usurper, rather

The affairs of Hungary.

[y] Sleid. 526. 529. F. Paul, 323. 338. Thuan. 286.

than the magnanimity of a mighty conqueror, deprived the young King of Hungary of the dominions which his father had left him, he had granted that unfortunate Prince the country of Transylvania, a province of his paternal kingdom. The government of this, together with the care of educating the young King, for he still allowed him to retain that title, though he had rendered it only an empty name, he committed to the Queen and Martinuzzi bishop of Waradin, whom the late King had appointed joint-guardians of his son, and regents of his dominions, at a time when those offices were of greater importance. This co-ordinate jurisdiction occasioned the same dissensions in a small principality as it would have excited in a great kingdom; an ambitious young Queen, possessed with an high opinion of her own capacity for governing, and an high-spirited prelate, fond of power, contending who should engross the greatest share in the administration. Each had their partizans among the nobles; but as Martinuzzi, by his great talents, began to acquire the ascendant, Isabella turned his own arts against him, and courted the protection of the Turks.

Martinuzzi favours Ferdinand's pretensions in that kingdom.

The neighbouring Bashas, jealous of the bishop's power as well as abilities, readily promised her the aid which she demanded, and would soon have obliged Martinuzzi to have given up to her the sole direction of affairs, if his ambition, fertile in expedients, had not suggested to him a new measure, and one that tended not only to preserve ferve but to enlarge his authority. Having concluded an agreement with the Queen, by the mediation of some of the nobles, who were solicitous to save their country from the calamities of a civil war, he secretly dispatched one of his confidents to Vienna, and entered into a negociation with Ferdinand. As it was no difficult matter to persuade Ferdinand, that the same man whose enmity and intrigues had driven him out of a great part of his Hungarian dominions, might, upon a reconciliation, become equally instrumental in recovering them, he listened eagerly to the first overtures of an union with that prelate. Martinuzzi allured him by such prospects of advantage, and engaged, with so much confidence, that he would prevail on the most powerful of the Hungarian nobles to take arms in his favour, that Ferdinand, notwithstanding his truce with Solyman, agreed to invade Transylvania. The command of the troops destined for that service, consisting of veteran Spanish and German soldiers, was given to Castaldo Marquis de Piadena, an officer formed by the famous Marquis de Pescara, whom he strongly resembled both in his enterprising genius for civil business, and in his great knowledge in the art of war. This army, more formidable by the discipline of the soldiers, and the abilities of the general, than by its numbers, was powerfully seconded by Martinuzzi and his faction among the Hungarians. As the Turkish Bashas, the Sultan himself being at the head of his army on the frontiers of Persia, could not afford

afford the Queen such immediate or effectual assistance as the exigency of her affairs required, she quickly lost all hopes of being able to retain any longer the authority which she possessed as regent, and even began to despair of her son's safety.

The success of his measures.

MARTINUZZI did not suffer this favourable opportunity of accomplishing his own designs to pass unimproved, and ventured, while she was in this state of dejection, to lay before her a proposal, which at any other time she would have rejected with disdain. He represented how impossible it was for her to resist Ferdinand's victorious arms; that even if the Turks should enable her to make head against them, she would be far from changing her condition to the better, and could not consider them as deliverers, but as masters, to whose commands she must submit; he conjured her, therefore, as she regarded her own dignity, the safety of her son, or the security of Christendom, rather to give up Transylvania to Ferdinand, and to make over to him her son's title to the crown of Hungary, than to allow both to be usurped by the inveterate enemy of the Christian faith. At the same time he promised her, in Ferdinand's name, a compensation for herself, as well as for her son, suitable to their rank, and proportional to the value of what they were to sacrifice. Isabella, deserted by some of her adherents, distrusting others, destitute of friends, and surrounded by Castaldo's and Martinuzzi's nuzzi's troops, subscribed these hard conditions, though with a reluctant hand. Upon this, she surrendered such places of strength as were still in her possession, she gave up all the ensigns of royalty, particularly a crown of gold, which, as the Hungarians believed, had descended from heaven, and conferred on him who wore it an undoubted right to the throne. As she could not bear to remain a private person, in a country where she had once enjoyed sovereign power, she instantly set out with her son for Silesia, in order to take possession of the principalities of Oppelen and Ratibor, the investiture of which Ferdinand had engaged to grant her son, and likewise to bestow one of his daughters upon him in marriage.

Appointed governor of that part of Hungary which was subject to Ferdinand.

UPON the resignation of the young King, Martinuzzi, and after his example the rest of the Transylvanian grandees, swore allegiance to Ferdinand; who, in order to testify his grateful sense of the zeal as well as success with which that prelate had served him, affected to distinguish him by every possible mark of favour and confidence. He appointed him governor of Transylvania, with almost unlimited authority; he publicly ordered Castaldo to pay the greatest deference to his opinion and commands; he increased his revenues, which were already very great, by new appointments; he nominated him archbishop of Gran, and prevailed on the Pope to raise him to the dignity of a Cardinal. All this ostentation

BOOK X.
1551.

of good-will, however, was void of sincerity, and calculated to conceal sentiments the most perfectly its reverse. Ferdinand dreaded Martinuzzi's abilities; distrusted his fidelity; and foresaw, that as his extensive authority enabled him to check any attempt towards circumscribing or abolishing the extensive privileges which the Hungarian nobility possessed, he would stand forth, on every occasion, the guardian of the liberties of his country, rather than act the part of a viceroy devoted to the will of his sovereign.

Ferdinand begins to form designs against him.

FOR this reason, he secretly gave it in charge to Castaldo, to watch his motions, to guard against his designs, and to thwart his measures. But Martinuzzi, either because he did not perceive that Castaldo was placed as a spy on his actions, or because he despised Ferdinand's insidious arts, assumed the direction of the war against the Turks with his usual tone of authority, and conducted it with great magnanimity, and no less success. He recovered some places of which the Infidels had taken possession; he rendered their attempts to reduce others abortive; and established Ferdinand's authority not only in Transylvania, but in the Bannat of Temeswar, and several of the countries adjacent. In carrying on these operations, he often differed in sentiments from Castaldo and his officers, and treated the Turkish prisoners with a degree not only of humanity, but even of generosity, which Castaldo loudly condemned. This was represented at Vienna as an

artful

artful method of courting the friendship of the Infidels, that, by securing their protection, he might shake off all dependence upon the sovereign whom he now acknowledged. Though Martinuzzi, in justification of his own conduct, contended that it was impolitic by unnecessary severities to exasperate an enemy prone to revenge, Castaldo's accusations gained credit with Ferdinand, prepossessed already against Martinuzzi, and jealous of every thing that could endanger his own authority in Hungary, in proportion as he knew it to be precarious and ill established. These suspicions Castaldo confirmed and strengthened, by the intelligence which he transmitted continually to his confidents at Vienna. By misrepresenting what was innocent, and putting the worst construction on what seemed dubious in Martinuzzi's conduct; by imputing to him designs which he never formed, and charging him with actions of which he was not guilty; he at last convinced Ferdinand, that, in order to preserve his Hungarian crown, he must cut off that ambitious prelate. But Ferdinand, foreseeing that it would be dangerous to proceed in the regular course of law against a subject of such exorbitant power as might enable him to set his sovereign at defiance, determined to employ violence, in order to obtain that satisfaction which the laws were too feeble to afford him.

He issued his orders accordingly to Castaldo, who willingly undertook that infamous service.

He is assassinated by his command.

Having

Having communicated the design to some Italian and Spanish officers whom he could trust, and concerted with them the plan of executing it, they entered Martinuzzi's apartment, early one morning, under pretence of presenting to him some dispatches which were to be sent off immediately to Vienna; and while he perused a paper with attention, one of their number struck him with his poignard in the throat. The blow was not mortal. Martinuzzi started up with the intrepidity natural to him, and grappling the assassin, threw him to the ground. But the other conspirators rushing in, an old man, unarmed, and alone, was unable long to sustain such an unequal conflict, and sunk under the wounds which he received from so many hands. The Transylvanians were restrained by dread of the foreign troops stationed in their country, from rising in arms, in order to take vengeance on the murderers of a prelate who had long been the object of their love as well as veneration. They spoke of the deed, however, with horror and execration; and exclaimed against Ferdinand, whom neither gratitude for recent and important services, nor reverence for a character considered as sacred and inviolable among Christians, could restrain from shedding the blood of a man, whose only crime was attachment to his native country. The nobles, detesting the jealous as well as cruel policy of a court, which, upon uncertain and improbable surmises, had given up a person, no less conspicuous for his merit than his rank, to be butchered by assassins, either retired

retired to their own estates, or if they continued with the Austrian army, grew cold to the service. The Turks, encouraged by the death of an enemy whose abilities they knew and dreaded, prepared to renew hostilities early in the spring; and instead of the security which Ferdinand had expected from the removal of Martinuzzi, it was evident that his territories in Hungary were about to be attacked with greater vigour, and defended with less zeal, than ever [a].

Maurice courts the protection of the French King.

By this time, Maurice having almost finished his intrigues and preparations, was on the point of declaring his intentions openly, and of taking the field against the Emperor. His first care, after he came to this resolution, was to disclaim that narrow and bigoted maxim of the confederates of Smalkalde, which had led them to shun all connexion with foreigners. He had observed how fatal this had been to their cause; and, instructed by their error, he was as eager to court the protection of Henry II. as they had been solicitous to prevent the interposition of Francis I. Happily for him, he found Henry in a disposition to listen to the first overture on his part, and in a situation which enabled him to bring the whole force of the French monarchy into action. Henry had long observed the progress of the Emperor's arms with jealousy, and wished to distin-

[a] Sleid. 535. Thuan. lib. ix. 309, &c. Istuanhaffi Hist. Regn. Hungarici, lib. xvi. 189, &c. Mem. de Ribier, ii. 871. Natalis Comitis Historia, lib. iv. 84, &c.

guish himself by entering the lifts against the same enemy, whom it had been the glory of his father's reign to oppose. He had laid hold on the first opportunity in his power of thwarting the Emperor's designs, by taking the Duke of Parma under his protection; and hostilities were already begun, not only in that dutchy but in Piedmont. Having terminated the war with England by a peace, no less advantageous to himself than honourable for his allies the Scots, the restless and enterprising courage of his nobles was impatient to display itself on some theatre of action more conspicuous than the petty operations in Parma or Piedmont afforded them.

His treaty with him. JOHN DE FIENNE, bishop of Bayonne, whom Henry had sent into Germany, under pretence of hiring troops to be employed in Italy, was empowered to conclude a treaty in form with Maurice and his associates. As it would have been very indecent in a King of France to have undertaken the defence of the Protestant church, the interests of religion, how much soever they might be affected by the treaty, were not once mentioned in any of the articles. Religious concerns, they pretended to commit entirely to the disposition of Divine Providence; the only motives assigned for their present confederacy against Charles, were to procure the Landgrave liberty, and to prevent the subversion of the ancient constitution and laws of the German Empire. In order to accomplish these ends, it was agreed,

that

that all the contracting parties should, at the same time, declare war against the Emperor; that neither peace nor truce should be made but by common consent, nor without including each of the confederates; that, in order to guard against the inconveniencies of anarchy, or of pretensions to joint command, Maurice should be acknowledged as head of the German confederates, with absolute authority in all military affairs; that Maurice and his associates should bring into the field seven thousand horse, with a proportional number of infantry; that, towards the subsistence of this army, during the three first months of the war, Henry should contribute two hundred and forty thousand crowns, and afterwards sixty thousand crowns a-month, as long as they continued in arms; that Henry should attack the Emperor on the side of Lorrain with a powerful army; that if it were found requisite to elect a new Emperor, such a person should be nominated as shall be agreeable to the King of France [b]. This treaty was concluded on the fifth of October, some time before Magdeburg surrendered, and the preparatory negociations were conducted with such profound secrecy, that, of all the Princes who afterwards acceded to it, Maurice communicated what he was carrying on to two only, John Albert, the reigning Duke of Mecklenburg, and William of Hesse, the Landgrave's eldest son. The league itself was no less anxiously

[b] Recueil des Traitez, tom. ii. 258. Thuan. lib. viii. 279.

concealed,

concealed, and with such fortunate care, that no rumour concerning it reached the ears of the Emperor or his ministers; nor do they seem to have conceived the most distant suspicion of such a transaction.

Solicits the aid of Edward VI. of England.

AT the same time, with a solicitude which was careful to draw some accession of strength from every quarter, Maurice applied to Edward VI. of England, and requested a subsidy of four hundred thousand crowns for the support of a confederacy formed in defence of the Protestant religion. But the factions which prevailed in the English court during the minority of that Prince, and which deprived both the councils and arms of the nation of their wonted vigour, left the English ministers neither time nor inclination to attend to foreign affairs, and prevented Maurice's obtaining that aid, which their zeal for the Reformation would have prompted them to grant him [c].

Demands once more that the Landgrave should be set at liberty.

December.

MAURICE, however, having secured the protection of such a powerful Monarch as Henry II. proceeded with great confidence, but with equal caution, to execute his plan. As he judged it necessary to make one effort more, in order to obtain the Emperor's consent that the Landgrave should be set at liberty, he sent a solemn embassy, in his own name, and in that of the Elector of Brandenburg, to Infpruck. After refuming, at

[c] Burnet's Hist. of the Reform. vol. ii. Append. 37.

great length, all the facts and arguments upon which they founded their claim, and representing, in the strongest terms, the peculiar engagements which bound them to be so assiduous in their solicitations, they renewed the request in behalf of the unfortunate prisoner, which they had so often preferred in vain. The Elector Palatine, the Duke of Wurtemberg, the Dukes of Mecklenburg, the Duke of Deuxponts, the Marquis of Brandenburg Bareith, and the Marquis of Baden, by their ambassadors, concurred with them in their suit. Letters were likewise delivered to the same effect from the King of Denmark, the Duke of Bavaria, and the Dukes of Lunenburg. Even the King of the Romans joined in this application, being moved with compassion towards the Landgrave in his wretched situation, or influenced, perhaps, by a secret jealousy of his brother's power and designs, which, since his attempt to alter the order of succession in the Empire, he had come to view with other eyes than formerly, and dreaded to a great degree.

But Charles, constant to his own system with regard to the Landgrave, eluded a demand urged by such powerful intercessors; and having declared that he would communicate his resolution concerning the matter to Maurice as soon as he arrived at Infpruck, where he was every day expected, he did not deign to descend into any more particular explication of his intentions [d]. This

---

[d] Sleid. 531. Thuan. lib. viii. 280.

BOOK X.
1551.

1552.
Maurice continues to amuse the Emperor.

application, though of no benefit to the Landgrave, was of great advantage to Maurice. It served to justify his subsequent proceedings, and to demonstrate the necessity of employing arms in order to extort that equitable concession, which his mediation or intreaty could not obtain. It was of use, too, to confirm the Emperor in his security, as both the solemnity of the application, and the solicitude with which so many Princes were drawn in to enforce it, led him to conclude that they placed all their hopes of restoring the Landgrave to liberty, in gaining his consent to dismiss him.

MAURICE employed artifices still more refined to conceal his machinations, to amuse the Emperor, and to gain time. He affected to be more solicitous than ever to find out some expedient for removing the difficulties with regard to the safe-conduct for the Protestant divines appointed to attend the council, so that they might repair thither without any apprehension of danger. His ambassadors at Trent had frequent conferences concerning this matter with the Imperial ambassadors in that city, and laid open their sentiments to them with the appearance of the most unreserved confidence. He was willing, at last, to have it believed, that he thought all differences with respect to this preliminary article were on the point of being adjusted; and in order to give credit to this opinion, he commanded Melancthon, together with his brethren, to set out on their

their journey to Trent. At the same time, he held a close correspondence with the Imperial court at Infpruck, and renewed on every occasion his professions not only of fidelity but of attachment to the Emperor. He talked continually of his intention of going to Infpruck in person; he gave orders to hire a house for him in that city, and to fit it up with the greatest dispatch for his reception [e].

But, profoundly skilled as Maurice was in the arts of deceit, and impenetrable as he thought the veil to be, under which he concealed his designs, there were several things in his conduct which alarmed the Emperor amidst his security, and tempted him frequently to suspect that he was meditating something extraordinary. As these suspicions took their rise from circumstances inconsiderable in themselves, or of an ambiguous as well as uncertain nature, they were more than counterbalanced by Maurice's address; and the Emperor would not, lightly, give up his confidence in a man, whom he had once trusted and loaded with favours. One particular alone seemed to be of such consequence, that he thought it necessary to demand an explanation with regard to it. The troops, which George of Mecklenburg had taken into pay after the capitulation of Magdeburg, having fixed their quarters in Thuringia, lived at discretion on the lands of the rich

The Emperor conceives some suspicion concerning his intentions.

[e] Arnoldi vita Maurit. ap. Menken, ii. 1229.

eccleſi-

ecclesiastics in their neighbourhood. Their licence and rapaciousness were intolerable. Such as felt or dreaded their exactions, complained loudly to the Emperor, and represented them as a body of men kept in readiness for some desperate enterprize. But Maurice, partly by extenuating the enormities of which they had been guilty, partly by representing the impossibility of disbanding these troops, or of keeping them to regular discipline, unless the arrears still due to them by the Emperor were paid, either removed the apprehensions which this had occasioned, or, as Charles was not in a condition to satisfy the demands of these soldiers, obliged him to be silent with regard to the matter [f].

Maurice prepares for action.

THE time of action was now approaching. Maurice had privately dispatched Albert of Brandenburg to Paris, in order to confirm his league with Henry, and to hasten the march of the French army. He had taken measures to bring his own subjects together on the first summons; he had provided for the security of Saxony, while he should be absent with the army; and he held the troops in Thuringia, on which he chiefly depended, ready to advance on a moment's warning. All these complicated operations were carried on without being discovered by the court at Inspruck, and the Emperor remained there in perfect tranquillity, busied entirely in counteracting the in-

[f] Sleid. 549. Thuan. 339.

trigues

trigues of the Pope's legate at Trent, and in settling the conditions on which the Proteftant divines fhould be admitted into the council, as if there had not been any tranfaction of greater moment in agitation.

THIS credulous fecurity in a Prince, who, by his fagacity in obferving the conduct of all around him, was commonly led to an excefs of diftruft, may feem unaccountable, and has been imputed to infatuation. But befides the exquifite addrefs with which Maurice concealed his intentions, two circumftances contributed to the delufion. The gout had returned upon Charles foon after his arrival at Infpruck, with an increafe of violence; and his conftitution being broken by fuch frequent attacks, he was feldom able to exert his natural vigour of mind, or to confider affairs with his ufual vigilance and penetration; and Granvelle, bifhop of Arras, his prime minifter, though one of the moft fubtle ftatefmen of that or perhaps of any age, was on this occafion the dupe of his own craft. He entertained fuch an high opinion of his own abilities, and held the political talents of the Germans in fuch contempt, that he defpifed all the intimations given him concerning Maurice's fecret machinations, or the dangerous defigns which he was carrying on. When the Duke of Alva, whofe dark fufpicious mind harboured many doubts concerning the Elector's fincerity, propofed calling him immediately to court to anfwer for his conduct, Granvelle

Circumftances which contributed to deceive the Emperor,

and his minifters,

velle replied with great scorn, That these apprehensions were groundless, and that a drunken German head was too gross to form any scheme which he could not easily penetrate and baffle. Nor did he assume this peremptory tone merely from confidence in his own discernment; he had bribed two of Maurice's ministers, and received from them frequent and minute information concerning all their master's motions. But through this very channel, by which he expected to gain access to all Maurice's counsels, and even to his thoughts, such intelligence was conveyed to him as completed his deception. Maurice fortunately discovered the correspondence of the two traitors with Granvelle, but instead of punishing them for their crime, he dexterously availed himself of their fraud, and turned his own arts against the bishop. He affected to treat these ministers with greater confidence than ever; he admitted them to his consultations; he seemed to lay open his heart to them; and taking care all the while to let them be acquainted with nothing but what it was his interest should be known, they transmitted to Inspruck such accounts as possessed Granvelle with a firm belief of his sincerity as well as good intentions [g]. The Emperor himself, in the fulness of security, was so little moved by a memorial, in name of the ecclesiastical electors, admonishing him to be on his guard against Maurice, that he made light of this intelligence; and

[g] Melvil's Memoirs, fol. edit. p. 12.

his anfwer to them abounds with declarations of his entire and confident reliance on the fidelity as well as attachment of that Prince [h].

BOOK X.
1552.

At laſt Maurice's preparations were completed, and he had the ſatisfaction to find that his intrigues and defigns were ſtill unknown. But, though now ready to take the field, he did not lay aſide the arts which he had hitherto employed; and by one piece of craft more, he deceived his enemies a few days longer. He gave out, that he was about to begin that journey to Infpruck of which he had ſo often talked, and he took one of the miniſters whom Granvelle had bribed, to attend him thither. After travelling poſt a few ſtages, he pretended to be indiſpoſed by the fatigue of the journey, and diſpatching the ſuſpected miniſters to make his apology to the Emperor for this delay, and to aſſure him that he would be at Infpruck within a few days; he mounted on horſeback, as ſoon as this ſpy on his actions was gone, rode full ſpeed towards Thuringia, joined his army, which amounted to twenty thouſand foot and five thouſand horſe, and put it immediatly in motion [i].

Maurice takes the field againſt the Emperor.

March 18.

[h] Sleid. 535.
[i] Melv. Mem. p. 13. Theſe circumſtances concerning the Saxon miniſters whom Granvelle had bribed, are not mentioned by the German hiſtorians; but as Sir James Melvil received his information from the Elector Palatine, and as they are perfectly agreeable to the reſt of Maurice's conduct, they may be confidered as authentic.

AT

BOOK X.

1552.
Publishes a manifesto justifying his conduct.

At the same time he published a manifesto containing his reasons for taking arms. These were three in number: That he might secure the Protestant religion, which was threatened with immediate destruction; That he might maintain the constitution and laws of the Empire, and save Germany from being subjected to the dominion of an absolute monarch; That he might deliver the Landgrave of Hesse from the miseries of a long and unjust imprisonment. By the first, he roused all the favourers of the Reformation, a party formidable by their zeal as well as numbers, and rendered desperate by oppression. By the second he interested all the friends of liberty, Catholics no less than Protestants, and made it their interest to unite with him in asserting the rights and privileges common to both. The third, besides the glory which he acquired by his zeal to fulfil his engagements to the unhappy prisoner, was become a cause of general concern, not only from the compassion which the Landgrave's sufferings excited, but from indignation at the injustice and rigour of the Emperor's proceedings against him. Together with Maurice's manifesto, another appeared in the name of Albert Marquis of Brandenburg Culmbach, who had joined him with a body of adventurers whom he had drawn together. The same grievances which Maurice had pointed out are mentioned in it, but with an excess of virulence and animosity suitable to the character of the Prince in whose name it was published.

THE

THE King of France added to these a manifesto in his own name; in which, after taking notice of the ancient alliance between the French and German nations, both descended from the same ancestors; and after mentioning the applications, which, in consequence of this, some of the most illustrious among the German Princes had made to him for his protection; he declared, that he now took arms to re-establish the ancient constitution of the Empire, to deliver some of its Princes from captivity, and to secure the privileges and independence of all the members of the Germanic body. In this manifesto, Henry assumed the extraordinary title of *Protector of the Liberties of Germany, and of its captive Princes*; and there was engraved on it a cap, the ancient symbol of freedom, placed between two daggers, in order to intimate to the Germans, that this blessing was to be acquired and secured by force of arms [i].

MAURICE had now to act a part entirely new, but his flexible genius was capable of accommodating itself to every situation. The moment he took arms, he was as bold and enterprising in the field, as he had been cautious and crafty in the cabinet. He advanced by rapid marches towards the Upper Germany. All the towns in his way opened their gates to him. He reinstated the

---

[i] Sleid. 549. Thuan. lib. x. 339. Mem. de Ribier, ii. 371.

magistrates whom the Emperor had deposed, and gave possession of the churches to the Protestant ministers whom he had ejected. He directed his march to Augsburg, and as the Imperial garrison, which was too inconsiderable to think of defending it, retired immediately, he took possession of that great city, and made the same changes there as in the towns through which he had passed [k].

The Emperor's astonishment and distress.

No words can express the Emperor's astonishment and consternation at events so unexpected. He saw a great number of the German Princes in arms against him, and the rest either ready to join them, or wishing success to their enterprize. He beheld a powerful Monarch united with them in close league, seconding their operations in person at the head of a formidable army, while he, through negligence and credulity, which exposed him no less to scorn than to danger, had neither made, nor was in condition to make, any effectual provision, either for crushing his rebellious subjects, or resisting the invasion of the foreign enemy. Part of his Spanish troops had been ordered into Hungary against the Turks; the rest had marched back to Italy upon occasion of the war in the dutchy of Parma. The bands of veteran Germans had been dismissed, because he was not able to pay them; or had entered into Maurice's service after the siege of Magdeburg; and he remained at Inspruck with a body of sol-

[k] Sleid. 555. Thuan. 342.

diers

diers hardly strong enough to guard his own person. His treasury was as much exhausted, as his
army was reduced. He had received no remittances for some time from the new world. He
had forfeited all credit with the merchants of Genoa and Venice, who refused to lend him money,
though tempted by the offer of exorbitant interest. Thus Charles, though undoubtedly the most
considerable potentate in Christendom, and capable of exerting the greatest strength, his power,
notwithstanding the violent attack made upon it,
being still unimpaired, found himself in a situation
which rendered him unable to make such a sudden
and vigorous effort as the juncture required, and
was necessary to have saved him from the present
danger.

IN this situation, the Emperor placed all his
hopes on negociating; the only resource of such
as are conscious of their own weakness. But
thinking it inconsistent with his dignity to make
the first advances to subjects who were in arms
against him, he avoided that indecorum by employing the mediation of his brother Ferdinand.
Maurice confiding in his own talents to conduct
any negociation in such a manner as to derive advantage from it, and hoping that, by the appearance of facility in hearkening to the first overture
of accommodation, he might amuse the Emperor, and tempt him to slacken the activity with
which he was now preparing to defend himself,
readily agreed to an interview with Ferdinand in
the

the town of Lintz in Austria; and having left his army to proceed on its march under the command of the duke of Mecklenburg, he repaired thither.

<small>Progress of the French army.</small>

MEANWHILE the King of France punctually fulfilled his engagements to his allies. He took the field early, with a numerous and well-appointed army, and marching directly into Lorrain, Toul and Verdun opened their gates at his approach. His forces appeared next before Metz, and that city, by a fraudulent stratagem of the Constable Montmorency, who having obtained permission to pass through it with a small guard, introduced as many troops as were sufficient to overpower the garrison, was likewise seized without bloodshed. Henry made his entry into all these towns with great pomp; he obliged the inhabitants to swear allegiance to him, and annexed those important conquests to the French Monarchy. He left a strong garrison in Metz. From thence he advanced towards Alsace, in order to attempt new conquests, to which the success that had hitherto attended his arms invited him [1].

<small>The negociations between the Emperor and Maurice of no effect.</small>

THE conference at Lintz did not produce any accommodation. Maurice, when he consented to it, seems to have had nothing in view but to amuse the Emperor; for he made such demands, both in behalf of his confederates and their ally

[1] Thuan. 349.

the French King, as he knew would not be accepted by a Prince, too haughty to submit, at once, to conditions dictated by an enemy. But, however firmly Maurice adhered during the negociation to the interests of his associates, or how steadily soever he kept in view the objects which had induced him to take arms, he often professed a strong inclination to terminate the differences with the Emperor in an amicable manner. Encouraged by this appearance of a pacific disposition, Ferdinand proposed a second interview at Passau on the twenty-sixth of May, and that a truce should commence on that day, and continue to the tenth of June, in order to give them leisure for adjusting all the points in dispute.

Maurice advances towards Inspruck. Upon this, Maurice rejoined his army on the ninth of May, which had now advanced to Gundelfingen. He put his troops in motion next morning; and as sixteen days yet remained for action before the commencement of the truce, he resolved, during that period, to venture upon an enterprize, the success of which would be so decisive, as to render the negociations at Passau extremely short, and entitle him to treat upon his own terms. He foresaw that the prospect of a cessation of arms, which was to take place so soon, together with the opinion of his earnestness to re-establish peace, with which he had artfully amused Ferdinand, could hardly fail of inspiring the Emperor with such false hopes, that he would naturally become remiss, and relapse into some degree of that security which had already been so fatal to him. Relying on this conjecture, he marched directly at the head of his army towards Infpruck, and advanced with the moſt rapid motion that could be given to ſo great a body of troops. On the eighteenth, he arrived at Fieſſen, a poſt of great conſequence, at the entrance into the Tyroleſe. There he found a body of eight hundred men, whom the Emperor had aſſembled, ſtrongly intrenched, in order to oppoſe his progreſs. He attacked them inſtantly with ſuch violence and impetuoſity, that they abandoned their lines precipitately, and, falling back on a ſecond body poſted near Ruten, communicated the panic terror with which they themſelves had been ſeized, to thoſe troops; ſo that they likewiſe took to flight, after a feeble reſiſtance.

Takes the caſtle of Ehrenbergh. ELATED with this ſuccefs, which exceeded his moſt ſanguine hopes, Maurice preſſed forward to Ehrenbergh, a caſtle ſituated on an high and ſteep precipice, which commanded the only paſs through the mountains. As this fort had been ſurrendered to the Proteſtants at the beginning of the Smalkaldic war, becauſe the garriſon was then too weak to defend it, the Emperor, ſenſible of its importance, had taken care, at this juncture, to throw into it a body of troops ſufficient to maintain it againſt the greateſt army. But a ſhepherd, in purſuing a goat which had ſtrayed from his flock, having diſcovered an unknown path by which it was poſſible to aſcend to the top of of the rock, came with this seasonable piece of intelligence to Maurice. A small band of chosen soldiers, under the command of George of Mecklenburg, was instantly ordered to follow this guide. They set out in the evening, and clambering up the rugged track with infinite fatigue as well as danger, they reached the summit unperceived; and at an hour which had been agreed on, when Maurice began the assault on the one side of the castle, they appeared on the other, ready to scale the walls, which were feeble in that place, because it had been hitherto deemed inaccessible. The garrison, struck with terror at the sight of an enemy on a quarter where they had thought themselves perfectly secure, immediately threw down their arms. Maurice, almost without bloodshed, and which was of greater consequence to him, without loss of time, took possession of a place, the reduction of which might have retarded him long, and have required the utmost efforts of his valour and skill [m].

Maurice was now only two days march from Inspruck, and without losing a moment he ordered his infantry to advance thither, having left his cavalry, which was unserviceable in that mountainous country, at Fiessen, to guard the mouth of the pass. He proposed to advance with such rapidity as to anticipate any accounts of the loss of Ehrenbergh, and to surprise the Emperor, to-

A mutiny of his troops retards his march.

[m] Arnoldi vita Maurit. 123.

gether with his attendants, in an open town incapable of defence. But juft as his troops began to move, a battalion of mercenaries mutinied, declaring that they would not ftir until they had received the gratuity, which, according to the cuftom of that age, they claimed as the recompence due to them for having taken a place by affault. It was with great difficulty, as well as danger, and not without fome confiderable lofs of time, that Maurice quieted this infurrection, and prevailed on the foldiers to follow him to a place where he promifed them fuch rich booty as would be an ample reward for all their fervices.

The Emperor flies in confufion from Infpruck.

To the delay, occafioned by this unforefeen accident, the Emperor owed his fafety. He was informed of the approaching danger late in the evening, and knowing that nothing could fave him but a fpeedy flight, he inftantly left Infpruck, without regarding the darknefs of the night, or the violence of the rain which happened to fall at that time; and notwithftanding the debility occafioned by the gout, which rendered him unable to bear any motion but that of a litter, he travelled by the light of torches, taking his way over the Alps, by roads almoft impaffable. His courtiers and attendants followed him with equal precipitation, fome of them on fuch horfes as they could haftily procure, many of them on foot, and all in the utmoft confufion. In this miferable plight, very unlike the pomp with which Charles had appeared during the five preceding years as the

the conqueror of Germany, he arrived at length with his dejected train at Villach in Carinthia, and scarcely thought himself secure even in that remote inaccessible corner.

Maurice entered Infpruck a few hours after the Emperor and his attendants had left it; and enraged that the prey should escape out of his hands when he was just ready to seize it, he pursued them some miles; but finding it impossible to overtake persons, to whom their fear gave speed, he returned to the town, and abandoned all the Emperor's baggage, together with that of his ministers, to be plundered by the soldiers; while he preserved untouched every thing belonging to the King of the Romans, either because he had formed some friendly connexion with that Prince, or because he wished to have it believed that such a connexion subsisted between them. As there now remained only three days to the commencement of the truce (with such nicety had Maurice calculated his operations), he set out for Paffau, that he might meet Ferdinand on the day appointed.

Maurice enters that town.

Before Charles left Infpruck, he withdrew the guards placed on the degraded Elector of Saxony, whom, during five years, he had carried about with him as a prisoner; and set him entirely at liberty, either with an intention to embarrass Maurice by letting loose a rival, who might difpute his title to his dominions and dignity,

The Emperor fets the Elector of Saxony at liberty.

BOOK X.
1552.

nity, or from a sense of the indecency of detaining him a prisoner, while he himself run the risk of being deprived of his own liberty. But that Prince, seeing no other way of escaping than that which the Emperor took, and abhorring the thoughts of falling into the hands of a kinsman, whom he justly considered as the author of all his misfortunes, chose rather to accompany Charles in his flight, and to expect the final decision of his fate from the treaty which was now approaching.

The council of Trent breaks up in great consternation.

These were not the only effects which Maurice's operations produced. It was no sooner known at Trent that he had taken arms, than a general consternation seized the fathers of the council. The German prelates immediately returned home, that they might provide for the safety of their respective territories. The rest were extremely impatient to be gone; and the legate, who had hitherto disappointed all the endeavours of the Imperial ambassadors to procure an audience in the council for the Protestant divines, laid hold with joy on such a plausible pretext for dismissing an assembly, which he had found it so difficult to govern. In a congregation held on the twenty-eighth of April, a decree was issued proroguing the council during two years, and appointing it to meet at the expiration of that time, if peace were then re-established in Europe[n]. This prorogation, however, continued

[n] F. Paul, 353.

no less than ten years; and the proceedings of the council, when re-assembled in the year one thousand five hundred and sixty-two, fall not within the period prescribed to this history.

The convocation of this assembly had been passionately desired by all the States and Princes in Christendom, who, from the wisdom as well as piety of prelates representing the whole body of the faithful, expected some charitable and efficacious endeavours towards composing the dissensions which unhappily had arisen in the church. But the several Popes by whose authority it was called, had other objects in view. They exerted all their power or policy to attain these; and by the abilities as well as address of their legates, by the ignorance of many of the prelates, and by the servility of the indigent Italian bishops, acquired such influence in the council, that they dictated all its decrees, and framed them not with an intention to restore unity and concord to the church, but to establish their own dominion, or to confirm those tenets, upon which they imagined that dominion to be founded. Doctrines, which had hitherto been admitted upon the credit of tradition alone, and received with some latitude of interpretation, were defined with a scrupulous nicety, and confirmed by the sanction of authority. Rites, which had formerly been observed only in deference to custom supposed to be ancient, were established by the decrees of the church, and declared to be essential parts of its worship,

worship. The breach, instead of being closed, was widened, and made irreparable. In place of any attempt to reconcile the contending parties, a line was drawn with such studied accuracy, as ascertained and marked out the distinction between them. This still serves to keep them at a distance; and, without some signal interposition of Divine Providence, must render the separation perpetual.

Character of the historians of this council.

Our knowledge of the proceedings of this assembly, is derived from three different authors. Father Paul of Venice wrote his history of the Council of Trent, while the memory of what had passed there was recent, and some who had been members of it were still alive. He has exposed the intrigues and artifices by which it was conducted, with a freedom and severity which have given a deep wound to the credit of the council. He has described its deliberations, and explained its decrees, with such perspicuity and depth of thought, with such various erudition and such force of reason, as have justly entitled his work to be placed among the most admired historical compositions. About half a century thereafter, the Jesuit Pallavicini published his history of the council, in opposition to that of Father Paul, and by employing all the force of an acute and refining genius to invalidate the credit, or to confute the reasonings of his antagonist, he labours to prove, by artful apologies for the proceedings of the council, and subtile interpretations of its decrees,

crees, that it deliberated with impartiality, and decided with judgment as well as candour. Vargas, a Spanish doctor of laws, who was appointed to attend the Imperial ambassadors at Trent, sent the bishop of Arras a regular account of the transactions there, explaining all the arts which the Legate employed to influence or overawe the council. His letters have been published, in which he inveighs against the papal court with that asperity of censure, which was natural to a man whose situation enabled him to observe its intrigues thoroughly, and who was obliged to exert all his attention and talents in order to disappoint them. But whichsoever of these authors an intelligent person takes for his guide, in forming a judgment concerning the spirit of the council, he must discover so much ambition as well as artifice among some of the members, so much ignorance and corruption among others; he must observe such a large infusion of human policy and passions, mingled with such a scanty portion of that simplicity of heart, sanctity of manners, and love of truth, which alone qualify men to determine what doctrines are worthy of God, and what worship is acceptable to him; that he will find it no easy matter to believe, that any extraordinary influence of the Holy Ghost hovered over this assembly, and dictated its decrees.

While Maurice was employed in negociating with the King of the Romans at Lintz, or in making war on the Emperor in the Tyrol, the French

The French endeavour to surprise Strasbourg;

French King had advanced into Alsace as far as Strasburgh; and having demanded leave of the Senate to march through the city, he hoped that, by repeating the same fraud which he had practised at Metz, he might render himself master of the place, and by that means secure a passage over the Rhine into the heart of Germany. But the Strasburghers, instructed and put on their guard by the credulity and misfortune of their neighbours, shut their gates; and having assembled a garrison of five thousand soldiers, repaired their fortifications, rased the houses in their suburbs, and determined to defend themselves to the utmost. At the same time they sent a deputation of their most respectable citizens to the King, in order to divert him from making any hostile attempt upon them. The Electors of Treves and Cologn, the Duke of Cleves, and other Princes in the neighbourhood, interposed in their behalf; beseeching Henry that he would not forget so soon the title which he had generously assumed; and instead of being the Deliverer of Germany, become its Oppressor. The Swiss Cantons seconded them with zeal, soliciting Henry to spare a city which had long been connected with their community in friendship and alliance.

but without success.

POWERFUL as this united intercession was, it would not have prevailed on Henry to forego a prize of so much value, if he had been in a condition to have seized it. But, in that age, the method

method of subsisting numerous armies at a distance from the frontiers of their own country, was imperfectly understood, and neither the revenues of Princes, nor their experience in the art of war, were equal to the great and complicated efforts which such an undertaking required. The French, though not far removed from their own frontier, began already to suffer from scarcity of provisions, and had no sufficient magazines collected to support them during a siege, which must necessarily have been of great length°. At the same time, the Queen of Hungary, governess of the Low Countries, had assembled a considerable body of troops, which, under the command of Martin de Rossem, laid waste Champagne, and threatened the adjacent provinces of France. These concurring circumstances obliged the King, though with reluctance, to abandon the enterprize. But being willing to acquire some merit with his allies, by this retreat which he could not avoid, he pretended to the Swiss that he had taken the resolution merely in compliance with their request P; and then, after giving orders that all the horses in his army should be led to drink in the Rhine, as a proof of his having pushed his conquests so far, he marched back towards Champagne.

WHILE the French King and the main army of the confederates were thus employed, Albert

° Thuan. 351, 352
P Sleid. 557. Brantome, tom. vii. 39.

of Brandenburg was entrusted with the command of a separate body of eight thousand men, consisting chiefly of mercenaries who had resorted to his standard, rather from the hope of plunder, than the expectation of regular pay. That Prince, seeing himself at the head of such a number of desperate adventurers, ready to follow wherever he should lead them, soon began to disdain a state of subordination, and to form such extravagant schemes of aggrandizing himself, as seldom occur, even to ambitious minds, unless when civil war or violent factions rouse them to bold exertions, by alluring them with immediate hopes of success. Full of these aspiring thoughts, Albert made war in a manner very different from the other confederates. He endeavoured to spread the terror of his arms by the rapidity of his motions, as well as the extent and rigour of his devastations; he exacted contributions wherever he came, in order to amass such a sum of money, as would put it in his power to keep his army together; he laboured to get possession of Nuremberg, Ulm, or some other of the free cities in Upper Germany, in which, as a capital, he might fix the seat of his power. But, finding these cities on their guard, and in a condition to resist his attacks, he turned all his rage against the popish ecclesiastics, whose territories he plundered with such wanton and merciless barbarity, as gave them a very unfavourable impression of the spirit of that reformation in religion, with zeal for which he pretended to be animated. The bishops

bishops of Bamburgh and Wurzburgh, by their situation, lay particularly exposed to his ravages; he obliged the former to transfer to him, in property, almost one half of his extensive diocese; and compelled the latter to advance a great sum of money in order to save his territories from ruin and desolation. During all those wild sallies, Albert paid no regard either to Maurice's orders, whose commands as Generalissimo of the league he had engaged to obey, or to the remonstrances of the other confederates; and manifestly discovered, that he attended only to his own private emolument, without any solicitude about the common cause, or the general objects which had induced them to take arms[q].

MAURICE having ordered his army to march back into Bavaria, and having published a proclamation enjoining the Lutheran clergy and instructors of youth, to resume the exercise of their functions in all the cities, schools, and universities from which they had been ejected, met Ferdinand at Passau on the twenty-sixth day of May. As matters of the greatest consequence to the future peace and independence of the Empire were to be settled in this congress, the eyes of all Germany were fixed upon it. Besides Ferdinand and the Imperial ambassadors, the Duke of Bavaria, the bishops of Saltzburgh and Aichstadt, the ministers of all the Electors, to-

[q] Sleid. 561. Thuan. 357.

BOOK X.
1552.

gether with deputies from most of the considerable Princes and free cities, resorted to Passau. Maurice, in the name of his associates, and the King of the Romans as the Emperor's representative, opened the negociation. The Princes who were present, together with the deputies of such as were absent, acted as intercessors or mediators between them.

The terms which Maurice proposed.

MAURICE, in a long discourse, explained the motives of his own conduct. After having enumerated all the unconstitutional and oppressive acts of the Emperor's administration, he, agreeably to the manifesto which he had published when he took arms against him, limited his demands to three articles: That the Landgrave of Hesse should be immediately set at liberty; That the grievances in the civil government of the Empire should be redressed; and that the Protestants should be allowed the public exercise of their religion without molestation. Ferdinand and the Imperial ambassadors discovering their unwillingness to gratify him with regard to all these points, the mediators wrote a joint letter to the Emperor, beseeching him to deliver Germany from the calamities of a civil war, by giving such satisfaction to Maurice and his party as might induce them to lay down their arms; and at the same time they prevailed upon Maurice to grant a prolongation of the truce for a short time, during which they undertook to procure the Emperor's final answer to his demands.

THIS

THIS request was presented to the Emperor in the name of all the Princes of the Empire, Popish as well as Protestant, in the name of such as had lent an helping hand to forward his ambitious schemes, as well as of those who had viewed the progress of his power with jealousy and dread. The uncommon and cordial unanimity with which they concurred at this juncture in enforcing Maurice's demands, and in recommending peace, flowed from different causes. Such as were most attached to the Roman Catholic church could not help observing, that the Protestant confederates were at the head of a numerous army, while the Emperor was but just beginning to provide for his own defence. They foresaw that great efforts would be required of them, and would be necessary on their part, in order to cope with enemies, who had been allowed to get the start so far, and to attain such formidable power. Experience had taught them, that the fruit of all these efforts would be reaped by the Emperor alone, and the more complete any victory proved which they should gain, the faster would they bind their own fetters, and render them the more intolerable. These reflections made them cautious how they contributed a second time, by their indiscreet zeal, to put the Emperor in possession of power which would be fatal to the liberties of their country. Notwithstanding the intolerant spirit of bigotry in that age, they chose rather that the Protestants should acquire that security for their religion which

1552. Powerfully supported by the Princes of the Empire.

which they demanded, than by affisting Charles to oppress them, to give such additional force to the Imperial prerogative, as would overturn the constitution of the Empire. To all these considerations, the dread of seeing Germany laid waste by a civil war added new force. Many states of the Empire already felt the destructive rage of Albert's arms, others dreaded it, and all wished for an accommodation between the Emperor and Maurice, which they hoped would save them from that cruel scourge.

The motives which influenced the Emperor at this juncture.

Such were the reasons that induced so many Princes, notwithstanding the variety of their political interests, and the opposition in their religious sentiments, to unite in recommending to the Emperor an accommodation with Maurice, not only as a salutary, but as a necessary measure. The motives which prompted Charles to desire it, were not fewer or of less weight. He was perfectly sensible of the superiority which the confederates had acquired through his own negligence; and he now felt the insufficiency of his own resources to oppose them. His Spanish subjects, disgusted at his long absence, and weary of endless wars, which were of little benefit to their country, refused to furnish him any considerable supply either of men or money; and although by his address or importunity he might have hoped to draw from them at last more effectual aid; that, he knew, was too distant to be of any service in the present exigency of his affairs. His treasury

treasury was drained; his veteran forces were dispersed or disbanded, and he could not depend much either on the fidelity or courage of the new levied soldiers whom he was collecting. There was no hope of repeating with success the same artifices which had weakened and ruined the Smalkaldic league. As the end at which he aimed was not known, he could no longer employ the specious pretexts which had formerly concealed his ambitious designs. Every Prince in Germany was alarmed and on his guard; and it was vain to think of blinding them a second time to such a degree, as to make one part of them instruments to enslave the other. The spirit of a confederacy, whereof Maurice was the head, experience had taught him to be very different from that of the league of Smalkalde; and from what he had already felt, he had no reason to flatter himself that its counsels would be as irresolute, or its efforts as timid and feeble. If he should resolve on continuing the war, he might be assured, that the most considerable states in Germany would take part in it against him; and a dubious neutrality was the utmost he could expect from the rest. While the confederates found full employment for his arms in one quarter, the King of France would seize the favourable opportunity, and push on his operations in another, with almost certain success. That monarch had already made conquests in the Empire, which Charles was no less eager to recover, than impatient to be revenged on him for aiding his malecontent subjects.

subjects. Though Henry had now retired from the banks of the Rhine, he had only varied the scene of hostilities, having invaded the Low-Countries with all his forces. The Turks, roused by the solicitations of the French King, as well as stimulated by resentment against Ferdinand for having violated the truce in Hungary, had prepared a powerful fleet to ravage the coasts of Naples and Sicily, which he had left almost defenceless, by calling thence the greatest part of the regular troops to join the army which he was now assembling.

Ferdinand zealous to promote an accommodation.

FERDINAND, who went in person to Villach, in order to lay before the Emperor the result of the conferences at Passau, had likewise reasons peculiar to himself for desiring an accommodation. These prompted him to second, with the greatest earnestness, the arguments which the Princes assembled there had employed in recommending it. He had observed, not without secret satisfaction, the fatal blow that had been given to the despotic power which his brother had usurped in the Empire. He was extremely solicitous to prevent Charles from recovering his former superiority, as he foresaw that ambitious Prince would immediately resume, with increased eagerness, and with a better chance of success, his favourite scheme of transmitting that power to his son, by excluding his brother from the right of succession to the Imperial throne. On this account he was willing to contribute towards circumscribing the Imperial authority, in order

to render his own poffeffion of it certain. Be-
fides, Solyman, exafperated at the lofs of Tran-
fylvania, and ftill more at the fraudulent arts by
which it had been feized, had ordered into the
field an army of an hundred thoufand men, which
having defeated a great body of Ferdinand's troops,
and taken feveral places of importance, threatened
not only to complete the conqueft of the province,
but to drive them out of that part of Hungary
which was ftill fubject to his jurifdiction. He
was unable to refift fuch a mighty enemy; the
Emperor, while engaged in a domeftic war, could
afford him no aid; and he could not even hope to
draw from Germany the contingent, either of
troops or money, ufually furnifhed to repel the in-
vafions of the Infidels. Maurice, having obferved
Ferdinand's perplexity with regard to this laft
point, had offered, if peace were re-eftablifhed on
a fecure foundation, that he would march in per-
fon with his troops into Hungary againft the
Turks. Such was the effect of this well-timed
propofal, that Ferdinand, deftitute of every other
profpect of relief, became the moft zealous advo-
cate whom the confederates could have employed
to urge their claims, and there was hardly any
thing that they could have demanded which he
would not have chofen to grant, rather than have
retarded a pacification, to which he trufted as the
only means of faving his Hungarian crown.

WHEN fo many caufes confpired in rendering an accommodation eligible, it might have been expected

BOOK X.
1552.

expected that it would have taken place immediately. But the inflexibility of the Emperor's temper, together with his unwillingness at once to relinquish objects which he had long pursued with such earnestness and assiduity, counterbalanced, for some time, the force of all the motives which disposed him to peace, and not only put that event at a distance, but seemed to render it uncertain. When Maurice's demands, together with the letter of the mediators at Passau, were presented to him, he peremptorily refused to redress the grievances which were pointed out, nor would he agree to any stipulation for the immediate security of the Protestant religion, but proposed referring both these to the determination of a future diet. On his part, he required that instant reparation should be made to all who, during the present war, had suffered either by the licentiousness of the confederate troops, or the exactions of their leaders.

Maurice's vigorous operations facilitate it.

MAURICE, who was well acquainted with the Emperor's arts, immediately concluded that he had nothing in view by these overtures but to amuse and deceive; and therefore, without listening to Ferdinand's intreaties, he left Passau abruptly, and joining his troops, which were encamped at Mergentheim, a city in Franconia, belonging to the knights of the Teutonic order, he put them in motion, and renewed hostilities. As three thousand men in the Emperor's pay had thrown themselves into Frankfort on the Maine, and

EMPEROR CHARLES V.

and might from thence infest the neighbouring country of Hesse, he marched towards that city, and laid siege to it in form. The briskness of this enterprize, and the vigour with which Maurice carried on his approaches against the town, gave such an alarm to the Emperor, as disposed him to lend a more favourable ear to Ferdinand's arguments in behalf of an accommodation. Firm and haughty as his nature was, he found it necessary to bend, and signified his willingness to make concessions on his part, if Maurice, in return, would abate somewhat of the rigour of his demands. Ferdinand, as soon as he perceived that his brother began to yield, did not desist from his importunities, until he prevailed on him to declare what was the utmost that he would grant for the security of the confederates. Having gained this difficult point, he instantly dispatched a messenger to Maurice's camp, and imparting to him the Emperor's final resolution, conjured him not to frustrate his endeavours for the re-establishment of peace; or, by an unseasonable obstinacy on his side, to disappoint the wishes of all Germany for that salutary event.

MAURICE, notwithstanding the prosperous situation of his affairs, was strongly inclined to listen to this advice. The Emperor, though over-reached and surprised, had now begun to assemble troops, and however slow his motions might be, while the first effects of his consternation remained, he was sensible that Charles must at last

BOOK X.

1552.
July 17.

Maurice desirous of an accommodation.

act with vigour proportional to the extent of his power and territories, and lead into Germany an army formidable by its numbers, and still more by the terror of his name, as well as the remembrance of his past victories. He could scarcely hope that a confederacy composed of so many members would continue to operate with union and perseverance sufficient to resist the consistent and well-directed efforts of an army, at the absolute disposal of a leader accustomed to command and to conquer. He felt already, although he had not hitherto experienced the shock of any adverse event, that he himself was the head of a disjointed body. He saw, from the example of Albert of Brandenburg, how difficult it would be, with all his address and credit, to prevent any particular member from detaching himself from the whole, and how impossible to recal him to his proper rank and subordination. This filled him with apprehensions for the common cause. Another consideration gave him no less disquiet with regard to his own particular interests. By setting at liberty the degraded Elector, and by repealing the act by which that Prince was deprived of his hereditary honours and dominions, the Emperor had it in his power to wound him in the most tender part. The efforts of a Prince beloved by his ancient subjects, and revered by all the Protestant party, in order to recover what had been unjustly taken from him, could hardly have failed of exciting commotions in Saxony, which would endanger all that he had acquired at the expence of so much dissimulation and artifice. It was no less in the Emperor's power to render vain all the solicitations of the confederates in behalf of the Landgrave. He had only to add one act of violence more to the injustice and rigour with which he had already treated him; and he had accordingly threatened the sons of that unfortunate Prince, that if they persisted in their present enterprize, instead of seeing their father restored to liberty, they should hear of his having suffered the punishment which his rebellion had merited [r].

The peace of Religion concluded at Passau.

HAVING deliberated upon all these points with his associates, Maurice thought it more prudent to accept of the conditions offered, though less advantageous than those which he had proposed, than again to commit all to the doubtful issue of war [s]. He repaired forthwith to Passau, and signed the treaty of peace; of which the chief articles were, That before the twelfth day of August, the confederates shall lay down their arms, and disband their forces; That on or before that day the Landgrave shall be set at liberty, and conveyed in safety to his castle of Rheinfels; That a diet shall be held within six months, in order to deliberate concerning the most proper and effectual method of preventing for the future all disputes and dissensions about religion; That, in the mean time, neither the Emperor, nor any other Prince, shall, upon any pretext whatever,

August 2.

[r] Sleid. 571.
[s] Sleid. Hist. 563, &c. Thuan. lib. x. 359, &c.

offer

offer any injury or violence to such as adhered to the confession of Augsburg, but allow them to enjoy the free and undisturbed exercise of their religion; That, in return, the Protestants shall not molest the Catholics either in the exercise of their ecclesiastical jurisdiction, or in performing their religious ceremonies; That the Imperial chamber shall administer justice impartially to persons of both parties, and Protestants be admitted indiscriminately with the Catholics to sit as judges in that court; That if the next diet should not be able to terminate the disputes with regard to religion, the stipulations in the present treaty in behalf of the Protestants shall continue for ever in full force and vigour; That none of the confederates shall be liable to any action on account of what had happened during the course of the war; That the consideration of those encroachments which had been made, as Maurice pretended, upon the constitution and liberties of the Empire, shall be remitted to the approaching diet; That Albert of Brandenburg shall be comprehended in the treaty, provided he shall accede to it, and disband his forces before the twelfth of August [i].

Reflections upon this peace and upon the conduct of Maurice.

SUCH was the memorable treaty of Passau, that overturned the vast fabrick, in erecting which Charles had employed so many years, and had exerted the utmost efforts of his power and policy;

[i] Receuil des Traitez, ii. 261.

that annulled all his regulations with regard to religion; defeated all his hopes of rendering the Imperial authority abfolute and hereditary in his family; and eftablifhed the Proteftant church, which had hitherto fubfifted precarioufly in Germany, through connivance, or by expedients, upon a firm and fecure bafis. Maurice reaped all the glory of having concerted and completed this unexpected revolution. It is a fingular circumftance, that the Reformation fhould be indebted for its fecurity and full eftablifhment in Germany, to the fame hand which had brought it to the brink of deftruction, and that both events fhould have been accomplifhed by the fame arts of diffimulation. The ends, however, which Maurice had in view, at thofe different junctures, feem to have been more attended to than the means by which he attained them; and he was now as univerfally extolled for his zeal and public fpirit as he had lately been condemned for his indifference and interefted policy. It is no lefs worthy of obfervation, that the French King, a monarch zealous for the Catholic faith, fhould employ his power in order to protect and maintain the Reformation in the Empire, at the very time when he was perfecuting his own Proteftant fubjects with all the fiercenefs of bigotry, and that the league for this purpofe, which proved fo fatal to the Romifh church, fhould be negociated and figned by a Roman Catholic bifhop. So wonderfully doth

the

the wisdom of God superintend and regulate the caprice of human passions, and render them subservient towards the accomplishment of his own purposes.

Little attention paid to the French King in this treaty.

LITTLE attention was paid to the interests of the French King during the negociations at Passau. Maurice and his associates, having gained what they had in view, discovered no great solicitude about an ally, whom, perhaps, they reckoned to be overpaid for the assistance which he had given them, by his acquisitions in Lorrain. A short clause which they procured to be inserted in the treaty, importing that the King of France might communicate to the confederates his particular pretensions or causes of hostility, which they would lay before the Emperor, was the only sign that they gave of their remembering how much they had been indebted to him for their success. Henry experienced the same treatment, which every Prince who lends his aid to the authors of a civil war may expect. As soon as the rage of faction began to subside, and any prospect of accommodation to open, his services were forgotten, and his associates made a merit with their sovereign, of the ingratitude with which they abandoned their protector. But how much soever Henry might be enraged at the perfidy of his allies, or at the impatience with which they hastened to make their peace with the Emperor, at his expence, he was perfectly sensible that

it

it was more his interest to keep well with the Germanic body, than to resent the indignities offered him by any particular members of it. For that reason he dismissed the hostages which he had received from Maurice and his associates, and affected to talk in the same strain as formerly, concerning his zeal for maintaining the ancient constitution and liberties of the Empire.

THE HISTORY OF THE REIGN OF THE EMPEROR CHARLES V.

BOOK XI.

AS soon as the treaty of Passau was signed, Maurice, in consequence of his engagements with Ferdinand, marched into Hungary at the head of twenty thousand men. But the great superiority of the Turkish armies, the frequent mutinies both of the Spanish and German soldiers, occasioned by their want of pay, together with the dissentions between Maurice and Castaldo, who was piqued at being obliged to resign the chief command to him, prevented his performing any thing in that country suitable to his former fame, or of great benefit to the King of the Romans [a].

[margin: BOOK XI. 1552. Aug. 3. Maurice marches into Hungary against the Turks.]

[a] Istuanhaffii Hist. Hungar. 288. Thuan. lib. x. 371.

1552.
The Landgrave of Hesse recovers his liberty.

When Maurice set out for Hungary, the Prince of Hesse parted from him with the forces under his command, and marched back into his own country, that he might be ready to receive his father upon his return, and give up to him the reins of government which he had held during his absence. But fortune was not yet weary of persecuting the Landgrave. A battalion of mercenary troops, which had been in the pay of Hesse, being seduced by Reifenberg their colonel, a soldier of fortune, ready to engage in any enterprise, secretly withdrew from the young Prince as he was marching homewards, and joined Albert of Brandenburgh, who still continued in arms against the Emperor, refusing to be included in the treaty of Passau. Unhappily for the Landgrave, an account of this reached the Netherlands, just as he was dismissed from the citadel of Mechlin where he had been confined, but before he had got beyond the frontiers of that country. The Queen of Hungary, who governed there in her brother's name, incensed at such an open violation of the treaty to which he owed his liberty, issued orders to arrest him, and committed him again to the custody of the same Spanish captain who had guarded him for five years with the most severe vigilance. Philip beheld all the horrors of his imprisonment renewed, and his spirits subsiding in the same proportion as they had risen during the short interval in which he had enjoyed liberty; he sunk into despair, and believed himself to be doomed to perpetual captivity.

tivity. But the matter being so explained to the Emperor, as fully satisfied him that the revolt of Reifenberg's mercenaries could be imputed neither to the Landgrave nor to his son, he gave orders for his release; and Philip at last obtained the liberty for which he had so long languished [b]. But though he recovered his freedom, and was reinstated in his dominions, his sufferings seem to have broken the vigour, and to have extinguished the activity of his mind: From being the boldest as well as most enterprising Prince in the Empire, he became the most timid and cautious, and passed the remainder of his days in a pacific indolence.

THE degraded Elector of Saxony, likewise, procured his liberty in consequence of the treaty of Passau. The Emperor having been obliged to relinquish all his schemes for extirpating the Protestant religion, had no longer any motive for detaining him a prisoner; and being extremely solicitous, at that juncture, to recover the confidence and good-will of the Germans, whose assistance was essential to the success of the enterprise which he meditated against the King of France, he, among other expedients for that purpose, thought of releasing from imprisonment a Prince whose merit entitled him no less to esteem, than his sufferings rendered him the object of compassion. John Frederick took possession ac-

Likewise the Elector of Saxony.

[b] Sleid. 573. Belcarii Comment. 834.

cordingly

cordingly of that part of his territories which had been reserved for him, when Maurice was invested with the Electoral dignity. As in this situation, he continued to display the same virtuous magnanimity for which he had been conspicuous in a more prosperous and splendid state, and which he had retained amidst all his sufferings, he maintained during the remainder of his life that high reputation to which he had so just a title.

The Emperor resolves to make war upon France.

THE loss of Metz, Toul, and Verdun, had made a deep impression on the Emperor. Accustomed to terminate all his operations against France with advantage to himself, he thought that it nearly concerned his honour not to allow Henry the superiority in this war, or to suffer his own administration to be stained with the infamy of having permitted territories of such consequence to be dismembered from the Empire. This was no less a point of interest than of honour. As the frontier of Champagne was more naked, and lay more exposed than that of any province in France, Charles had frequently, during his wars with that kingdom, made inroads upon that quarter with great success and effect; but if Henry were allowed to retain his late conquests, France would gain such a formidable barrier on that side, as to be altogether secure, where formerly she had been weakest. On the other hand, the Empire had now lost as much, in point of security, as France had acquired; and being stripped of the defence which those cities afforded it, lay open
to

EMPEROR CHARLES V.

to be invaded on a quarter, where all the towns having been hitherto confidered as interior, and remote from any enemy, were but flightly fortified. Thefe confiderations determined Charles to attempt recovering the three towns of which Henry had made himfelf mafter; and the preparations which he had made againft Maurice and his affociates, enabled him to carry his refolution into immediate execution.

As foon, then, as the peace was concluded at Paffau, he left his inglorious retreat at Villach, and advanced to Augfburg, at the head of a confiderable body of Germans which he had levied, together with all the troops which he had drawn out of Italy and Spain. To thefe he added feveral battalions, which having been in the pay of the confederates, entered into his fervice when difmiffed by them; and he prevailed likewife on fome Princes of the Empire to join him with their vaffals. In order to conceal the deftination of this formidable army, and to guard againft alarming the French King, fo as to put him on preparing for the defence of his late conquefts, he gave out that he was to march forthwith into Hungary, in order to fecond Maurice in his operations againft the Infidels. When he began to advance towards the Rhine, and could no longer employ that pretext, he tried a new artifice, and fpread a report, that he took this route in order to chaftife Albert of Brandenburg, whofe cruel exactions in that part

His preparations for this purpofe.

of the Empire called loudly for his interpofition to check them.

The precautions of the French for the defence of Metz.

But the French having grown acquainted, at laft, with arts by which they had been fo often deceived, viewed all Charles's motions with diftruft. Henry immediately difcerned the true object of his vaft preparations, and refolved to defend the important conquefts which he had gained with vigour equal to that with which they were about to be attacked. As he forefaw that the whole weight of the war would be turned againft Metz, by whofe fate that of Toul and Verdun would be determined, he nominated Francis of Lorrain, Duke of Guife, to take the command in that city during the fiege, the iffue of which would equally affect the honour and intereft of his country. His choice could not have fallen upon any perfon more worthy of that truft. The Duke of Guife poffeffed, in a high degree, all the talents of courage, fagacity, and prefence of mind, which render men eminent in military command. He was largely endowed with that magnanimity of foul which delights in bold enterprifes, and afpires to fame by fplendid and extraordinary actions. He repaired with joy to the dangerous ftation affigned him, as to a theatre on which he might difplay his great qualities under the immediate eye of his countrymen, all ready to applaud him. The martial genius of the French nobility in that age, which confidered it as the greateft reproach to remain inactive,

The Duke of Guife appointed governor of the town.

when

when there was any opportunity of fignalifing their courage, prompted great numbers to follow a leader who was the darling as well as the pattern of every one that courted military fame. Several Princes of the blood, many noblemen of the higheft rank, and all the young officers who could obtain the King's permiffion, entered Metz as volunteers. By their prefence they added fpirit to the garrifon, and enabled the Duke of Guife to employ, on every emergency, perfons eager to diftinguifh themfelves, and fit to conduct any fervice.

BOOK XI.

1552.

But with whatever alacrity the Duke of Guife undertook the defence of Metz, he found every thing, upon his arrival there, in fuch a fituation, as might have induced any perfon of lefs intrepid courage to defpair of defending it with fuccefs. The city was of great extent, with large fuburbs; the walls were in many places feeble and without ramparts; the ditch narrow; and the old towers, which projected inftead of baftions, were at too great diftance from each other to defend the fpace between them. For all thefe defects he endeavoured to provide the beft remedy which the time would permit. He ordered the fuburbs, without fparing the monafteries or churches, not even that of St. Arnulph, in which feveral Kings of France had been buried, to be levelled with the ground; but in order to guard againft the imputation of impiety, to which fuch a violation

Prepares for a vigorous defence.

of so many sacred edifices, as well as of the ashes of the dead, might expose him, he executed this with much religious ceremony. Having ordered all the holy vestments and utensils, together with the bones of the Kings, and other persons deposited in these churches, to be removed, they were carried in solemn procession to a church within the walls, he himself walking before them bare-headed, with a torch in his hand. He then pulled down such houses as stood near the walls, cleared and enlarged the ditch, repaired the ruinous fortifications, and erected new ones. As it was necessary that all these works should be finished with the utmost expedition, he laboured at them with his own hands: the officers and volunteers imitated his example, and the soldiers submitted with cheerfulness to the most severe and fatiguing service, when they saw that their superiors did not decline to bear a part in it. At the same time he compelled all useless persons to leave the place; he filled the magazines with provisions and military stores; he burnt the mills, and destroyed the corn and forage for several miles round the town. Such were his popular talents, as well as his arts of acquiring an ascendant over the minds of men, that the citizens seconded him with no less ardour than the soldiers; and every other passion being swallowed up in the zeal to repulse the enemy, with which he inspired them, they beheld the ruin of their estates, together with the havoc which he made among

among their public and private buildings, without any emotion of resentment[c].

Meantime the Emperor, having collected all his forces, continued his march towards Metz. As he passed through the cities on the Rhine, he saw the dismal effects of that licentious and wasteful war which Albert had carried on in these parts. Upon his approach, that Prince, though at the head of twenty thousand men, withdrew into Lorrain, as if he had intended to join the French King, whose arms he had quartered with his own in all his standards and ensigns. Albert was not in a condition to cope with the Imperial troops[d], which amounted at least to sixty thousand men, forming one of the most numerous and best appointed armies which had been brought into the field during that age, in any of the wars among Christian Princes.

The chief command, under the Emperor, was committed to the Duke of Alva, assisted by the Marquis de Marignano, together with the most experienced of the Italian and Spanish generals. As it was now towards the end of October, these intelligent officers represented the great danger of beginning, at such an advanced season, a siege which could not fail to prove very tedious. But Charles adhered to his own opinion with his usual obstinacy, and being confident that he had made

[c] Thuan. xi. 387.   [d] Natal. Comitis, Hist. 127.

such

such preparations, and taken such precautions, as would ensure success, he ordered the city to be invested. As soon as the Duke of Alva appeared, a large body of the French sallied out and attacked his van-guard with great vigour, put it in confusion, and killed or took prisoners a considerable number of men. By this early specimen which they gave of the conduct of their officers, as well as the valour of their troops, they shewed the Imperialists what an enemy they had to encounter, and how dear every advantage must cost them. The place, however, was completely invested, the trenches were opened, and the other works begun.

<small>Both parties endeavour to gain Albert of Brandenburg.</small>

THE attention both of the besiegers and besieged was turned for some time towards Albert of Brandenburg, and they strove with emulation which should gain that Prince, who still hovered in the neighbourhood, fluctuating in all the uncertainty of irresolution, natural to a man, who, being swayed by no principle, was allured different ways by contrary views of interest. The French tempted him with offers extremely beneficial; the Imperialists scrupled at no promise which they thought might allure him. After much hesitation he was gained by the Emperor, from whom he expected to receive advantages which were both more immediate and more permanent. As the French King, who began to suspect his intentions, had appointed a body of troops under the Duke of Aumale, brother to the Duke

Duke of Guife, to watch his motions, Albert fell upon them unexpectedly with fuch vigour that he routed them entirely, killed many of the officers, wounded Aumale himfelf, and took him prifoner. Immediately after this victory, he marched in triumph to Metz, and joined his army to that of the Emperor. Charles, in reward for this fervice, and the great acceffion of ftrength which he brought him, granted Albert a formal pardon of all paft offences, and confirmed him in the poffeffion of the territories which he had violently ufurped during the war [e].

The Duke of Guife, though deeply affected with his brother's misfortune, did not remit, in any degree, the vigour with which he defended the town. He haraffed the befiegers by frequent fallies, in which his officers were fo eager to diftinguifh themfelves, that his authority being hardly fufficient to reftrain the impetuofity of their courage, he was obliged at different times to fhut the gates, and to conceal the keys, in order to prevent the Princes of the blood, and noblemen of the firft rank, from expofing themfelves to danger in every fally. He repaired in the night what the enemy's artillery had beat down during the day, or erected behind the ruined works new fortifications of almoft equal ftrength. The Imperialifts, on their part, pufhed on the attack with great fpirit, and carried forward, at once,

The gallant behaviour of the Duke of Guife and his garrifon.

[e] Sleid. 575. Thuan. lib. xi. 389. 392.

approaches

approaches against different parts of the town. But the art of attacking fortified places was not then arrived at that degree of perfection to which it was carried towards the close of the sixteenth century, during the long war in the Netherlands. The besiegers, after the unwearied labour of many weeks, found that they had made but little progress; and although their batteries had made breaches in different places, they saw, to their astonishment, works suddenly appear, in demolishing which their fatigues and dangers would be renewed. The Emperor, enraged at the obstinate resistance which his army met with, left Thionville, where he had been confined by a violent fit of the gout, and though still so infirm that he was obliged to be carried in a litter, he repaired to the camp; that, by his presence, he might animate the soldiers, and urge on the attack with greater spirit. Upon his arrival, new batteries were erected, and new efforts were made with redoubled ardour.

The distress of the Imperial army. BUT, by this time, winter had set in with great rigour; the camp was alternately deluged with rain or covered with snow; at the same time provisions were become extremely scarce, as a body of French cavalry which hovered in the neighbourhood, often interrupted the convoys, or rendered their arrival difficult and uncertain. Diseases began to spread among the soldiers, especially among the Italians and Spaniards, unaccustomed to such inclement weather; great numbers

bers were disabled from serving, and many died. At length, such breaches were made as seemed practicable, and Charles resolved to hazard a general assault, in spite of all the remonstrances of his generals against the imprudence of attacking a numerous garrison, conducted and animated by the most gallant of the French nobility, with an army weakened by diseases, and disheartened with ill success. The Duke of Guise, suspecting the Emperor's intentions from the extraordinary movements which he observed in the enemy's camp, ordered all his troops to their respective posts. They appeared immediately on the walls, and behind the breaches, with such a determined countenance, so eager for the combat, and so well prepared to give the assailants a warm reception, that the Imperialists, instead of advancing to the charge when the word of command was given, stood motionless in a timid dejected silence. The Emperor, perceiving that he could not trust troops whose spirits were so much broken, retired abruptly to his quarters, complaining that he was now deserted by his soldiers, who deserved no longer the name of men [f].

Deeply as this behaviour of his troops mortified and affected Charles, he would not hear of abandoning the siege, though he saw the necessity of changing the method of attack. He suspended

[f] Thuan. 397.

the fury of his batteries, and propofed to proceed by the more fecure but tedious method of fapping. But as it ftill continued to rain or to fnow almoft inceffantly, fuch as were employed in this fervice endured incredible hardfhips: and the Duke of Guife, whofe induftry was not inferior to his valour, difcovering all their mines, counterworked them, and prevented their effect. At laft, Charles finding it impoffible to contend any longer with the feverity of the feafon, and with enemies whom he could neither overpower by force, nor fubdue by art, while at the fame time a contagious diftemper raged among his troops, and cut off daily great numbers of the officers as well as foldiers, yielded to the folicitations of his generals, who conjured him to fave the remains of his army by a timely retreat; "Fortune," fays he, "I now perceive, refembles other females, and choofes to confer her favours on young men, while fhe turns her back on thofe who are advanced in years."

Dec. 26. Obliged to raife the fiege.

UPON this, he gave orders immediately to raife the fiege, and fubmitted to the difgrace of abandoning the enterprife, after having continued fifty-fix days before the town, during which time he had loft upwards of thirty thoufand men, who died of difeafes, or were killed by the enemy. The Duke of Guife, as foon as he perceived the intention of the Imperialifts, fent out feveral bodies both of cavalry and infantry to infeft their rear, to pick up ftragglers, and to feize every opportunity of attacking them with advantage. Such was the confusion with which they made their retreat, that the French might have haraffed them in the moft cruel manner. But when they fallied out, a fpectacle prefented itfelf to their view, which extinguifhed at once all hoftile rage, and melted them into tendernefs and compaffion. The Imperial camp was filled with the fick and wounded, with the dead and the dying. In all the different roads by which the army retired, numbers were found, who, having made an effort to efcape, beyond their ftrength, were left, when they could go no farther, to perifh without affiftance. This they received from their enemies, and were indebted to them for all the kind offices which their friends had not the power to perform. The Duke of Guife immediately ordered proper refrefhments for fuch as were dying of hunger; he appointed furgeons to attend the fick and wounded; he removed fuch as could bear it into the adjacent villages; and thofe who would have fuffered by being carried fo far, he admitted into the hofpitals which he had fitted up in the city for his own foldiers. As foon as they recovered, he fent them home under an efcort of foldiers, and with money to bear their charges. By thefe acts of humanity, which were uncommon in that age, when war was carried on with greater rancour and ferocity than at prefent, the Duke of Guife completed the fame which he had acquired by his gallant and fuccefsful defence of Metz, and engaged thofe whom he had vanquifhed

Ruin of the Imperial army, and humanity of the French.

quished to vie with his own countrymen in extolling his name [g].

Bad situation of the Emperor's affairs in Italy.

To these calamities in Germany, were added such unfortunate events in Italy, as rendered this the most disastrous year in the Emperor's life. During his residence at Villach, Charles had applied to Cosmo di Medici for the loan of two hundred thousand crowns. But his credit at that time was so low, that in order to obtain this inconsiderable sum, he was obliged to put him in possession of the principality of Piombino, and by giving up that, he lost the footing which he had hitherto maintained in Tuscany, and enabled Cosmo to assume, for the future, the tone and deportment of a Prince altogether independent. Much about the time that his indigence constrained him to part with this valuable territory, he lost Siena, which was of still greater consequence, through the ill conduct of Don Diego de Mendoza [h].

The revolt of Siena.

SIENA, like most of the great cities in Italy, had long enjoyed a republican government, under the protection of the Empire; but being torn in pieces by the dissentions between the nobility and the people, which divided all the Italian commonwealths, the faction of the people, which gained

---

[g] Sleid. 575. Thuan. lib. xi. 389, &c. Pere Daniel, Hist. de France, tom. iii. 392. Pere Daniel's account of this siege is taken from the journal of the Sieur de Salignac, who was present. Natal. Comit. Hist. 129.

[h] Thuan. lib. xi. 376.

the ascendant, besought the Emperor to become the guardian of the administration which they had established, and admitted into their city a small body of Spanish soldiers, whom he had sent to countenance the execution of the laws, and to preserve tranquillity among them. The command of these troops was given to Mendoza, at that time ambassador for the Emperor at Rome, who persuaded the credulous multitude, that it was necessary for their security against any future attempt of the nobles, to allow him to build a citadel in Siena; and as he flattered himself that by means of this fortress he might render the Emperor master of the city, he pushed on the works with all possible dispatch. But he threw off the mask too soon. Before the fortifications were completed, he began to indulge his natural haughtiness and severity of temper, and to treat the citizens with great insolence. At the same time the soldiers in garrison being paid as irregularly as the Emperor's troops usually were, lived almost at discretion upon the inhabitants, and were guilty of many acts of licence and oppression.

These injuries awakened the Sienese to a sense of their danger. As they saw the necessity of exerting themselves, while the unfinished fortifications of the citadel left them any hopes of success, they applied to the French ambassador at Rome, who readily promised them his master's protection and assistance. At the same time, for-

The Sienese court the assistance of France.

getting

getting their domestic animosities when such a mortal blow was aimed at the liberty and existence of the republic, they sent agents to the exiled nobles, and invited them to concur with them in saving their country from the servitude with which it was threatened. As there was not a moment to lose, measures were concerted speedily, but with great prudence; and were executed with equal vigour. The citizens rose suddenly in arms; the exiles flocked into the town from different parts with all their partisans, and what troops they could draw together; and several bodies of mercenaries in the pay of France appeared to support them. The Spaniards, though surprised, and much inferior in number, defended themselves with great courage; but seeing no prospect of relief, and having no hopes of maintaining their station long in a half-finished fortress, they soon gave it up. The Sienese, with the utmost alacrity, levelled it with the ground, that no monument might remain of that odious structure, which had been raised in order to enslave them. At the same time renouncing all connexion with the Emperor, they sent ambassadors to thank the king of France as the restorer of their liberty, and to entreat that he would secure to them the perpetual enjoyment of that blessing, by continuing his protection to their republic [i].

[i] Pecci Memorie de Siena, vol. iii. p. 230. 261. Thuan. 375. 377, &c. Paruta. Hist. Venet. 267. Mem. de Ribier, 424, &c.

To these misfortunes, one still more fatal had almost succeeded. The severe administration of Don Pedro de Toledo, viceroy of Naples, having filled that kingdom with murmuring and disaffection, the Prince of Salerno, the head of the malecontents, had fled to the court of France, where all who bore ill-will to the Emperor or his ministers were sure of finding protection and assistance. That nobleman, in the usual style of exiles, boasting much of the number and power of his partisans, and of his great influence with them, prevailed on Henry to think of invading Naples, from an expectation of being joined by all those with whom the Prince of Salerno held correspondence, or who were dissatisfied with Toledo's government. But though the first hint of this enterprise was suggested by the Prince of Salerno, Henry did not choose that its success should entirely depend upon his being able to fulfil the promises which he had made. He applied for aid to Solyman, whom he courted, after his father's example, as his most vigorous auxiliary against the Emperor, and solicited him to second his operations, by sending a powerful fleet into the Mediterranean. It was not difficult to obtain what he requested of the Sultan, who, at this time, was highly incensed against the house of Austria, on account of the proceedings in Hungary. He ordered an hundred and fifty ships to be equipped, that they might sail towards the coast of Naples, at whatever time Henry should name, and might co-operate with the French troops in their attempts upon that kingdom.

dom. The command of this fleet was given to the corsair Dragut, an officer trained up under Barbarossa, and scarcely inferior to his master in courage, in talents, or in good fortune. He appeared on the coast of Calabria at the time which had been agreed on, landed at several places, plundered and burnt several villages; and at last, casting anchor in the bay of Naples, filled that city with consternation. But as the French fleet, detained by some accident, which the contemporary historians have not explained, did not join the Turks according to concert, they, after waiting twenty days, without hearing any tidings of it, set sail for Constantinople, and thus delivered the viceroy of Naples from the terror of an invasion which he was not in a condition to have resisted [k].

1553. The Emperor sensibly affected with the state of his affairs.

As the French had never given so severe a check to the Emperor in any former campaign, they expressed immoderate joy at the success of their arms. Charles himself, accustomed to a long series of prosperity, felt the calamity most sensibly, and retired from Metz into the Low-Countries, much dejected with the cruel reverse of fortune which affected him in his declining age, when the violence of the gout had increased to such a pitch, as entirely broke the vigour of his constitution, and rendered him peevish, difficult of access, and often incapable of applying to

[k] Thuan. 375 380. Mem. de Ribier, ii. 403. Gianone.

business.

business. But whenever he enjoyed any interval of ease, all his thoughts were bent on revenge; and he deliberated, with the greatest solicitude, concerning the most proper means of annoying France, and of effacing the stain which had obscured the reputation and glory of his arms. All the schemes concerning Germany, which had engrossed him so long, being disconcerted by the peace of Passau, the affairs of the empire became only secondary objects of attention; and enmity to France was the predominant passion which chiefly occupied his mind.

The turbulent ambition of Albert of Brandenburg excited violent commotions, which disturbed the Empire during this year. That Prince's troops having shared in the calamities of the siege of Metz, were greatly reduced in number. But the Emperor, prompted by gratitude for his distinguished services on that occasion, or perhaps with a secret view of fomenting divisions among the Princes of the Empire, having paid up all the money due to him, he was enabled with that sum to hire so many of the soldiers dismissed from the Imperial army, that he was soon at the head of a body of men as numerous as ever. The bishops of Bamberg and Wurtzburg having solicited the Imperial chamber to annul, by its authority, the iniquitous conditions which Albert had compelled them to sign, that court unanimously found all their engagements with him to be void in their own nature, because they had

The violent proceedings of Albert of Brandenburg.

BOOK XI.

1553.

been extorted by force; enjoined Albert to renounce all claim to the performance of them; and, if he should persist in such an unjust demand, exhorted all the Princes of the Empire to take arms against him as a disturber of the public tranquillity. To this decision, Albert opposed the confirmation of his transactions with the two prelates, which the Emperor had granted him as the reward of his having joined the Imperial army at Metz; and in order to intimidate his antagonists, as well as to convince them of his resolution not to relinquish his pretensions, he put his troops in motion, that he might secure the territory in question. Various endeavours were employed, and many expedients proposed, in order to prevent the kindling a new war in Germany. But the same warmth of temper which rendered Albert turbulent and enterprizing, inspiring him with the most sanguine hopes of success, even in his wildest undertakings, he disdainfully rejected all reasonable overtures of accommodation.

He is condemned by the Imperial chamber.

Upon this, the Imperial chamber issued its decree against him, and required the Elector of Saxony, together with several other Princes mentioned by name, to take arms in order to carry it into execution. Maurice, and those associated with him, were not unwilling to undertake this service. They were extremely solicitous to maintain public order by supporting the authority of the Imperial chamber, and saw the necessity of

giving

giving a timely check to the usurpations of an ambitious Prince, who had no principle of action but regard to his own interest, and no motive to direct him but the impulse of ungovernable passions. They had good reason to suspect, that the Emperor encouraged Albert in his extravagant and irregular proceedings, and secretly afforded him assistance, that, by raising him up to rival Maurice in power, he might, in any future broil, make use of his assistance to counterbalance and control the authority which the other had acquired in the Empire [1].

THESE considerations united the most powerful Princes in Germany in a league against Albert, of which Maurice was declared generalissimo. This formidable confederacy, however, wrought no change in Albert's sentiments; but as he knew that he could not resist so many Princes, if he should allow them time to assemble their forces, he endeavoured, by his activity, to deprive them of all the advantages which they might derive from their united power and numbers; and for that reason marched directly against Maurice, the enemy whom he dreaded most. It was happy for the allies that the conduct of their affairs was committed to a Prince of such abilities. He, by his authority and example, had inspired them with vigour; and having carried on their preparations

April 2. A confederacy formed against him, of which Maurice was head.

---

[1] Sleid. 585. Mem. de Ribier, ii. 442. Arnoldi vita Maurit. ap. Menken, ii. 1242.

BOOK XI.
1553.

with a degree of rapidity of which confederate bodies are feldom capable, he was in condition to face Albert before he could make any confiderable progrefs.

He attacks Albert,

THEIR armies, which were nearly equal in number, each confifting of twenty-four thoufand men, met at Sieverhaufen, in the duchy of Lunenburgh; and the violent animofity againft each other, which poffeffed the two leaders, did not fuffer them to continue long inactive. The troops, inflamed with the fame hoftile rage, marched fiercely to the combat; they fought with the greateft obftinacy; and as both generals were capable of availing themfelves of every favourable occurrence, the battle remained long doubtful, each gaining ground upon the other alternately. At laft victory declared for Maurice, who was fuperior in cavalry, and Albert's army fled in confufion, leaving four thoufand dead in the field, and their camp, baggage, and artillery, in the hands of the conquerors. The allies bought their victory dear, their beft troops fuffered greatly, two fons of the Duke of Brunfwick, a Duke of Lunenburgh, and many other perfons of diftinction, were among the number of the flain [m]. But all thefe were foon forgotten; for Maurice himfelf, as he led up to a fecond charge a body of horfe which had been broken, receiv-

June 9.

and defeats his army;

but is killed in the battle.

[m] Hiftoria pugnæ infelicis inter Maurit. & Albert. Thom. Wintzero auctore apud Scard. ii. 559. Sleid. 583. Rufcelli epiftres aux Princes, 154. Arnoldi vita Maurit. 1245.

ed

EMPEROR CHARLES V.

ed a wound with a piftol-bullet in the belly, of which he died two days after the battle, in the thirty-fecond year of his age, and in the fixth after his attaining the electoral dignity.

Of all the perfonages who have appeared in the hiftory of this active age, when great occurrences and fudden revolutions called forth extraordinary talents to view, and afforded them full opportunity to difplay themfelves, Maurice may juftly be confidered as the moft remarkable. If his exorbitant ambition, his profound diffimulation, and his unwarrantable ufurpation of his kinfman's honours and dominions, exclude him from being praifed as a virtuous man; his prudence in concerting his meafures, his vigour in executing them, and the uniform fuccefs with which they were attended, entitle him to the appellation of a great Prince. At an age when impetuofity of fpirit commonly predominates over political wifdom, when the higheft effort even of a genius of the firft order is to fix on a bold fcheme, and to execute it with promptitude and courage, he formed and conducted an intricate plan of policy, which deceived the moft artful Monarch in Europe. At the very juncture when the Emperor had attained to almoft unlimited defpotifm, Maurice, with power feemingly inadequate to fuch an undertaking, compelled him to relinquifh all his ufurpations, and eftablifhed not only the religious but civil liberties of Germany on fuch foundations as have hitherto remained

mained unshaken. Although, at one period of his life, his conduct excited the jealousy of the Protestants, and at another drew on him the resentment of the Roman Catholics, such was his masterly address, that he was the only Prince of the age who, in any degree, possessed the confidence of both, and whom both lamented as the most able as well as faithful guardian of the constitution and laws of his country.

Albert continues the war.

THE consternation which Maurice's death occasioned among his troops, prevented them from making the proper improvement of the victory which they had gained. Albert, whose active courage, and profuse liberality, rendered him the darling of such military adventurers as were little solicitous about the justice of his cause, soon reassembled his broken forces, and made fresh levies with such success, that he was quickly at the head of fifteen thousand men, and renewed his depredations with additional fury. But Henry of Brunswick having taken the command of the allied troops, defeated him in a second battle, scarcely less bloody than the former. Even then his courage did not sink, nor were his resources exhausted. He made several efforts, and some of them very vigorous, to retrieve his affairs: But being laid under the ban of the Empire by the Imperial chamber; being driven by degrees out of all his hereditary territories, as well as those which he had usurped; being forsaken by many of his officers, and overpowered by the number

Sept. 12.

number of his enemies, he fled for refuge into France. After having been, for a considerable time, the terror and scourge of Germany, he lingered out some years in an indigent and dependent state of exile, the miseries of which his restless and arrogant spirit endured with the most indignant impatience. Upon his death without issue, his territories, which had been seized by the Princes who took arms against him, were restored, by a decree of the Emperor, to his collateral heirs of the house of Brandenburgh [n].

1553: He is driven out of Germany.

January 12, 1557.

MAURICE having left only one daughter, who was afterwards married to William Prince of Orange, by whom she had a son who bore his grandfather's name, and inherited the great talents for which he was conspicuous, a violent dispute arose concerning the succession to his honours and territories. John Frederick, the degraded elector, claimed the electoral dignity, and that part of his patrimonial estate of which he had been violently stripped after the Smalkaldick war. Augustus, Maurice's only brother, pleaded his right not only to the hereditary possessions of their family, but to the electoral dignity, and to the territories which Maurice had acquired. As Augustus was a Prince of considerable abilities, as well as of great candour and gentleness of manners, the states of Saxony, forgetting the merits and sufferings of their for-

Maurice's brother Augustus succeeds him in the electoral dignity.

[n] Sleid. 592. 594. 599. Struv. Corp. Hist. Germ. 1075.

mer

mer master, declared warmly in his favour. His pretensions were powerfully supported by the King of Denmark, whose daughter he had married, and zealously espoused by the King of the Romans, out of regard to Maurice's memory. The degraded Elector, though secretly favoured by his ancient enemy the Emperor, was at last obliged to relinquish his claim, upon obtaining a small addition to the territories which had been allotted to him, together with a stipulation, securing to his family the eventual succession, upon a failure of male heirs in the Albertine line. That unfortunate, but magnanimous Prince, died next year, soon after ratifying this treaty of agreement; and the electoral dignity is still possessed by the descendants of Augustus[o].

Hostilities in the Low-Countries.

DURING these transactions in Germany, war was carried on in the Low-Countries with considerable vigour. The Emperor, impatient to efface the stain which his ignominious repulse at Metz left upon his military reputation, had an army early in the field, and laid siege to Terouane. Though the town was of such importance, that Francis used to call it one of the two pillars on which a King of France might sleep with security, the fortifications were in bad repair: Henry, trusting to what had happened at Metz, thought nothing more was necessary to render all the efforts of the enemy abortive, than to reinforce the gar-

[o] Sleid. 587. Thuan. 409. Struv. Corp. Hist. Germ.

rifon with a confiderable number of the young nobility. But d'Efsè, a veteran officer who commanded them, being killed, and the Imperialifts pufhing the fiege with great vigour and perfeverance, the place was taken by affault. That it might not fall again into the hands of the French, Charles ordered not only the fortifications but the town itfelf to be rafed, and the inhabitants to be difperfed in the adjacent cities. Elated with this fuccefs, the Imperialifts immediately invefted Hefdin, which, though defended with great bravery, was likewife taken by affault, and fuch of the garrifon as efcaped the fword were made prifoners. The Emperor entrufted the conduct of this fiege to Emanuel Philibert of Savoy, Prince of Piedmont, who, on that occafion, gave the firft difplay of thofe great talents for military command, which foon entitled him to be ranked among the firft generals of the age, and facilitated his reeftablifhment in his hereditary dominions, the greater part of which having been over-run by Francis in his expeditions into Italy, were ftill retained by Henry [p].

THE lofs of thefe towns, together with fo many perfons of diftinction, either killed or taken by the enemy, was no inconfiderable calamity to France, and Henry felt it very fenfibly; but he was ftill more mortified at the Emperor's having recovered his wonted fuperiority in the field fo foon

The progrefs of the Imperialifts difquiets the French King.

[p] Thuan. 411. Haræi Annales Brabant. 669.

after

after the blow at Metz, which the French had represented as fatal to his power. He was ashamed too, of his own remissness and excessive security at the opening of the campaign; and in order to repair that error, he assembled a numerous army, and led it into the Low-Countries.

Roused at the approach of such a formidable enemy, Charles left Brussels, where he had been shut up so closely during seven months, that it came to be believed in many parts of Europe that he was dead; and though he was so much debilitated by the gout that he could hardly bear the motion of a litter, he hastened to join his army. The eyes of all Europe were turned with expectation towards those mighty and exasperated rivals, between whom a decisive battle was now thought unavoidable. But Charles having prudently declined to hazard a general engagement, and the violence of the autumnal rains rendering it impossible for the French to undertake any siege, they retired, without having performed any thing suitable to the great preparations which they had made [q].

The Imperialists unsuccessful in Italy.

The Imperial arms were not attended with the same success in Italy. The narrowness of the Emperor's finances seldom allowed him to act with vigour in two different places at the same time; and having exerted himself to the utmost in order

[q] Haræus, 672. Thuan. 414.

to make a great effort in the Low-Countries, his operations on the other ſide of the Alps were proportionally feeble. The viceroy of Naples, in conjunction with Coſmo di Medici, who was greatly alarmed at the introduction of French troops into Siena, endeavoured to become maſter of that city. But, inſtead of reducing the Sieneſe, the Imperialiſts were obliged to retire abruptly, in order to defend their own country, upon the appearance of the Turkiſh fleet, which threatened the coaſt of Naples; and the French not only eſtabliſhed themſelves more firmly in Tuſcany, but, by the aſſiſtance of the Turks, conquered a great part of the iſland of Corſica, ſubject at that time to the Genoeſe[r].

and in Hungary,

The affairs of the houſe of Auſtria declined no leſs in Hungary during the courſe of this year. As the troops which Ferdinand kept in Tranſylvania received their pay very irregularly, they lived almoſt at diſcretion upon the inhabitants; and their inſolence and rapaciouſneſs greatly diſguſted all ranks of men, and alienated them from their new ſovereign, who, inſtead of protecting, plundered his ſubjects. Their indignation at this, added to their deſire of revenging Martinuzzi's death, wrought ſo much upon a turbulent nobility impatient of injury, and upon a fierce people prone to change, that they were ripe for a revolt. At that very juncture, their

[r] Thuan. 417

late

late Queen Isabella, together with her son, appeared in Transylvania. Her ambitious mind could not bear the solitude and inactivity of a private life; and repenting quickly of the cession which she had made of the crown in the year one thousand five hundred and fifty-one, she left the place of her retreat, hoping that the dissatisfaction of the Hungarians with the Austrian government would prompt them once more to recognise her son's right to the crown. Some noblemen of great eminence declared immediately in his favour. The Basha of Belgrade, by Solyman's order, espoused his cause, in opposition to Ferdinand; the Spanish and German soldiers, instead of advancing against the enemy, mutinied for want of pay, declaring that they would march back to Vienna; so that Castaldo, their general, was obliged to abandon Transylvania to Isabella and the Turks, and to place himself at the head of the mutineers, that by his authority he might restrain them from plundering the Austrian territories through which they passed[s].

Solyman's domestic distresses.

FERDINAND's attention was turned so entirely towards the affairs of Germany, and his treasures so much exhausted by his late efforts in Hungary, that he made no attempt to recover this valuable province, although a favourable opportunity for that purpose presented itself, as Solyman was then engaged in a war with Persia, and involved be-

[s] Thuan. 430.

fides in domestic calamities which engrossed and disturbed his mind. Solyman, though distinguished by many accomplishments from the other Ottoman Princes, had all the passions peculiar to that violent and haughty race. He was jealous of his authority, sudden as well as furious in his anger, and susceptible of all that rage and love, which reigns in the East, and often produces the wildest and most tragical effects. His favourite mistress was a Circassian slave of exquisite beauty, who bore him a son called Mustapha, whom, both on account of his birth-right and his merit, he destined to be the heir of his crown. Roxalana, a Russian captive, soon supplanted the Circassian, and gained the Sultan's heart. Having the address to retain the conquest which she had made, she kept possession of his love without any rival for many years, during which she brought him several sons and one daughter. All the happiness, however, which she derived from the unbounded sway that she had acquired over a monarch whom one half of the world revered or dreaded, was embittered by perpetual reflections on Mustapha's accession to the throne, and the certain death of her sons, who, she foresaw, would be immediately sacrificed, according to the barbarous jealousy of Turkish policy, to the safety of the new Emperor. By dwelling continually on this melancholy idea, she came gradually to view Mustapha as the enemy of her children, and to hate him with more than a stepmother's ill-will. This prompted her to wish his destruc-

BOOK XI.

1553.

The tragical history of his son Mustapha.

deftruction, in order to fecure for one of her own fons the throne which was deftined for him. Nor did fhe want either ambition to attempt fuch a high enterprize, or the arts requifite for carrying it into execution. Having prevailed on the Sultan to give her only daughter in marriage to Ruftan the Grand Vifier, fhe difclofed her fcheme to that crafty minifter, who perceiving that it was his own intereft to co-operate with her, readily promifed his affiftance towards aggrandizing that branch of the royal line to which he was fo nearly allied.

As foon as Roxalana had concerted her meafures with this able confident, fhe began to affect a wonderful zeal for the Mahometan religion, to which Solyman was fuperftitioufly attached, and propofed to found and endow a royal mofque, a work of great expence, but deemed by the Turks meritorious in the higheft degree. The Mufti whom fhe confulted, approved much of her pious intention; but, having been gained and inftructed by Ruftan, told her, that fhe being a flave could derive no benefit herfelf from that holy deed, for all the merit of it would accrue to Solyman, the mafter whofe property fhe was. Upon this fhe feemed to be overwhelmed with forrow, and to fink into the deepeft melancholy, as if fhe had been difgufted with life and all its enjoyments. Solyman, who was abfent with the army, being informed of this dejection of mind, and of the caufe from which it proceeded, difcovered

covered all the solicitude of a lover to remove it, and by a writing under his hand declared her a free woman. Roxalana having gained this point, proceeded to build the mosque, and re-assumed her usual gaiety of spirit. But when Solyman, on his return to Constantinople, sent an eunuch, according to the custom of the seraglio, to bring her to partake of his bed, she, seemingly with deep regret, but in the most peremptory manner, declined to follow the eunuch, declaring that what had been an honour to her while a slave, became a crime as she was now a free woman, and that she would not involve either the Sultan or herself in the guilt that must be contracted by such an open violation of the law of their prophet. Solyman, whose passion this difficulty, as well as the affected delicacy which gave rise to it, heightened and inflamed, had recourse immediately to the Mufti for his direction. He replied, agreeably to the Koran, that Roxalana's scruples were well founded; but added, artfully, in words which Rustan had taught him to use, that it was in the Sultan's power to remove these difficulties, by espousing her as his lawful wife. The amorous monarch closed eagerly with the proposal, and solemnly married her, according to the form of the Mahometan ritual; though, by doing so, he disregarded a maxim of policy which the pride of the Ottoman blood had taught all the Sultans since Bajazet I. to consider as inviolable. From his time, none of the Turkish monarchs had married, because, when he was vanquished and taken

taken prisoner by Tamerlane, his wife had been abused with barbarous insolence by the Tartars. That no similar calamity might again subject the Ottoman family to the same disgrace, the Sultans admitted none to their beds but slaves, whose dishonour could not bring any such stain upon their house.

But the more uncommon the step was, the more it convinced Roxalana, of the unbounded influence which she had acquired over the Sultan's heart; and emboldened her to prosecute, with greater hope of success, the scheme that she had formed in order to destroy Mustapha. This young Prince having been entrusted by his father, according to the practice of the Sultans in that age, with the government of several different provinces, was at that time invested with the administration in Diarbequir, the ancient Mesopotamia, which Solyman had wrested from the Persians, and added to his empire. In all these different commands, Mustapha had conducted himself with such cautious prudence as could give no offence to his father, though, at the same time, he governed with so much moderation as well as justice, and displayed such valour and generosity, as rendered him equally the favourite of the people and the darling of the soldiery.

There was no room to lay any folly or vice to his charge, that could impair the high opinion which his father entertained of him. Roxalana's male-

malevolence was more refined; fhe turned his virtues againft him, and made ufe of thefe as engines for his deftruction. She often mentioned, in Solyman's prefence, the fplendid qualities of his fon; fhe celebrated his courage, his liberality, his popular arts, with malicious and exaggerated praife. As foon as fhe perceived that the Sultan heard thefe encomiums, which were often repeated, with uneafinefs; that fufpicion of his fon began to mingle itfelf with his former efteem; and that by degrees he came to view him with jealoufy and fear; fhe introduced, as by accident, fome difcourfe concerning the rebellion of his father Selim againft Bajazet his grandfather: fhe took notice of the bravery of the veteran troops under Muftapha's command, and of the neighbourhood of Diarbequir to the territories of the Perfian Sophi, Solyman's mortal enemy. By thefe arts, whatever remained of paternal tendernefs was gradually extinguifhed, and fuch paffions were kindled in the breaft of the Sultan, as gave all Roxalana's malignant fuggeftions the colour not only of probability but of truth. His fufpicions and fear of Muftapha fettled into deep-rooted hatred. He appointed fpies to obferve and report all his words and actions; he watched and ftood on his guard againft him as his moft dangerous enemy.

Having thus alienated the Sultan's heart from Muftapha, Roxalana ventured upon another ftep. She

She entreated Solyman to allow her own sons the liberty of appearing at court, hoping that by gaining access to their father, they might, by their good qualities and dutiful deportment, insinuate themselves into that place in his affections which Mustapha had formerly held; and, though what she demanded was contrary to the practice of the Ottoman family in that age, the uxorious monarch granted her request. To all these female intrigues Rustan added an artifice still more subtle, which completed the Sultan's delusion, and heightened his jealousy and fear. He wrote to the Bashaws of the provinces adjacent to Diarbequir, instructing them to send him regular intelligence of Mustapha's proceedings in his government, and to each of them he gave a private hint, flowing in appearance from his zeal for their interest, that nothing would be more acceptable to the Sultan than to receive favourable accounts of a son whom he destined to sustain the glory of the Ottoman name. The Bashaws, ignorant of his fraudulent intention, and eager to pay court to their sovereign at such an easy price, filled their letters with studied but fatal panegyrics of Mustapha, representing him as a Prince worthy to succeed such an illustrious father, and as endowed with talents which might enable him to emulate, perhaps to equal, his fame. These letters were industriously shewn to Solyman, at the seasons when it was known that they would make the deepest impression. Every expression

expreſſion in recommendation of his ſon wounded him to the heart; he ſuſpected his principal officers of being ready to favour the moſt deſperate attempts of a Prince whom they were ſo fond of praiſing; and fancying that he ſaw them already aſſaulting his throne with rebellious arms, he determined, while it was yet in his power, to anticipate the blow, and to ſecure his own ſafety by his ſon's death.

For this purpoſe, though under pretence of renewing the war againſt Perſia, he ordered Ruſtan to march towards Diarbequir at the head of a numerous army, and to rid him of a ſon whoſe life he deemed inconſiſtent with his own ſafety. But that crafty miniſter did not chooſe to be loaded with the odium of having executed this cruel order. As ſoon as he arrived in Syria he wrote to Solyman, that the danger was ſo imminent as called for his immediate preſence; that the camp was full of Muſtapha's emiſſaries; that many of the ſoldiers were corrupted; that the affections of all leaned towards him; that he had diſcovered a negociation which had been carried on with the Sophi of Perſia in order to marry Muſtapha with one of his daughters; that he already felt his own talents as well as authority to be inadequate to the exigencies of ſuch an arduous conjuncture; that the Sultan alone had ſagacity to diſcern what reſolution ſhould be taken in thoſe circumſtances, and power to carry that reſolution into execution.

This charge of courting the friendship of the Sophi, Roxalana and Ruftan had referved as the laft and moft envenomed of all their calumnies. It operated with the violence which they expected from Solyman's inveterate abhorrence of the Perfians, and threw him into the wildeft tranfports of rage. He fet out inftantly for Syria, and haftened thither with all the precipitation and impatience of fear and revenge. As foon as he joined his army near Aleppo, and had concerted meafures with Ruftan, he fent a Chiaus, or meffenger of the court, to his fon, requiring him to repair immediately to his prefence. Muftapha, though no ftranger to his ftep-mother's machinations, or to Ruftan's malice, or to his father's violent temper, yet relying on his own innocence, and hoping to difcredit the accufations of his enemies by the promptitude of his obedience, followed the meffenger without delay to Aleppo. The moment he arrived in the camp, he was introduced into the Sultan's tent. As he entered it, he obferved nothing that could give him any alarm; no additional crowd of attendants, no body of armed guards, but the fame order and filence which always reign in the Sultan's apartments. In a few minutes, however, feveral mutes appeared, at the fight of whom Muftapha, knowing what was his doom, cried with a loud voice, " Lo, my death!" and attempted to fly. The mutes rufhed forward to feize him; he refifted and ftruggled, demanding with the utmoft earneftnefs to fee the Sultan; and defpair, together with

with the hope of finding protection from the foldiers, if he could escape out of the tent, animated him with such extraordinary strength, that, for some time, he baffled all the efforts of the executioners. Solyman was within hearing of his son's cries, as well as of the noise which the struggle occasioned. Impatient of this delay of his revenge, and struck with terror at the thoughts of Mustapha's escaping, he drew aside the curtain which divided the tent, and thrusting in his head, darted a fierce look towards the mutes, and, with wild and threatening gestures, seemed to condemn their sloth and timidity. At sight of his father's furious and unrelenting countenance, Mustapha's strength failed, and his courage forsook him; the mutes fastened the bow-string about his neck, and in a moment put an end to his life.

The dead body was exposed before the Sultan's tent. The soldiers gathered round it, and contemplating that mournful object with astonishment, and sorrow, and indignation, were ready, if a leader had not been wanting, to have broke out into the wildest excesses of rage. After giving vent to the first expressions of their grief, they retired each man to his tent, and shutting themselves up, bewailed in secret the cruel fate of their favourite; nor was there one of them who tasted food, or even water, during the remainder of that day. Next morning the same solitude and silence reigned in the camp; and Solyman, being afraid that some dreadful storm would follow this

sullen

sullen calm, in order to appease the enraged soldiers, deprived Rustan of the seals, ordered him to leave the camp, and raised Achmet, a gallant officer much beloved in the army, to the dignity of Visier. This change, however, was made in concert with Rustan himself; that crafty minister suggesting it as the only expedient which could save himself or his master. But within a few months, when the resentment of the soldiers began to subside, and the name of Mustapha to be forgotten, Achmet was strangled by the Sultan's command, and Rustan reinstated in the office of Visier. Together with his former power, he reassumed the plan for exterminating the race of Mustapha which he had concerted with Roxalana; and as they were afraid that an only son whom Mustapha had left, might grow up to avenge his death, they redoubled their activity, and by employing the same arts against him which they had practised against his father, they inspired Solyman with the same fears, and prevailed on him to issue orders for putting to death that young innocent Prince. These orders were executed with barbarous zeal, by an eunuch, who was dispatched to Bursa, the place where the Prince resided; and no rival was left to dispute the Ottoman throne with the sons of Roxalana[t].

[t] Augerii Gislenii Busbequii Legationis Turcicæ Epistolæ iv. Franc. 1615. p. 37. Thuan. lib. 12. p. 432. Mem. de Ribier, ii. 457. Maurocenii Histor. Veneta, lib. vii. p. 60.

SUCH

Such tragical scenes, productive of so deep distress, seldom occur but in the history of the great monarchies of the East, where the warmth of the climate seems to give every emotion of the heart its greatest force, and the absolute power of sovereigns accustoms and enables them to gratify all their passions without controul. While this interesting transaction in the court of Solyman engaged his whole attention, Charles was pursuing, with the utmost ardour, a new scheme for aggrandizing his family. About this time, Edward the Sixth of England, after a short reign, in which he displayed such virtues as filled his subjects with sanguine hopes of being happy under his government, and made them bear with patience all that they suffered from the weakness, the dissensions, and the ambition of the ministers who assumed the administration during his minority, was seized with a lingering distemper which threatened his life. The Emperor no sooner received an account of this, than his ambition, always attentive to seize every opportunity of acquiring an increase of power, or of territories, to his son, suggested the thought of adding England to his other kingdoms, by the marriage of Philip with the Princess Mary, the heir of Edward's crown. Being apprehensive however, that his son, who was then in Spain, might decline a match with a Princess in her thirty-eighth year, and eleven years older than himself[u]; Charles determined

1553. Charles projects a marriage between his son and Mary of England.

[u] Palav. Hist. Concil. Trid. v. ii. c. 13. p. 150.

notwith-

BOOK XI.

1553.

To which Philip gives his confent.

notwithstanding his own age and infirmities, to make offer of himself as a husband to his cousin.

The sentiments of Mary and of the English with regard to it.

But though Mary was so far advanced in years, and destitute of every charm either of person or of manners that could win affection, or command esteem, Philip, without hesitation, gave his consent to the match proposed by his father, and was willing, according to the usual maxim of Princes, to sacrifice his inclination to his ambition. In order to ensure the success of his scheme, the Emperor, even before Edward's death, began to take such steps as might facilitate it. Upon Edward's demise, Mary mounted the throne of England; the pretensions of the lady Jane Gray proving as unfortunate as they were ill founded[x]. Charles sent immediately a pompous embassy to London to congratulate Mary on her accession to the throne, and to propose the alliance with his son. The Queen, dazzled with the prospect of marrying the heir of the greatest Monarch in Europe; fond of uniting more closely with her mother's family, to which she had been always warmly attached; and eager to secure the powerful aid which she knew would be necessary towards carrying on her favourite scheme of re-establishing the Romish religion in England, listened in the most favourable manner to the proposal. Among her subjects, it met with a very different reception. Philip, it was well known, contended for

[x] Carte's Hist. of England, iii. 287.

all the tenets of the church of Rome with a fan-guinary zeal which exceeded the meafure even of Spanifh bigotry: this alarmed all the numerous partifans of the Reformation. The Caftilian haughtinefs and referve were far from being acceptable to the Englifh, who, having feveral times feen their throne occupied by perfons who were born fubjects, had become accuftomed to an unceremonious and familiar intercourfe with their fovereigns. They could not think, without the utmoft uneafinefs, of admitting a foreign Prince to that influence in their councils, which the hufband of their Queen would naturally poffefs. They dreaded, both from Philip's overbearing temper, and from the maxims of the Spanifh monarchy which he had imbibed, that he would infufe ideas into the Queen's mind, dangerous to the liberties of the nation, and would introduce foreign troops and money into the kingdom, to affift her in any attempt againft them.

FULL of thefe apprehenfions, the Houfe of Commons, though in that age extremely obfequious to the will of their Monarchs, prefented a warm addrefs againft the Spanifh match; many pamphlets were publifhed, reprefenting the dangerous confequences of the alliance with Spain, and defcribing Philip's bigotry and arrogance in the moft odious colours. But Mary, inflexible in all her refolutions, paid no regard to the remonftrances of her Commons, or to the fentiments

The Houfe of Commons remonftrate againft it.

ments of the people. The Emperor, having secured, by various arts, the ministers whom she trusted most, they approved warmly of the match, and large sums were remitted by him in order to gain the rest of the council. Cardinal Pole, whom the Pope, immediately upon Mary's accession, had dispatched as his legate into England, in order to reconcile his native country to the see of Rome, was detained by the Emperor's command at Dillinghen in Germany, lest by his presence he should thwart Philip's pretensions, and employ his interest in favour of his kinsman Courtnay Earl of Devonshire, whom the English ardently wished their sovereign to choose for a husband [y].

The marriage treaty concluded,

As the negociation did not admit of delay, it was carried forward with the greatest rapidity, the Emperor agreeing, without hesitation, to every article in favour of England, which Mary's ministers either represented as necessary to soothe the people and reconcile them to the match, or that was suggested by their own fears and jealousy of a foreign master. The chief articles were, that Philip, during his marriage with the Queen, should bear the title of King of England, but the entire administration of affairs, as well as the sole disposal of all revenues, offices, and benefices, should remain with the Queen; that the heirs of the marriage should, together with the crown of

1554. January 12.

[y] Carte, iii. 288.

England,

England, inherit the dutchy of Burgundy and the Low-Countries; that if Prince Charles, Philip's only son by a former marriage, should die without issue, his children by the Queen, whether male or female, should succeed to the crown of Spain, and all the Emperor's hereditary dominions; that, before the consummation of the marriage, Philip should swear solemnly, that he would retain no domestic who was not a subject of the Queen, and would bring no foreigners into the kingdom that might give umbrage to the English; that he would make no alteration in the constitution or laws of England; that he would not carry the Queen, or any of the children born of this marriage, out of the kingdom; that if the Queen should die before him without issue, he would immediately leave the crown to the lawful heir, without claiming any right of administration whatever; that in consequence of this marriage, England should not be engaged in any war subsisting between France and Spain; and that the alliance between France and England should remain in full force [z].

But this treaty, though both the Emperor and Mary's ministers employed their utmost address in framing it so as to please the English, was far from quieting their fears and jealousies. They saw that words and promises were a feeble secu-

[z] Rymer's Fœd. vol. xv. 377. 393. Mem. de Ribier, ii. 498.

rity against the encroachments of an ambitious Prince, who, as soon as he got possession of the power and advantages which the Queen's husband must necessarily enjoy, could easily evade any of the articles which either limited his authority or obstructed his schemes. They were convinced that the more favourable the conditions of the present treaty were to England, the more Philip would be tempted hereafter to violate them. They dreaded that England, like Naples, Milan, and the other countries annexed to Spain, would soon feel the dominion of that crown to be intolerably oppressive, and be constrained, as they had been, to waste its wealth and vigour in wars wherein it had no interest, and from which it could derive no advantage. These sentiments prevailed so generally, that every part of the kingdom was filled with discontent at the match, and with indignation against the advisers of it.

Wyat's insurrection. Sir Thomas Wyat, a gentleman of some note, and of good intentions towards the public, took advantage of this, and roused the inhabitants of Kent to arms, in order to save their country from a foreign yoke. Great numbers resorted in a short time to his standard; he marched to London with such rapidity, and the Queen was so utterly unprovided for defence, that the aspect of affairs was extremely threatening; and if any nobleman of distinction had joined the malecontents, or had Wyat possessed talents equal, in any degree, to the boldness of his enterprize, the insurrection must have proved fatal to Mary's power. But

But all Wyat's measures were concerted with so little prudence, and executed with such irresolution, that many of his followers forsook him; the rest were dispersed by an handful of soldiers; and he himself was taken prisoner, without having made any effort worthy of the cause that he had undertaken, or suitable to the ardour with which he engaged in it. He suffered the punishment due to his rashness and rebellion. The Queen's authority was confirmed and increased by her success in defeating this inconsiderate attempt to abridge it. The lady Jane Gray, whose title the ambition of her relations had set up in opposition to that of the Queen, was, notwithstanding her youth and innocence, brought to the scaffold. The lady Elizabeth, the Queen's sister, was observed with the most jealous attention. The treaty of marriage was ratified by the parliament.

PHILIP landed in England with a magnificent retinue, celebrated his nuptials with great solemnity; and though he could not lay aside his natural severity and pride, or assume gracious and popular manners, he endeavoured to conciliate the favour of the English nobility by his extraordinary liberality. Lest that should fail of acquiring him such influence in the government of the kingdom as he aimed at obtaining, the Emperor kept a body of twelve thousand men on the coast of Flanders, in readiness to embark for England, and to support his son in all his enterprizes.

The marriage celebrated.

BOOK XI.

1554.
Mary's measures to overturn the Protestant religion in England.

EMBOLDENED by all these favourable circumstances, Mary pursued the scheme of extirpating the Protestant religion out of her dominions, with the most precipitate zeal. The laws of Edward the Sixth, in favour of the Reformation, were repealed; the Protestant clergy ejected; all the forms and rites of the Popish worship were re-established; the nation was solemnly absolved from the guilt which it had contracted during the period of its apostacy, and was publicly reconciled to the church of Rome by Cardinal Pole, who, immediately after the Queen's marriage, was permitted to continue his journey to England, and to exercise his legatine functions with the most ample power. Not satisfied with having overturned the Protestant church, and re-establishing the ancient system on its ruins, Mary insisted that all her subjects should conform to the same mode of worship which she preferred; should profess their faith in the same creed which she had approved; and abjure every practice or opinion that was deemed repugnant to either of them. Powers altogether unknown in the English constitution, were vested in certain persons appointed to take cognizance of heresy, and they proceeded to exercise them with more than inquisitorial severity. The prospect of danger, however, did not intimidate the principal teachers of the Protestant doctrines, who believed that they were contending for truths of the utmost consequence to the happiness of mankind. They boldly avowed their sentiments, and were condemned to that cruel death which the church of Rome reserves for its enemies. This shocking punishment was inflicted with that barbarity which the rancour of false zeal alone can inspire. The English, who are inferior in humanity to no people in Europe, and remarkable for the mildness of their public executions, beheld, with astonishment and horror, persons who had filled the most respectable stations in their church, and who were venerable on account of their age, their piety, and their literature, condemned to endure torments to which their laws did not subject even the most atrocious criminals.

The obstacles which she had to surmount.

THIS extreme rigour did not accomplish the end at which Mary aimed. The patience and fortitude with which these martyrs for the Reformation submitted to their sufferings, the heroic contempt of death expressed by persons of every rank, and age, and sex, confirmed many more in the Protestant faith, than the threats of their enraged persecutors could frighten into apostacy. The business of such as were entrusted with trying heretics multiplied continually, and appeared to be as endless as it was odious. The Queen's ablest ministers became sensible how impolitic, as well as dangerous, it was to irritate the people by the frequent spectacle of public executions, which they detested as no less unjust than cruel. Even Philip was so thoroughly convinced of her having run to an excess of rigour, that on this occasion he assumed a part to which

BOOK XI.
1554.

The English jealous of Philip.

he was little accustomed, becoming an advocate for moderation and lenity ª.

But, notwithstanding this attempt to ingratiate himself with the English, they discovered a constant jealousy and distrust of all his intentions; and when some members, who had been gained by the court, ventured to move in the House of Commons that the nation ought to assist the Emperor, the Queen's father-in-law, in his war against France, the proposal was rejected with general dissatisfaction. A motion which was made, that the parliament should give its consent that Philip might be publicly crowned as the Queen's husband, met with such a cold reception, that it was instantly withdrawn ᵇ.

The French King alarmed at the match between Philip and Mary.

The King of France had observed the progress of the Emperor's negociation in England with much uneasiness. The great accession of territories as well as reputation which his enemy would acquire by the marriage of his son with the Queen of such a powerful kingdom, was obvious and formidable. He easily foresaw that the English, notwithstanding all their fears and precautions, would be soon drawn in to take part in the quarrels on the continent, and be compelled to act in subserviency to the Emperor's ambitious schemes. For this reason, Henry had given it

ª Godwin's Annals of Q. Mary ap. Kennet, v. ii. p. 329. Burnet's Hist. of Refor. ii. 298. 305.
ᵇ Carte's Hist. of England, iii. 314.

in charge to his ambassador at the court of London, to employ all his address in order to defeat or retard the treaty of marriage; and as there was not, at that time, any Prince of the blood in France, whom he could propose to the Queen as a husband, he instructed him to co-operate with such of the English as wished their sovereign to marry one of her own subjects. But the Queen's ardour and precipitation in closing with the first overtures in favour of Philip, having rendered all his endeavours ineffectual, Henry was so far from thinking it prudent to give any aid to the English malecontents, though earnestly solicited by Wyat and their other leaders, who tempted him to take them under his protection, by offers of great advantage to France, that he commanded his ambassador to congratulate the Queen in the warmest terms upon the suppression of the insurrection.

NOTWITHSTANDING these external professions, Henry dreaded so much the consequence of this alliance, which more than compensated for all the Emperor had lost in Germany, that he determined to carry on his military operations, both in the Low-Countries and in Italy, with extraordinary vigour, in order that he might compel Charles to accept of an equitable peace, before his daughter-in-law could surmount the aversion of her subjects to a war on the continent, and prevail on them to assist the Emperor either with money or troops. For this purpose he exerted

His preparations for a vigorous campaign.

BOOK XI.
1554.

erted himself to the utmost in order to have a numerous army early assembled on the frontiers of the Netherlands, and while one part of it laid waste the open country of Artois, the main body, under the Constable Montmorency, advanced towards the provinces of Liege and Hainault by the forest of Ardennes.

The progress of his arms.

THE campaign was opened with the siege of Mariemburgh, a town which the Queen of Hungary, the governess of the Low-Countries, had fortified at great expence; but, being destitute of a sufficient garrison, it surrendered in six days. Henry, elated with this success, put himself at the head of his army, and investing Bouvines, took it by assault, after a short resistance. With equal facility he became master of Dinant; and then turning to the left, bent his march towards the province of Artois. The large sums which the Emperor had remitted into England had so exhausted his treasury, as to render his preparations at this juncture slower and more dilatory than usual. He had no body of troops to make head against the French at their first entrance into his territories; and though he drew together all the forces in the country in the utmost hurry, and gave the command of them to Emanuel Philibert of Savoy, they were in no condition to face an enemy so far superior in number. The Prince of Savoy, however, by his activity and good conduct, made up for his want of troops. By watching all the motions of the French at a distance,

June 28.

The Emperor little able to obstruct it.

tance, and by chufing his own pofts with fkill, he put it out of their power either to form any fiege of confequence, or to attack him. Want of fubfiftence foon obliged them to fall back towards their own frontiers, after having burnt all the open towns, and having plundered the country through which they marched with a cruelty and licence more becoming a body of light troops than a royal army led by a great monarch.

But Henry, that he might not difmifs his army without attempting fome conqueft adequate to the great preparations, as well as fanguine hopes, with which he had opened the campaign, invefted Renti, a place deemed in that age of great importance, as, by its fituation on the confines of Artois and the Boulonnois, it covered the former province, and protected the parties which made incurfions into the latter. The town, which was ftrongly fortified and provided with a numerous garrifon, made a gallant defence; but being warmly preffed by a powerful army, it muft foon have yielded. The Emperor, who at that time enjoyed a fhort interval of eafe from the gout, was fo folicitous to fave it, that, although he could bear no other motion but that of a litter, he inftantly put himfelf at the head of his army, which having received feveral reinforcements was now ftrong enough to approach the enemy. The French were eager to decide the fate of Renti by a battle,

The French inveft Renti.

a battle, and expected it from the Emperor's arrival in his camp; but Charles avoided a general action with great industry, and as he had nothing in view but to save the town, he hoped to accomplish that, without exposing himself to the consequences of such a dangerous and doubtful event.

An action between the two armies. Aug. 13.

Notwithstanding all his precautions, a dispute, about a post which both armies endeavoured to seize, brought on an engagement which proved almost general. The Duke of Guise, who commanded the wing of the French which stood the brunt of the combat, displayed valour and conduct worthy of the defender of Metz; the Imperialists after an obstinate struggle were repulsed; the French remained masters of the post in dispute, and if the Constable, either from his natural caution and slowness, or from unwillingness to support a rival whom he hated, had not delayed bringing up the main body to second the impression which Guise had made, the route of the enemy must have been complete. The Emperor, notwithstanding the loss which he had sustained, continued in the same camp; and the French, being straightened for provisions, and finding it impossible to carry on the siege in the face of an hostile army, quitted their intrenchments. They retired openly, courting the enemy to approach, rather than shunning an engagement.

But

But Charles, having gained his end, suffered them to march off unmolested. As soon as his troops entered their own country, Henry threw garrisons into the frontier towns, and dismissed the rest of the army. This encouraged the Imperialists to push forward with a considerable body of troops into Picardy, and by laying waste the country with fire and sword, they endeavoured to revenge themselves for the ravages which the French had committed in Hainault and Artois[c]. But, as they were not able to reduce any place of importance, they gained nothing more than the enemy had done by this cruel and inglorious method of carrying on the war.

1554. The Imperialists invade Picardy.

The arms of France were still more unsuccessful in Italy. The footing which the French had acquired in Siena, occasioned much uneasiness to Cosmo di Medici, the most sagacious and enterprizing of all the Italian Princes. He dreaded the neighbourhood of a powerful people, to whom all who favoured the ancient republican government in Florence would have recourse, as to their natural protectors, against that absolute authority which the Emperor had enabled him to usurp; he knew how odious he was to the French, on account of his attachment to the Imperial party, and he foresaw that, if they were permitted to gather strength in Siena, Tuscany would soon feel the effects of their resentment.

Affairs of Italy.

Cosmo di Medici's schemes with regard to Siena.

[c] Thuan. 460, &c. Haræi Ann. Brab. 674.

For thefe reafons, he wifhed with the utmoft folicitude for the expulfion of the French out of
the Sienefe, before they had time to eftablifh
themfelves thoroughly in the country, or to receive
fuch reinforcements from France as would render
it dangerous to attack them. As this, however,
was properly the Emperor's bufinefs, who was
called by his intereft as well as honour to dif-
lodge thofe formidable intruders into the heart of
his dominions, Cofmo laboured to throw the whole
burden of the enterprize on him; and on that account had given no affiftance, during the former
campaign, but by advancing fome fmall fums of
money towards the payment of the Imperial
troops.

He negociates with the Emperor.

But as the defence of the Netherlands en-
groffed all the Emperor's attention, and his remittances into England had drained his treafury,
it was obvious that his operations in Italy would
be extremely feeble; and Cofmo plainly perceived, that if he himfelf did not take part openly
in the war, and act with vigour, the French
would fcarcely meet with any annoyance. As his
fituation rendered this refolution neceffary and
unavoidable, his next care was to execute it in
fuch a manner, that he might derive from it fome
other advantage, befide that of driving the
French out of his neighbourhood. With this
view, he difpatched an envoy to Charles, offering to declare war againft France, and to reduce
Siena at his own charges, on condition that he
fhould

should be repaid whatever he should expend in the enterprize, and be permitted to retain all his conquests until his demands were fully satisfied. Charles, to whom, at this juncture, the war against Siena was an intolerable burden, and who had neither expedient nor resource that could enable him to carry it on with proper vigour, closed gladly with this overture; and Cosmo, well acquainted with the low state of the Imperial finances, flattered himself that the Emperor, finding it impossible to reimburse him, would suffer him to keep quiet possession of whatever places he should conquer[d].

FULL of these hopes, he made great preparations for war, and as the French King had turned the strength of his arms against the Netherlands, he did not despair of assembling such a body of men as would prove more than a sufficient match for any force which Henry could bring into the field in Italy. He endeavoured, by giving one of his daughters to the Pope's nephew, to obtain assistance from the holy see, or at least to secure his remaining neutral. He attempted to detach the Duke of Orsini, whose family had been long attached to the French party, from his ancient confederates, by bestowing on him another of his daughters; and what was of greater consequence than either of these, he engaged John James Medecino, Marquis of Marignano, to take the

Enters into war with France.

Gives the command of his army to Medecino.

[d] Adriani Istoria de suoi tempi, vol. i, 662.

command

command of his army[e]. This officer, from a very low condition in life, had raised himself, through all the ranks of service, to high command, and had displayed talents, and acquired reputation in war, which entitled him to be placed on a level with the greatest generals in that martial age. Having attained a station of eminence so disproportionate to his birth, he laboured with a fond solicitude to conceal his original obscurity, by giving out that he was descended of the family of Medici, to which honour the casual resemblance of his name was his only pretension. Cosmo, happy that he could gratify him at such an easy rate, flattered his vanity in this point, acknowledged him as a relation, and permitted him to assume the arms of his family: Medecino, eager to serve the head of that family of which he now considered himself as a branch, applied with wonderful zeal and assiduity to raise troops; and as, during his long service, he had acquired great credit with the leaders of those mercenary bands which formed the strength of Italian armies, he engaged the most eminent of them to follow Cosmo's standard.

Peter Strozzi entrusted with the command of the French army in Italy.

To oppose this able general, and the formidable army which he had assembled, the King of France made choice of Peter Strozzi, a Florentine nobleman, who had resided long in France as an exile, and who had risen by his merit to

[e] Adriani Istoria, vol. i. p. 663.

high reputation, as well as command in the army. He was the fon of Philip Strozzi, who, in the year one thoufand five hundred and thirty-feven, had concurred with fuch ardour in the attempt to expel the family of Medici out of Florence, in order to re-eſtabliſh the ancient republican form of government; and who had periſhed in the undertaking. The fon inherited the implacable averfion to the Medici, as well as the fame enthufiaſtic zeal for the liberty of Florence, which had animated his father, whofe death he was impatient to revenge. Henry flattered himfelf that his army would make rapid progrefs under a general whofe zeal to promote his intereſt was roufed and feconded by fuch powerful paffions; efpecially as he had allotted him, for the fcene of action, his native country, in which he had many powerful partifans, ready to facilitate all his operations.

BUT how fpecious foever the motives might appear which induced Henry to make this choice, it proved fatal to the interefts of France in Italy. Cofmo, as foon as he heard that the mortal enemy of his family was appointed to take the command in Tufcany, concluded that the King of France aimed at fomething more than the protection of the Sienefe, and faw the neceffity of making extraordinary efforts, not merely to reduce Siena, but to fave himfelf from deſtruction [f].

The improdence of this choice.

[f] Pecci Memorie di Siena, vol. iv. p. 103, &c.

At the same time, the Cardinal of Ferrara, who had the entire direction of the French affairs in Italy, considered Strozzi as a formidable rival in power, and in order to prevent his acquiring any increase of authority from success, he was extremely remiss in supplying him either with money to pay his troops, or with provisions to support them. Strozzi himself, blinded by his resentment against the Medici, pushed on his operations with the impetuosity of revenge, rather than with the caution and prudence becoming a great general.

The battle of Marciano.

At first, however, he attacked several towns in the territory of Florence with such vigour as obliged Medecino, in order to check his progress, to withdraw the greater part of his army from Siena, which he had invested before Strozzi's arrival in Italy. As Cosmo sustained the whole burden of military operations, the expence of which must soon have exhausted his revenues; as neither the viceroy of Naples nor governor of Milan were in condition to afford him any effectual aid; and as the troops which Medecino had left in the camp before Siena could attempt nothing against it during his absence; it was Strözzi's business to have protracted the war, and to have transferred the seat of it into the territories of Florence; but the hope of ruining his enemy by one decisive blow, precipitated him

August 3. into a general engagement not far from Marciano. The armies were nearly equal in number;

ber; but a body of Italian cavalry, in which Strozzi placed great confidence, having fled without making any resistance, either through the treachery or cowardice of the officers who commanded it, his infantry remained exposed to the attacks of all Medecino's troops. Encouraged, however, by Strozzi's presence and example, who, after receiving a dangerous wound in endeavouring to rally the cavalry, placed himself at the head of the infantry, and manifested an admirable presence of mind, as well as extraordinary valour, they stood their ground with great firmness, and repulsed such of the enemy as ventured to approach them. But those gallant troops being surrounded at last on every side, and torn in pieces by a battery of cannon which Medecino brought to bear upon them, the Florentine cavalry broke in on their flanks, and a general rout ensued. Strozzi, faint with the loss of blood, and deeply affected with the fatal consequences of his own rashness, found the utmost difficulty in making his escape with a handful of men [g].

MEDECINO returned immediately to the siege of Siena with his victorious forces, and as Strozzi could not, after the greatest efforts of activity, collect as many men as to form the appearance of a regular army, he had leisure to carry on his approaches against the town without molestation.

[g] Pecci Memorie della Siena, vol. iv. p. 157.

But the Sienese, instead of sinking into despair upon this cruel disappointment of their only hope of obtaining relief, prepared to defend themselves to the utmost extremity, with that undaunted fortitude which the love of liberty alone can inspire. This generous resolution was warmly seconded by Monluc, who commanded the French garrison in the town. The active and enterprising courage which he had displayed on many occasions, had procured him this command; and as he had ambition which aspired at the highest military dignities, without any pretensions to attain them but what he could derive from merit, he determined to distinguish his defence of Siena by extraordinary efforts of valour and perseverance. For this purpose, he repaired and strengthened the fortifications with unwearied industry; he trained the citizens to the use of arms, and accustomed them to go through the fatigues and dangers of service in common with the soldiers; and as the enemy were extremely strict in guarding all the avenues to the city, he husbanded the provisions in the magazines with the most parsimonious œconomy, and prevailed on the soldiers, as well as the citizens, to restrict themselves to a very moderate daily allowance for their subsistence. Medecino, though his army was not numerous enough to storm the town by open force, ventured twice to assault it by surprise; but he was received each time with so much spirit, and repulsed with such loss, as discouraged him from repeating the attempt,

EMPEROR CHARLES V.

tempt, and left him no hopes of reducing the town but by famine.

<small>BOOK XI.
1554.</small>

With this view, he fortified his own camp with great care, occupied all the posts of strength round the place, and having entirely cut off the besieged from any communication with the adjacent country, he waited patiently until necessity should compel them to open their gates. But their enthusiastic zeal for liberty made the citizens despise the distresses occasioned by the scarcity of provisions, and supported them long under all the miseries of famine: Monluc, by his example and exhortations, taught his soldiers to vie with them in patience and abstinence; and it was not until they had withstood a siege of ten months, until they had eaten up all the horses, dogs, and other animals in the place, and were reduced almost to their last morsel of bread, that they proposed a capitulation. Even then they demanded honourable terms; and as Cosmo, though no stranger to the extremity of their condition, was afraid that despair might prompt them to venture upon some wild enterprize, he immediately granted them conditions more favourable than they could have expected.

<small>Medecino converts the siege into a blockade.</small>

<small>1555.</small>

The capitulation was made in the Emperor's name, who engaged to take the republic of Siena under the protection of the Empire; he promised to maintain the ancient liberties of the city, to

<small>April 22. The town obliged by famine to capitulate.</small>

Vol. IV.   M   allow

allow the magistrates the full exercise of their former authority, to secure the citizens in the undisturbed possession of their privileges and property; he granted an ample and unlimited pardon to all who had born arms against him; he reserved to himself the right of placing a garrison in the town, but engaged not to rebuild the citadel without the consent of the citizens. Monluc and his French garrison were allowed to march out with all the honours of war.

Medecino observed the articles of capitulation, as far as depended on him, with great exactness. No violence or insult whatever was offered to the inhabitants, and the French garrison was treated with all the respect due to their spirit and bravery. *Many of the Sienese retire to Monté-Alcino;* But many of the citizens suspecting, from the extraordinary facility with which they had obtained such favourable conditions, that the Emperor, as well as Cosmo, would take the first opportunity of violating them, and disdaining to possess a precarious liberty, which depended on the will of another, abandoned the place of their nativity, and accompanied the French to Monté-Alcino, Porto Ercole, and other small towns in the territory of the republic. *and establish a free government there.* They established, in Monté-Alcino, the same model of government to which they had been accustomed at Siena, and appointing magistrates with the same titles and jurisdiction, solaced themselves with this image of their ancient liberty.

The

EMPEROR CHARLES V.

THE fears of the Sienese concerning the fate of their country were not imaginary, or their suspicion of the Emperor and Cosmo ill-founded; for no sooner had the Imperial troops taken possession of the town, than Cosmo, without regarding the articles of capitulation, not only displaced the magistrates who were in office, and nominated new ones devoted to his own interest, but commanded all the citizens to deliver up their arms to persons whom he appointed to receive them. They submitted to the former from necessity, though with all the reluctance and regret which men accustomed to liberty feel in obeying the first commands of a master. They did not yield the same tame obedience to the latter; and many persons of distinction, rather than degrade themselves from the rank of freemen to the condition of slaves, by surrendering their arms, fled to their countrymen at Monté-Alcino, and chose to endure all the hardships, and encounter all the dangers which they had reason to expect in that new station, where they had fixed the seat of their republic.

BOOK XI.
1555.
Hardships to which the citizens of Siena were subjected.

COSMO, not reckoning himself secure while such numbers of implacable and desperate enemies were settled in his neighbourhood, and retained any degree of power, solicited Medecino to attack them in their different places of retreat, before they had time to recruit their strength and spirits, after the many calamities which they had suffered. He prevailed on him, though his army

Cosmo attacks those who had retired.

was much weakened by hard duty during the siege of Siena, to invest Porto Ercole; and the fortifications being both slight and incomplete, the besieged were soon compelled to open their gates. An unexpected order, which Medecino received from the Emperor to detach the greater part of his troops into Piedmont, prevented farther operations, and permitted the Sienese exiles to reside for some time undisturbed in Monté-Alcino. But their unhappy countrymen who remained at Siena, were not yet at the end of their sufferings; for the Emperor, instead of adhering to the articles of capitulation, granted his son Philip the investiture of that city and all its dependencies; and Francis de Toledo, in the name of their new master, proceeded to settle the civil and military government, treated them like a conquered people, and subjected them to the Spanish yoke, without paying any regard whatever to their privileges or ancient form of government [h].

Operations in Piedmont.

THE Imperial army in Piedmont had been so feeble for some time, and its commander so inactive, that the Emperor, in order to give vigour to his operations in that quarter, found it necessary not only to recal Medecino's troops from Tuscany while in the career of conquest, but to

[h] Sleid. 617. Thuan. lib. xv. 526. 537. Joan. Camerarii adnot. rer. præcipuarum ab anno 1550 ad 1561 ap. Freherum, vol. iii. p. 564. Pecci Memorie della Siena, iv. 64, &c.

employ

employ in Piedmont a general of such reputation and abilities, as might counterbalance the great military talents of the Marechal Brissac, who was at the head of the French forces in that country.

He pitched on the Duke of Alva for that purpose; but that choice was as much the effect of a court intrigue, as of his opinion with respect to the Duke's merit. Alva had long made court to Philip with the utmost assiduity, and had endeavoured to work himself into his confidence by all the insinuating arts of which his haughty and inflexible nature was capable. As he nearly resembled that Prince in many features of his character, he began to gain much of his good-will. Ruy Gomez de Silva, Philip's favourite, who dreaded the progress which this formidable rival made in his master's affections, had the address to prevail with the Emperor to name Alva to this command. The Duke, though sensible that he owed this distinction to the malicious arts of an enemy, who had no other aim than to remove him at a distance from court, was of such punctilious honour, that he would not decline a command that appeared dangerous and difficult, but, at the same time, was so haughty, that he would not accept of it but on his own terms, insisting on being appointed the Emperor's Vicar-general in Italy, with the supreme military command in all the Imperial and Spanish territories in that country. Charles granted all his demands;

Charles appoints the Duke of Alva generalissimo there.

and

and he took poffeffion of his new dignity with almoft unlimited authority.

His firft operations, however, were neither proportioned to his former reputation and the extenfive powers with which he was invefted, nor did they come up to the Emperor's expectations. Briffac had under his command an army which, though inferior in number to the Imperialifts, was compofed of chofen troops, which having grown old in fervice in that country, where every town was fortified, and every caftle capable of being defended, were perfectly acquainted with the manner of carrying on war there. By their valour, and his own good conduct, Briffac not only defeated all the attempts of the Imperialifts, but added new conquefts to the territories of which he was formerly mafter. Alva, after having boafted, with his ufual arrogance, that he would drive the French out of Piedmont, in a few weeks, was obliged to retire into winter-quarters, with the mortification of being unable to preferve entire that part of the country of which the Emperor had hitherto kept poffeffion [i].

As the operations of this campaign in Piedmont were indecifive, thofe in the Netherlands were inconfiderable, neither the Emperor nor King of France being able to bring into the field an army ftrong enough to undertake any enter-

[i] Thuan. lib. xv. 529. Guichenon Hift. de Savoye, tom. i. 670.

prize of moment. But what Charles wanted in force, he endeavoured to supply by a bold stratagem, the success of which would have been equal to that of the most vigorous campaign. During the siege of Metz, Leonard, Father Guardian of a convent of Franciscans in that city, had insinuated himself far into the esteem and favour of the Duke of Guise, by his attachment to the French. Being a man of an active and intriguing spirit, he had been extremely useful both in animating the inhabitants to sustain with patience all the hardships of the siege, and in procuring intelligence of the enemies designs and motions. The merit of those important services, together with the warm recommendations of the Duke of Guise, secured him such high confidence with Vielleville, who was appointed governor of Metz when Guise left the town, that he was permitted to converse or correspond with whatever persons he thought fit, and nothing that he did created any suspicion. This monk, from the levity natural to bold and projecting adventurers; or from resentment against the French, who had not bestowed on him such rewards as he thought due to his own merit; or tempted by the unlimited confidence which was placed in him, to imagine that he might carry on and accomplish any scheme with perfect security, formed a design of betraying Metz to the Imperialists.

1555. A conspiracy to betray Metz to the Imperialists.

He communicated his intention to the Queen-dowager of Hungary, who governed the Low-Countries in the name of her brother. She approving, without any scruple, an act of treachery, from which the Emperor might derive such signal advantage, assisted the Father Guardian in concerting the most proper plan for ensuring its success. They agreed, that the Father Guardian should endeavour to gain his monks to concur in promoting the design; that he should introduce into the convent a certain number of chosen soldiers, disguised in the habit of friars; that when every thing was ripe for execution, the governor of Thionville should march towards Metz in the night with a consideable body of troops, and attempt to scale the ramparts; that while the garrison was employed in resisting the assailants, the monks should set fire to the town in different places; that the soldiers who lay concealed should sally out of the convent, and attack those who defended the ramparts in the rear. Amidst the universal terror and confusion which events so unexpected would occasion, it was not doubted but that the Imperialists might become masters of the town. As a recompence for this service the Father Guardian stipulated that he should be appointed bishop of Metz, and ample rewards were promised to such of his monks as should be most active in co-operating with him.

The Father Guardian accomplished what he had undertaken to perform with great secrecy and dispatch. By his authority and arguments, as well as by the prospect of wealth or honours which he set before his monks, he prevailed on all of them to enter into the conspiracy. He introduced into the convent, without being suspected, as many soldiers as were thought sufficient. The governor of Thionville, apprized in due time of the design, had assembled a proper number of troops for executing it; and the moment approached, which probably would have wrested from Henry the most important of all his conquests.

Its progress.

But, happily for France, on the very day that was fixed for striking the blow, Vielleville, an able and vigilant officer, received information from a spy whom he entertained at Thionville, that certain Franciscan friars resorted frequently thither, and were admitted to many private conferences with the governor, who was carrying on preparations for some military enterprize with great dispatch, but with a most mysterious secrecy. This was sufficient to awaken Vielleville's suspicions. Without communicating these to any person, he instantly visited the convent of Franciscans; detected the soldiers who were concealed there; and forced them to discover as much as they knew concerning the nature of the enterprize. The Father Guardian, who had gone

Is discovered.

to Thionville that he might put the last hand to his machinations, was seized at the gate as he returned; and he, in order to save himself from the rack, revealed all the circumstances of the conspiracy.

A body of Imperialists defeated.

VIELLEVILLE, not satisfied with having seized the traitors, and having frustrated their schemes, was solicitous to take advantage of the discoveries which he had made, so as to be revenged on the Imperialists. For this purpose he marched out with the best troops in his garrison, and placing these in ambush near the road, by which the Father Guardian had informed him that the governor of Thionville would approach Metz, he fell upon the Imperialists with great fury, as they advanced in perfect security, without suspecting any danger to be near. Confounded at this sudden attack, by an enemy whom they expected to surprise, they made little resistance; and a great part of the troops employed in this service, among whom were many persons of distinction, was killed or taken prisoners. Before next morning, Vielleville returned to Metz in triumph.

The conspirators punished.

No resolution was taken for some time concerning the fate of the Father Guardian and his monks, the framers and conductors of this dangerous conspiracy. Regard for the honour of a body so numerous and respectable as the Franciscans, and unwillingness to afford a subject of triumph

triumph to the enemies of the Romish church by their disgrace, seem to have occasioned this delay. But at length, the necessity of inflicting exemplary punishment upon them, in order to deter others from venturing to commit the same crime, became so evident, that orders were issued to proceed to their trial. The guilt was made apparent by the clearest evidence; and sentence of death was passed upon the Father Guardian, together with twenty monks. On the evening previous to the day fixed for their execution, the gaoler took them out of the dungeons in which they had hitherto been confined separately, and shut them all up in one great room, that they might confess their sins one to another, and join together in preparing for a future state. But as soon as they were left alone, instead of employing themselves in the religious exercises suitable to their condition, they began to reproach the Father Guardian, and four of the senior monks who had been most active in seducing them, for their inordinate ambition, which had brought such misery on them, and such disgrace upon their order. From reproaches they proceeded to curses and execrations, and at last, in a frenzy of rage and despair, they fell upon them with such violence, that they murdered the Father Guardian on the spot, and so disabled the other four, that it became necessary to carry them next morning in a cart, together with the dead body of the Father Guardian, to the place of execution. Six of the youngest

youngest were pardoned, the rest suffered the punishment which their crime merited[k].

A fruitless negociation in order to establish peace.

Though both parties, exhausted by the length of the war, carried it on in this languishing manner, neither of them shewed any disposition to listen to overtures of peace. Cardinal Pole indeed laboured with all the zeal becoming his piety and humanity, to re-establish concord among the Princes of Christendom. He had not only persuaded his mistress, the Queen of England, to enter warmly into his sentiments, and to offer her mediation to the contending powers, but had prevailed both on the Emperor and King of France to send their plenipotentiaries to a village between Gravelines and Ardres. He himself, together with Gardiner bishop of Winchester, repaired thither in order to preside as mediators in the conferences which were to be held for adjusting all the points in difference. But though each of the monarchs committed this negociation to some of their ministers, in whom they placed the greatest confidence, it was soon evident that they came together with no sincere desire of accommodation. Each proposed articles so extravagant that they could have no hopes of their being accepted. Pole, after exerting in vain all his zeal and address, in order to persuade

May 21.

[k] Thuan. lib. xv. p. 522. Belcar. Com. Rer. Gal. 866. Memoirs du Marech. Vielleville, par M. Charloix, tom. iii. p. 249. &c. p. 347. Par. 1757.

them

them to relinquish such extravagant demands, and to consent to the substitution of more equal conditions, became sensible of the folly of wasting time, in attempting to re-establish concord between those, whom their obstinacy rendered irreconcilable, broke off the conference, and returned to England [1].

Affairs of Germany.

During these transactions in other parts of Europe, Germany enjoyed such profound tranquillity, as afforded the Diet full leisure to deliberate, and to establish proper regulations concerning a point of the greatest consequence to the internal peace of the Empire. By the treaty of Passau in one thousand five hundred and fifty-two, it had been referred to the next Diet of the Empire to confirm and perfect the plan of religious pacification, which was there agreed upon. The terror and confusion with which the violent commotions excited by Albert of Brandenburg had filled Germany, as well as the constant attention which Ferdinand was obliged to give to the affairs of Hungary, had hitherto prevented the holding a Diet, though it had been summoned, soon after the conclusion of the treaty, to meet at Augsburg.

Diet held at Augsburg, and Ferdinand's speech in it.

But as a Diet was now necessary on many accounts, Ferdinand about the beginning of this year had repaired to Augsburg. Though few of

[1] Thuan. lib. xv. p. 523. Mem. de Ribier, tom. ii. p. 613.

the Princes were present either in person or by their deputies, he opened the assembly by a speech, in which he proposed a termination of the dissensions to which the new tenets and controversies with regard to religion had given rise, not only as the first and great business of the Diet, but as the point which both the Emperor and he had most at heart. He represented the innumerable obstacles which the Emperor had to surmount before he could procure the convocation of a general council, as well as the fatal accidents which had for some time retarded, and had at last suspended the consultations of that assembly. He observed, that experience had already taught them how vain it was to expect any remedy for evils, which demanded immediate redress from a general council, the assembling of which would either be prevented, or its deliberations be interrupted by the dissensions and hostilities of the Princes of Christendom: That a national council in Germany, which, as some imagined, might be called with greater ease, and deliberate with more perfect security, was an assembly of an unprecedented nature, the jurisdiction of which was uncertain in its extent, and the form of its proceedings undefined: That in his opinion there remained but one method for composing their unhappy differences, which, though it had been often tried without success, might yet prove effectual if it were attempted with a better and more pacific spirit than had appeared on former occasions, and that was to choose a few men of learning,

ing, abilities, and moderation, who, by discussing the disputed articles, in an amicable conference, might explain them in such a manner as to bring the contending parties either to unite in sentiment, or to differ with charity.

Suspicions and fears of the Protestants.

This speech being printed in common form, and dispersed over the Empire, revived the fears and jealousies of the Protestants; Ferdinand, they observed with much surprise, had not once mentioned, in his address to the Diet, the treaty of Passau, the stipulations which they considered as the great security of their religious liberty. The suspicions to which this gave rise were confirmed by the accounts which they daily received of the extreme severity with which Ferdinand treated their Protestant brethren in his hereditary dominions; and, as it was natural to consider his actions as the surest indication of his intentions, this diminished their confidence in those pompous professions of moderation and of zeal for the re-establishment of concord, to which his practice seemed to be so repugnant.

These increased by the arrival of a nuncio from the Pope to the Diet.

The arrival of the cardinal Morone, whom the Pope had appointed to attend the Diet as his nuncio, completed their conviction, and left them no room to doubt that some dangerous machination was forming against the peace or safety of the Protestant church. Julius, elated with the unexpected return of the English nation from apostacy, began to flatter himself, that the spirit of mutiny and revolt having now spent its force, the happy period was come when the church might resume its ancient authority, and be obeyed by the people with the same tame submission as formerly. Full of these hopes he had sent Morone to Augsburg, with instructions to employ his eloquence to excite the Germans to imitate the laudable example of the English, and his political address in order to prevent any decree of the Diet to the detriment of the catholic faith. As Morone inherited from his father, the chancellor of Milan, uncommon talents for negociation and intrigue, he could hardly have failed of embarrassing the measures of the Protestants in the Diet, or of defeating whatever they aimed at obtaining in it for their farther security.

The death of Julius III.

BUT an unforeseen event delivered them from all the danger which they had reason to apprehend from Morone's presence. Julius, by abandoning himself to pleasures and amusements, no less unbecoming his age than his character, having contracted such habits of dissipation, that any serious occupation, especially if attended with difficulty, became an intolerable burden to him, had long resisted the solicitations of his nephew to hold a consistory, because he expected there a violent opposition to his schemes in favour of that young man. But when all the pretexts which he could invent for eluding this request were exhausted, and at the same time his indolent aversion

sion to business continued to grow upon him, he feigned indisposition rather than yield to his nephew's importunity; and that he might give the deceit a greater colour of probability, he not only confined himself to his apartment, but changed his usual diet and manner of life. By persisting too long in acting this ridiculous part, he contracted a real disease, of which he died in a few days, leaving his infamous minion the Cardinal de Monte to bear his name, and to disgrace the dignity which he had conferred upon him [m]. As soon as Moronè heard of his death, he set out abruptly from Augsburg, where he had resided only a few days, that he might be present at the election of a new Pontiff.

March 23.

The nuncio sets out for Rome.

ONE cause of their suspicions and fears being thus removed, the Protestants soon became sensible that their conjectures concerning Ferdinand's intentions, however specious, were ill-founded, and that he had no thoughts of violating the articles favourable to them in the treaty of Passau. Charles, from the time that Maurice had defeated all his schemes in the Empire, and overturned the great system of religious and civil despotism, which he had almost established there, gave little attention to the internal government of Germany, and permitted his brother to pursue

Ferdinand's reasons for wishing to satisfy the Protestants.

---

[m] Onuphr. Panvinius de Vitis Pontificum, p. 320. Thuan. lib. xv. 517.

VOL. IV.   N   whatever

whatever measures he judged most salutary and expedient. Ferdinand, less ambitious and enterprising than the Emperor, instead of resuming a plan, which he, with power and resources so far superior, had failed of accomplishing, endeavoured to attach the Princes of the Empire to his family by an administration uniformly moderate and equitable. To this he gave, at present, particular attention, because his situation at this juncture rendered it necessary to court their favour and support with more than usual assiduity.

Charles had resumed his plan of altering the succession to the Empire.

CHARLES had again resumed his favourite project of acquiring the Imperial crown for his son Philip, the prosecution of which, the reception it had met with when first proposed had obliged him to suspend, but had not induced him to relinquish. This led him warmly to renew his request to his brother, that he would accept of some compensation for his prior right of succession, and sacrifice that to the grandeur of the house of Austria. Ferdinand, who was as little disposed as formerly to give such an extraordinary proof of self-denial, being sensible that, in order to defeat this scheme, not only the most inflexible firmness on his part, but a vigorous declaration from the Princes of the Empire in behalf of his title, were requisite; was willing to purchase their favour by gratifying them in every point that they deemed interesting or essential.

At

AT the same time he stood in need of immediate and extraordinary aid from the Germanic body, as the Turks, after having wrested from him great part of his Hungarian territories, were ready to attack the provinces still subject to his authority with a formidable army, against which he could bring no equal force into the field. For this aid from Germany he could not hope, if the internal peace of the Empire were not established on a foundation solid in itself, and which should appear, even to the Protestants, so secure and so permanent, as might not only allow them to engage in a distant war with safety, but might encourage them to act in it with vigour.

[margin: 1555. The Turks were ready to invade Hungary.]

A STEP taken by the Protestants themselves, a short time after the opening of the Diet, rendered him still more cautious of giving them any new cause of offence. As soon as the publication of Ferdinand's speech awakened the fears and suspicions which have been mentioned, the Electors of Saxony and Brandenburg, together with the Landgrave of Hesse, met at Naumburgh, and confirming the ancient treaty of confraternity which had long united their families, they added to it a new article, by which the contracting parties bound themselves to adhere to the confession of Augsburg, and to maintain the doctrine which it contained in their respective dominions [n].

[margin: He is alarmed at some steps taken by the Protestants.]

[n] Chytræi Saxonia, 480.

1555.
Ferdinand zealous to promote an accommodation.

FERDINAND, influenced by all these considerations, employed his utmost address in conducting the deliberations of the diet, so as not to excite the jealousy of a party on whose friendship he depended, and whose enmity, as they had not only taken the alarm, but had begun to prepare for their defence, he had so much reason to dread. The members of the Diet readily agreed to Ferdinand's proposal of taking the state of religion into consideration, previous to any other business. But, as soon as they entered upon it, both parties discovered all the zeal and animosity which a subject so interesting naturally engenders, and which the rancour of controversy, together with the violence of civil war, had inflamed to the highest pitch.

The pretensions of the Catholics and Protestants.

THE Protestants contended, that the security which they claimed in consequence of the treaty of Passau should extend, without limitation, to all who had hitherto embraced the doctrine of Luther, or who should hereafter embrace it. The Catholics, having first of all asserted the Pope's right as the supreme and final judge with respect to all articles of faith, declared, that though, on account of the present situation of the Empire, and for the sake of peace, they were willing to confirm the toleration granted by the treaty of Passau, to such as had already adopted the new opinions; they must insist that this indulgence should not be extended either to those cities which had conformed to the Interim, or to such ecclesiastics as fhould for the future apoftatize from the church of Rome. It was no eafy matter to reconcile fuch oppofite pretenfions, which were fupported, on each fide, by the moft elaborate arguments, and the greateft acrimony of expreffion, that the abilities or zeal of theologians long exercifed in difputation could fuggeft. Ferdinand however, by his addrefs and perfeverance; by foftening fome things on each fide; by putting a favourable meaning upon others; by reprefenting inceffantly the neceffity as well as the advantages of concord; and by threatening, on fome occafions, when all other confiderations were difregarded, to diffolve the Diet, brought them at length to a conclufion in which they all agreed.

CONFORMABLY to this, a Recefs was framed, approved of, and publifhed with the ufual formalities. The following are the chief articles which it contained: That fuch Princes and cities as have declared their approbation of the Confeffion of Augfburg, fhall be permitted to profefs the doctrine and exercife the worfhip which it authorifes, without interruption or moleftation from the Emperor, the King of the Romans, or any power or perfon whatfoever; That the Proteftants, on their part, fhall give no difquiet to the Princes and States who adhere to the tenets and rites of the church of Rome; That, for the future, no attempt fhall be made towards terminating religious differences, but by the gentle

Sept. 25. The peace of religion eftablifhed.

gentle and pacific methods of perfuasion and conference; That the Popish ecclesiastics shall claim no spiritual jurisdiction in such states as receive the Confession of Augsburg; That such as had seized the benefices or revenues of the church, previous to the treaty of Passau, shall retain possession of them, and be liable to no prosecution in the Imperial chamber on that account; That the supreme civil power in every state shall have right to establish what form of doctrine and worship it shall deem proper, and if any of its subjects refuse to conform to these, shall permit them to remove with all their effects whithersoever they shall please; That if any prelate or ecclesiastic shall hereafter abandon the Romish religion, he shall instantly relinquish his diocese or benefice, and it shall be lawful for those in whom the right of nomination is vested, to proceed immediately to an election, as if the office were vacant by death or translation, and to appoint a successor of undoubted attachment to the ancient system [b].

Reflections on the progress of the principles of toleration.

SUCH are the capital articles in this famous Recess, which is the basis of religious peace in Germany, and the bond of union among its various states, the sentiments of which are so extremely different with respect to points the most interesting as well as important. In our age and nation, to which the idea of Toleration is fa-

[b] Sleid. 620. F. Paul, 368. Pallav. P. II. 161.

miliar

miliar, and its beneficial effects well known, it may seem strange, that a method of terminating their dissensions, so suitable to the mild and charitable spirit of the Christian religion, did not sooner occur to the contending parties. But this expedient, however salutary, was so repugnant to the sentiments and practice of Christians during many ages, that it did not lie obvious to discovery. Among the ancient heathens, all whose deities were local and tutelary, diversity of sentiment concerning the object or rites of religious worship seems to have been no source of animosity, because the acknowledging veneration to be due to any one God, did not imply denial of the existence or the power of any other God; nor were the modes and rites of worship established in one country incompatible with those which other nations approved of and observed. Thus the errors in their system of theology were of such a nature as to be productive of concord; and notwithstanding the amazing number of their deities, as well as the infinite variety of their ceremonies, a sociable and tolerating spirit subsisted almost universally in the pagan world.

But when the Christian revelation declared one Supreme Being to be the sole object of religious veneration, and prescribed the form of worship most acceptable to him, whoever admitted the truth of it held, of consequence, every other system of religion, as a deviation from what was established by divine authority, to be false and impious. Hence

Hence arose the zeal of the first converts to the Christian faith in propagating its doctrines, and the ardour with which they laboured to overturn every other form of worship. They employed, however, for this purpose no methods but such as suited the nature of religion. By the force of powerful arguments, they convinced the understandings of men; by the charms of superior virtue, they allured and captivated their hearts. At length the civil power declared in favour of Christianity; and though numbers, imitating the example of their superiors, crowded into the church, many still adhered to their ancient superstitions. Enraged at their obstinacy, the ministers of religion, whose zeal was still unabated, though their sanctity and virtue were much diminished, forgot so far the nature of their own mission, and of the arguments which they ought to have employed, that they armed the Imperial power against these unhappy men, and as they could not persuade, they tried to compel them to believe.

At the same time, controversies concerning articles of faith multiplied, from various causes, among Christians themselves, and the same unhallowed weapons which had first been used against the enemies of their religion, were turned against each other. Every zealous disputant endeavoured to interest the civil magistrate in his cause, and each in his turn employed the secular arm to crush or to exterminate his opponents.
Not

Not long after, the bishops of Rome put in their claim to infallibility in explaining articles of faith, and deciding points in controversy; and, bold as the pretension was, they, by their artifices and perseverance, imposed on the credulity of mankind, and brought them to recognise it. To doubt or to deny any doctrine to which these unerring instructors had given the sanction of their approbation, was held to be not only a resisting of truth, but an act of rebellion against their sacred authority: and the secular power, of which by various arts they had acquired the absolute direction, was instantly employed to avenge both.

Thus Europe had been accustomed, during many centuries, to see speculative opinions propagated or defended by force; the charity and mutual forbearance which Christianity recommends with so much warmth, were forgotten, the sacred rights of conscience and of private judgment were unheard of, and not only the idea of toleration, but even the word itself, in the sense now affixed to it, was unknown. A right to extirpate error by force, was universally allowed to be the prerogative of such as possessed the knowledge of truth; and as each party of Christians believed that they had got possession of this invaluable attainment, they all claimed and exercised, as far as they were able, the rights which it was supposed to convey. The Roman Catholics, as their system rested on the decisions of an infallible judge, never doubted that truth was on their side, and openly called on the civil power to repel the impious and heretical innovators who had risen up against it. The Protestants, no less confident that their doctrine was well founded, required, with equal ardour, the Princes of their party to check such as presumed to impugn it. Luther, Calvin, Cranmer, Knox, the founders of the reformed church in their respective countries, as far as they had power and opportunity, inflicted the same punishments upon such as called in question any article in their creeds, which were denounced against their own disciples by the church of Rome. To their followers, and perhaps to their opponents, it would have appeared a symptom of diffidence in the goodness of their cause, or an acknowledgment that it was not well founded, if they had not employed in its defence all those means which it was supposed truth had a right to employ.

It was towards the close of the seventeenth century before Toleration, under its present form, was admitted first into the republic of the United Provinces, and from thence introduced into England. Long experience of the calamities flowing from mutual persecution, the influence of free government, the light and humanity acquired by the progress of science, together with the prudence and authority of the civil magistrate, were all requisite in order to establish a regulation, so repugnant to the ideas which all the different sects had adopted, from mistaken conceptions concerning

cerning the nature of religion and the rights of truth, or which all of them had derived from the erroneous maxims established by the church of Rome.

Advantages of the religious peace to the Lutherans;

THE Recess of Augsburg, it is evident, was founded on no such liberal and enlarged sentiments concerning freedom of religious inquiry, or the nature of Toleration. It was nothing more than a scheme of pacification, which political considerations alone had suggested to the contending parties, and regard for their mutual tranquillity and safety had rendered necessary. Of this there can be no stronger proof than an article in the Recess itself, by which the benefits of the pacification are declared to extend only to the Catholics on the one side, and to such as adhered to the confession of Augsburg on the other. The followers of Zuinglius and Calvin remained, in consequence of that exclusion, without any protection from the rigour of the laws denounced against heretics. Nor did they obtain any legal security, until the treaty of Westphalia, near a century after this period, provided, that they should be admitted to enjoy, in as ample a manner as the Lutherans, all the advantages and protection which the Recess of Augsburg affords.

BUT if the followers of Luther were highly pleased with the security which they acquired by this Recess, such as adhered to the ancient system had no less reason to be satisfied with that article

and to the Catholics.

in it, which preserved entire to the Roman Catholic church the benefices of such ecclesiastics as should hereafter renounce its doctrines. This article, known in Germany by the name of the *Ecclesiastical Reservation*, was apparently so conformable to the idea and to the rights of an established church, and it seemed so equitable to prevent revenues, which had been originally appropriated for the maintenance of persons attached to a certain system, from being alienated to any other purpose, that the Protestants, though they foresaw its consequences, were obliged to relinquish their opposition to it. As the Roman Catholic Princes of the Empire have taken care to see this article exactly observed in every case where there was an opportunity of putting it in execution, it has proved the great barrier of the Romish church in Germany against the Reformation; and as, from this period, the same temptation of interest did not allure ecclesiastics to relinquish the established system, there have been few of that order, who have loved truth with such disinterested and ardent affection, as, for its sake, to abandon the rich benefices which they had in possession.

Marcellus II. elected Pope. April 9.

DURING the sitting of the diet, Marcellus Cervino, Cardinal of Santo Croce, was elected Pope in room of Julius. He, in imitation of Adrian, did not change his name on being exalted to the papal chair. As he equalled that Pontiff in purity of intention, while he excelled him much in the

His character.

the arts of government, and still more in knowledge of the state and genius of the papal court; as he had capacity to discern what reformation it needed, as well as what it could bear; such regulations were expected from his virtue and wisdom, as would have removed many of its grossest and most flagrant corruptions, and have contributed towards reconciling to the church such as, from indignation at these enormities, had abandoned its communion. But this excellent Pontiff was only shown to the church, and immediately snatched away. The confinement in the conclave had impaired his health, and the fatigue of tedious ceremonies upon his accession, together with too intense and anxious application of mind to the schemes of improvement which he meditated, exhausted so entirely the vigour of his feeble constitution, that he sickened on the twelfth, and died on the twentieth day after his election [p].

His death.

All the refinements in artifice and intrigue, peculiar to conclaves, were displayed in that which was held for electing a successor to Marcellus; the Cardinals of the Imperial and French factions labouring, with equal ardour, to gain the necessary number of suffrages for one of their own party. But, after a struggle of no long duration, though conducted with all the warmth and eagerness natural to men contending for so great an object, they united in chusing John Peter Caraffa,

The election of Paul IV.

May 23.

[p] Thuan. 520. F. Paul, 365. Onuph. Panvin. 321, &c.

the eldest member of the sacred college, and the son of Count Montorio, a nobleman of an illustrious family in the kingdom of Naples. The address and influence of Cardinal Farnese, who favoured his pretensions, Caraffa's own merit, and perhaps his great age, which soothed all the disappointed candidates with the near prospect of a new vacancy, concurred in bringing about this speedy union of suffrages. In order to testify his respect for the memory of Paul III. by whom he had been created Cardinal, as well as his gratitude to the family of Farnese, he assumed the name of Paul IV.

His rise and character.

THE choice of a prelate of such a singular character, and who had long held a course extremely different from that which usually led to the dignity now conferred upon him, filled the Italians, who had nearest access to observe his manners and deportment, with astonishment, and kept them in suspense and solicitude with regard to his future conduct. Paul, though born in a rank of life which, without any other merit, might have secured to him the highest ecclesiastical preferments, had, from his early years, applied to study with all the assiduity of a man who had nothing but his personal attainments to render him conspicuous. By means of this, he not only acquired profound skill in scholastic theology, but added to that a considerable knowledge of the learned languages and of polite literature, the study of which had been lately revived in Italy, and was purfued at this time with great ardour. His mind however, naturally gloomy and fevere, was more formed to imbibe the four fpirit of the former, than to receive any tincture of elegance or liberality of fentiment from the latter; fo that he acquired rather the qualities and paffions of a reclufe ecclefiaftic, than the talents neceffary for the conduct of great affairs. Accordingly, when he entered into orders, although feveral rich benefices were beftowed upon him, and he was early employed as nuncio in different courts, he foon became difgufted with that courfe of life, and languifhed to be in a fituation more fuited to his tafte and temper. With this view, he refigned at once all his ecclefiaftical preferments, and having inftituted an order of regular priefts, whom he denominated Theatines, from the name of the archbifhopric which he had held, he affociated himfelf as a member of their fraternity, conformed to all the rigorous rules to which he had fubjected them, and preferred the folitude of a monaftic life, with the honour of being the founder of a new order, to all the great objects which the court of Rome prefented to his ambition.

In this retreat he remained for many years, until Paul III. induced by the fame of his fanctity and knowledge, called him to Rome, in order to confult with him concerning the meafures which might be moft proper and effectual for fuppreffing herefy, and re-eftablifhing the ancient authority of the church. Having thus allured

him

him from his solitude, the Pope, partly by his entreaties, and partly by his authority, prevailed on him to accept of a Cardinal's hat, to re-assume the benefices which he had resigned, and to return again into the usual path of ecclesiastical ambition which he seemed to have relinquished. But, during two successive Pontificates, under the first of which the court of Rome was the most artful and interested, and under the second the most dissolute of any in Europe, Caraffa retained his monastic austerity. He was an avowed and bitter enemy not only of all innovation in opinion, but of every irregularity in practice; he was the chief instrument in establishing the formidable and odious tribunal of the Inquisition in the papal territories; he appeared a violent advocate on all occasions for the jurisdiction and discipline of the church, and a severe censurer of every measure which seemed to flow from motives of policy or interest, rather than from zeal for the honour of the ecclesiastical order, and the dignity of the Holy See. Under a prelate of such a character, the Roman courtiers expected a severe and violent Pontificate, during which the principles of sound policy would be sacrificed to the narrow prejudices of priestly zeal; while the people of Rome were apprehensive of seeing the sordid and forbidding rigour of monastic manners substituted in place of the magnificence to which they had long been accustomed in the papal court. These apprehensions Paul was extremely solicitous to remove. At his first entrance

entrance upon the administration, he laid aside that austerity which had hitherto distinguished his person and family, and when the master of his household inquired in what manner he would chuse to live, he haughtily replied, "As becomes a great Prince." He ordered the ceremony of his coronation to be conducted with more than usual pomp; and endeavoured to render himself popular by several acts of liberality and indulgence towards the inhabitants of Rome [q].

His natural severity of temper, however, would have soon returned upon him, and would have justified the conjectures of the courtiers, as well as the fears of the people, if he had not, immediately after his election, called to Rome two of his nephews, the sons of his brother the Count of Montorio. The eldest he promoted to be Governor of Rome. The youngest, who had hitherto served as a soldier of fortune in the armies of Spain or France, and whose disposition as well as manners were still more foreign from the clerical character than his profession, he created a Cardinal, and appointed him legate of Bologna, the second office in power and dignity which a Pope can bestow. These marks of favour, no less sudden than extravagant, he accompanied with the most unbounded confidence and attachment, and forgetting all his former severe maxims, he seemed

[q] Platina, p. 327. Castaldo Vita di Paolo IV. Rom. 1615. p. 70.

to have no other object than the aggrandizing of his nephews. Their ambition, unfortunately for Paul, was too aspiring to be satisfied with any moderate acquisition. They had seen the family of Medici raised by the interest of the Popes of that house to supreme power in Tuscany; Paul III. had, by his abilities and address, secured the dutchies of Parma and Placentia to the family of Farnese. They aimed at some establishment for themselves, no less considerable and independent; and as they could not expect that the Pope would carry his indulgence towards them so far as to secularize any part of the patrimony of the church, they had no prospect of attaining what they wished, but by dismembering the Imperial dominions in Italy, in hopes of seizing some portion of them. This alone they would have deemed a sufficient reason for sowing the seeds of discord between their uncle and the Emperor.

But Cardinal Caraffa had, besides, private reasons which filled him with hatred and enmity to the Emperor. While he served in the Spanish troops he had not received such marks of honour and distinction as he thought due to his birth and merit. Disgusted with this ill-usage, he had abruptly quitted the Imperial service; and entering into that of France, he had not only met with such a reception as soothed his vanity, and attached him to the French interest, but by contracting an intimate friendship with Strozzi, who commanded the French army in Tuscany, he had imbibed

imbibed a mortal antipathy to the Emperor as the great enemy to the liberty and independence of the Italian states. Nor was the Pope himself indisposed to receive impressions unfavourable to the Emperor. The opposition given to his election by the Cardinals of the Imperial faction, left in his mind deep resentment, which was heightened by the remembrance of ancient injuries from Charles or his ministers.

Of this his nephews took advantage, and employed various devices, in order to exasperate him beyond a possibility of reconciliation. They aggravated every circumstance which could be deemed any indication of the Emperor's dissatisfaction with his promotion; they read to him an intercepted letter, in which Charles taxed the Cardinals of his party with negligence or incapacity in not having defeated Paul's election: They pretended, at one time, to have discovered a conspiracy formed by the Imperial minister and Cosmo di Medici against the Pope's life; they alarmed him, at another, with accounts of a plot for assassinating themselves. By these artifices, they kept his mind, which was naturally violent, and become suspicious from old age, in such perpetual agitation, as precipitated him into measures which otherwise he would have been the first person to condemn[r]. He seized some of the Cardi-

They endeavour to alienate the Pope from the Emperor.

[r] Ripamontii Hist. Patriæ, lib. iii. 1146. ap. Græv. Thes. vol. ii. Mem. de Ribier, ii. 615. Adriani Istor. i. 906.

nals who were most attached to the Emperor, and confined them in the castle of St. Angelo; he persecuted the Colonnas and other Roman barons, the ancient retainers to the Imperial faction, with the utmost severity; and discovering on all occasions his distrust, fear, or hatred of the Emperor, he began at last to court the friendship of the French King, and seemed willing to throw himself absolutely upon him for support and protection.

Induce him to court the King of France.

THIS was the very point to which his nephews wished to bring him as most favourable to their ambitious schemes; and as the accomplishment of these depended on their uncle's life, whose advanced age did not admit of losing a moment unnecessarily in negociations, instead of treating at second-hand with the French ambassador at Rome, they prevailed on the Pope to dispatch a person of confidence directly to the court of France, with such overtures on his part as they hoped would not be rejected. He proposed an alliance offensive and defensive between Henry and the Pope; that they should attack the dutchy of Tuscany and the kingdom of Naples with their united forces; and if their arms should prove successful, that the ancient republican form of government should be re-established in the former, and the investiture of the latter should be granted to one of the French King's sons, after reserving a certain territory which should be annexed to the patrimony of the church, together with an independent

pendent and princely establishment for each of the Pope's nephews.

Constable Montmorency opposes the alliance with the Pope.

The King, allured by these specious projects, gave a most favourable audience to the envoy. But when the matter was proposed in council, the constable Montmorency, whose natural caution and aversion to daring enterprises increased with age and experience, remonstrated with great vehemence against the alliance. He put Henry in mind how fatal to France every expedition into Italy had been during three successive reigns, and if such an enterprise had proved too great for the nation even when its strength and finances were entire, there was no reason to hope for success, if it should be attempted now, when both were exhausted by extraordinary efforts during wars, which had lasted, with little interruption, almost half a century. He represented the manifest imprudence of entering into engagements with a Pope of fourscore, as any system which rested on no better foundation than his life, must be extremely precarious, and upon the event of his death, which could not be distant, the face of things, together with the inclination of the Italian States, must instantly change, and the whole weight of the war be left upon the King alone. To these considerations he added the near prospect which they now had of a final accommodation with the Emperor, who, having taken the resolution of retiring from the world, wished to transmit his kingdoms in peace to his son; and he concluded with representing the absolute certainty of drawing the arms of England upon France, if it should appear that the re-establishment of tranquillity in Europe was prevented by the ambition of its Monarch.

<small>The Duke of Guise favours it.</small>

These arguments, weighty in themselves, and urged by a minister of great authority, would probably have determined the King to decline any connexion with the Pope. But the Duke of Guise, and his brother the Cardinal of Lorrain, who delighted no less in bold and dangerous undertakings than Montmorency shunned them, declared warmly for an alliance with the Pope. The Cardinal expected to be entrusted with the conduct of the negociations in the court of Rome to which this alliance would give rise; the Duke hoped to obtain the command of the army which would be appointed to invade Naples; and considering themselves as already in these stations, vast projects opened to their aspiring and unbounded ambition. Their credit, together with the influence of the King's mistress, the famous Diana of Poitiers, who was, at that time, entirely devoted to the interest of the family of Guise, more than counterbalanced all Montmorency's prudent remonstrances, and prevailed on an inconsiderate Prince to listen to the overtures of the Pope's envoy.

<small>Cardinal of Lorrain sent to negociate with the Pope.</small>

The Cardinal of Lorrain, as he had expected, was immediately sent to Rome with full powers to to conclude the treaty, and to concert measures for carrying it into execution. Before he could reach that city, the Pope, either from reflecting on the danger and uncertain issue of all military operations, or through the address of the Imperial ambassador, who had been at great pains to soothe him, had not only begun to lose much of the ardour with which he had commenced the negociation with France, but even discovered great unwillingness to continue it. In order to rouse him from this fit of despondency, and to rekindle his former rage, his nephews had recourse to the arts which they had already practised with so much success. They alarmed him with new representations of the Emperor's hostile intentions, with fresh accounts which they had received of threats uttered against him by the Imperial ministers, and with new discoveries which they pretended to have made of conspiracies formed, and just ready to take effect against his life.

But these artifices, having been formerly tried, would not have operated a second time with the same force, nor have made the impression which they wished, if Paul had not been excited by an offence of that kind which he was least able to bear. He received advice of the Recess of the Diet of Augsburg, and of the toleration which was thereby granted to the Protestants; and this threw him at once into such transports of passion against the Emperor and King of the Romans, as carried him headlong into all the violent measures

Paul enraged at the proceedings of the Diet of Augsburg;

of his nephews. Full of high ideas with respect to the papal prerogative, and animated with the fiercest zeal against heresy, he considered the liberty of deciding concerning religious matters, which had been assumed by an assembly composed chiefly of laymen, as a presumptuous and unpardonable encroachment on that jurisdiction which belonged to him alone; and regarded the indulgence which had been given to the Protestants as an impious act of that power which the Diet had usurped. He complained loudly of both to the Imperial ambassador. He insisted that the Recess of the Diet should immediately be declared illegal and void. He threatened the Emperor and King of the Romans, in case they should either refuse or delay to gratify him in this particular, with the severest effects of his vengeance. He talked in a tone of authority and command which might have suited a pontiff of the twelfth century, when a papal decree was sufficient to have shaken, or to have overturned, the throne of the greatest Monarch in Europe; but which was altogether improper in that age, especially when addressed to the minister of a Prince who had so often made pontiffs more formidable than Paul feel the weight of his power. The ambassador, however, heard all his extravagant propositions and menaces with much patience, and endeavoured to soothe him, by putting him in mind of the extreme distress to which the Emperor had been reduced at Inspruck, of the engagements which he had come under to the Protestants, in order to extricate himself, of the necessity of fulfilling thefe, and of accommodating his conduct to the fituation of his affairs. But weighty as thefe confiderations were, they made no impreffion on the mind of the haughty and bigoted pontiff, who inftantly replied, That he would abfolve him by his apoftolic authority from thofe impious engagements, and even command him not to perform them; that in carrying on the caufe of God and of the church, no regard ought to be had to the maxims of worldly prudence and policy; and that the ill fuccefs of the Emperor's fchemes in Germany might juftly be deemed a mark of the divine difpleafure againft him, on account of his having paid little attention to the former, while he regulated his conduct entirely by the latter. Having faid this, he turned from the ambaffador abruptly without waiting for a reply.

His nephews took care to applaud and cherifh thefe fentiments, and eafily wrought up his arrogant mind, fraught with all the monkifh ideas concerning the extent of the papal fupremacy, to fuch a pitch of refentment againft the houfe of Auftria, and to fuch an high opinion of his own power, that he talked continually of his being the fucceffor of thofe who had depofed Kings and Emperors; that he was exalted as head over them all, and would trample fuch as oppofed him under his feet. In this difpofition the Cardinal of Lorrain found the Pope, and eafily perfuaded him to fign a treaty, which had for its object

and exafperated by his nephews.

Dec. 15. concludes a treaty with France.

object the ruin of a Prince, against whom he was so highly exasperated. The stipulations in the treaty were much the same as had been proposed by the Pope's envoy at Paris; and it was agreed to keep the whole transaction secret until their united forces should be ready to take the field [s].

The Emperor resolves to resign his hereditary dominions. During the negociation of this treaty at Rome and Paris, an event happened which seemed to render the fears that had given rise to it vain, and the operations which were to follow upon it unnecessary. This was the Emperor's resignation of his hereditary dominions to his son Philip; together with his resolution to withdraw entirely from any concern in business or the affairs of this world, in order that he might spend the remainder of his days in retirement and solitude. Though it requires neither deep reflection nor extraordinary discernment to discover that the state of royalty is not exempt from cares and disappointment; though most of those who are exalted to a throne find solicitude, and satiety, and disgust to be their perpetual attendants in that envied pre-eminence; yet, to descend voluntarily from the supreme to a subordinate station, and to relinquish the possession of power in order to attain the enjoyment of happiness, seems to be an effort too great for the human mind. Several instances, indeed, occur in history, of Mo-

---

[s] Pallav. lib. xiii. p. 163. F. Paul, 365. Thuan. lib. xv. 525. lib. xvi. 540. Mem. de Ribier, ii. 609, &c.

narchs who have quitted a throne, and have ended their days in retirement. But they were either weak Princes who took this refolution rafhly, and repented of it as foon as it was taken; or unfortunate Princes, from whofe hands fome ftronger rival had wrefted their fceptre, and compelled them to defcend with reluctance into a private ftation. Dioclefian is perhaps the only Prince capable of holding the reins of government, who ever refigned them from deliberate choice, and who continued during many years to enjoy the tranquillity of retirement without fetching one penitent figh, or cafting back one look of defire, towards the power or dignity which he had abandoned.

No wonder, then, that Charles's refignation fhould fill all Europe with aftonifhment, and give rife, both among his contemporaries, and among the hiftorians of that period, to various conjectures concerning the motives which determined a Prince, whofe ruling paffion had been uniformly the love of power, at the age of fifty-fix, when objects of ambition continue to operate with full force on the mind, and are purfued with the greateft ardour, to take a refolution fo fingular and unexpected. But while many authors have imputed it to motives fo frivolous and fantaftical, as can hardly be fuppofed to influence any reafonable mind; while others have imagined it to be the refult of fome profound fcheme of policy;

The motives of this refignation.

hiftohistorians more intelligent, and better informed, neither ascribe it to caprice, nor search for mysterious secrets of state, where simple and obvious causes will fully account for the Emperor's conduct. Charles had been attacked early in life with the gout, and notwithstanding all the precautions of the most skilful physicians, the violence of the distemper increased as he advanced in age, and the fits became every year more frequent, as well as more severe. Not only was the vigour of his constitution broken, but the faculties of his mind were impaired by the excruciating torments which he endured. During the continuance of the fits, he was altogether incapable of applying to business, and even when they began to abate, as it was only at intervals that he could attend to what was serious, he gave up a great part of his time to trifling and even childish occupations, which served to relieve or to amuse his mind, enfeebled and worn out with excess of pain. Under these circumstances, the conduct of such affairs as occurred of course, in governing so many kingdoms, was a burden more than sufficient; but to push forward and complete the vast schemes, which the ambition of his more active years had formed, or to keep in view and carry on the same great system of policy, extending to every nation in Europe, and connected with the operations of every different court, were functions which so far exceeded his strength, that they oppressed and overwhelmed

his

his mind. As he had been long accustomed to view the business of every department, whether civil, or military, or ecclesiastical, with his own eyes, and to decide concerning it according to his own ideas, it gave him the utmost pain when he felt his infirmities increase so fast upon him, that he was obliged to commit the conduct of all affairs to his ministers. He imputed every misfortune which befel him, and every miscarriage that happened, even when the former was unavoidable and the latter accidental, to his inability to take the inspection of business himself. He complained of his hard fortune, in being opposed, in his declining years, to a rival, who was in the full vigour of life, and that while Henry could take and execute all his resolutions in person, he should now be reduced, both in council and in action, to rely on the talents and exertions of other men. Having thus grown old before his time, he wisely judged it more decent to conceal his infirmities in some solitude, than to expose them any longer to the public eye; and prudently determined not to forfeit the fame, or lose the acquisitions of his better years, by struggling, with a vain obstinacy, to retain the reins of government, when he was no longer able to hold them with steadiness, or to guide them with address*.

But

---

* Dom Levesque, in his memoirs of Cardinal Granvelle, gives a reason for the Emperor's resignation, which, as far as I recollect, is not mentioned by any other historian. He says,
that

BOOK XI.

1555.
Circumstances which had retarded it.

But though Charles had revolved this scheme in his mind for several years, and had communicated it to his sisters the dowager Queens of France and Hungary, who not only approved of his intention, but offered to accompany him to whatever place of retreat he should chuse; several things had hitherto prevented his carrying it into execution. He could not think of loading his son with the government of so many king-

---

that the Emperor having ceded the government of the kingdom of Naples and the dutchy of Milan to his son, upon his marriage with the Queen of England; Philip, notwithstanding the advice and intreaties of his father, removed most of the ministers and officers whom he had employed in those countries, and appointed creatures of his own, to fill the places which they held. That he aspired openly, and with little delicacy, to obtain a share in the administration of affairs in the Low-Countries. That he endeavoured to thwart the Emperor's measures, and to limit his authority, behaving towards him sometimes with inattention, and sometimes with haughtiness. That Charles finding that he must either yield on every occasion to his son, or openly contend with him, in order to avoid either of these, which were both disagreeable and mortifying to a father, he took the resolution of resigning his crowns, and of retiring from the world, vol. i. p. 24, &c. Dom Levesque derived his information concerning these curious facts, which he relates very briefly, from the original papers of Cardinal Granvelle. But as that vast collection of papers, which has been preserved and arranged by M. l'Abbé Boizot of Besançon, though one of the most valuable historical monuments of the sixteenth century, and which cannot fail of throwing much light on the transactions of Charles V. is not published, I cannot determine what degree of credit should be given to this account of Charles's resignation. I have therefore taken no notice of it in relating this event.

doms, until he should attain such maturity of age, and of abilities, as would enable him to sustain that weighty burden. But as Philip had now reached his twenty-eighth year, and had been early accustomed to business, for which he discovered both inclination and capacity, it can hardly be imputed to the partiality of paternal affection, that his scruples, with regard to this point, were entirely removed; and that he thought he might place his son, without further hesitation or delay, on the throne which he himself was about to abandon. His mother's situation had been another obstruction in his way. For although she had continued almost fifty years in confinement, and under the same disorder of mind which concern for her husband's death had brought upon her, yet the government of Spain was still vested in her jointly with the Emperor; her name was inserted together with his in all the public instruments issued in that kingdom; and such was the fond attachment of the Spaniards to her, that they would probably have scrupled to recognise Philip as their sovereign, unless she had consented to assume him as her partner on the throne. Her utter incapacity for business rendered it impossible to obtain her consent. But her death, which happened this year, removed this difficulty; and as Charles, upon that event, became sole monarch of Spain, it left the succession open to his son. The war with France had likewise been a reason for retaining the administration of affairs in his own hand, as he was extremely

solicitous

solicitous to have terminated it, that he might have given up his kingdoms to his son at peace with all the world. But as Henry had discovered no disposition to close with any of his overtures, and had even rejected proposals of peace, which were equal and moderate, in a tone that seemed to indicate a fixed purpose of continuing hostilities, he saw that it was vain to wait longer in expectation of an event, which, however desirable, was altogether uncertain.

The formalities with which he executed it.

As this, then, appeared to be the proper juncture for executing the scheme which he had long meditated, Charles resolved to resign his kingdoms to his son, with a solemnity suitable to the importance of the transaction, and to perform this last act of sovereignty with such formal pomp, as might leave a lasting impression on the minds not only of his subjects but of his successor. With this view he called Philip out of England, where the peevish temper of his Queen, which increased with her despair of having issue, rendered him extremely unhappy; and the jealousy of the English left him no hopes of obtaining the direction of their affairs. Having assembled the States of the Low-Countries at Brussels, on the twenty-fifth of October, Charles seated himself, for the last time, in the chair of state, on one side of which was placed his son, and on the other his sister the Queen of Hungary, regent of the Netherlands, with a splendid retinue of the princes of the Empire and grandees of Spain

standing

standing behind him. The president of the council of Flanders, by his command, explained, in a few words, his intention in calling this extraordinary meeting in the States. He then read the instrument of resignation, by which Charles surrendered to his son Philip all his territories, jurisdiction, and authority in the Low-Countries, absolving his subjects there from their oath of allegiance to him, which he required them to transfer to Philip his lawful heir, and to serve him with the same loyalty and zeal which they had manifested, during so long a course of years, in support of his government.

CHARLES then rose from his seat, and leaning on the shoulder of the Prince of Orange, because he was unable to stand without support, he addressed himself to the audience, and from a paper which he held in his hand, in order to assist his memory, he recounted, with dignity, but without ostentation, all the great things which he had undertaken and performed since the commencement of his administration. He observed, that, from the seventeenth year of his age, he had dedicated all his thoughts and attention to public objects, reserving no portion of his time for the indulgence of his ease, and very little for the enjoyment of private pleasure; that either in a pacific or hostile manner, he had visited Germany nine times, Spain six times, France four times, Italy seven times, the Low-Countries ten times, England twice, Africa as often, and had made

made eleven voyages by sea; that while his health permittted him to discharge his duty, and the vigour of his constitution was equal, in any degree, to the arduous office of governing such extensive dominions, he had never shunned labour, nor repined under fatigue; that now when his health was broken, and his vigour exhausted by the rage of an incurable distemper, his growing infirmities admonished him to retire, nor was he so fond of reigning, as to retain the sceptre in an impotent hand, which was no longer able to protect his subjects, or to secure to them the happiness which he wished they should enjoy; that instead of a sovereign worn out with diseases, and scarcely half alive, he gave them one in the prime of life, accustomed already to govern, and who added to the vigour of youth all the attention and sagacity of maturer years; that if, during the course of a long administration, he had committed any material error in government, or if, under the pressure of so many and great affairs, and amidst the attention which he had been obliged to give to them, he had either neglected or injured any of his subjects, he now implored their forgiveness; that, for his part, he should ever retain a grateful sense of their fidelity and attachment, and would carry the remembrance of it along with him to the place of his retreat, as his sweetest consolation, as well as the best reward for all his services, and in his last prayers to Almighty God would pour forth his most earnest petitions for their welfare.

THEN

Then turning towards Philip, who fell on his knees and kissed his father's hand, "If," says he, "I had left you by my death this rich inheritance, to which I have made such large additions, some regard would have been justly due to my memory on that account; but now, when I voluntarily resign to you what I might have still retained, I may well expect the warmest expressions of thanks on your part. With these, however, I dispense, and shall consider your concern for the welfare of your subjects, and your love of them, as the best and most acceptable testimony of your gratitude to me. It is in your power, by a wise and virtuous administration, to justify the extraordinary proof which I, this day, give of my paternal affection, and to demonstrate that you are worthy of the confidence which I repose in you. Preserve an inviolable regard for religion; maintain the Catholic faith in its purity; let the laws of your country be sacred in your eyes; encroach not on the rights and privileges of your people; and if the time should ever come, when you shall wish to enjoy the tranquillity of private life, may you have a son endowed with such qualities, that you can resign your sceptre to him, with as much satisfaction as I give up mine to you."

As soon as Charles had finished this long address to his subjects and to their new sovereign, he sunk into the chair, exhausted and ready to faint with the fatigue of such an extraordinary effort.

effort. During his difcourfe, the whole audience melted into tears, fome from admiration of his magnanimity, others foftened by the expreffions of tendernefs towards his fon, and of love to his people; and all were affected with the deepeft forrow at lofing a fovereign, who, during his adminiftration, had diftinguifhed the Netherlands, his native country, with particular marks of his regard and attachment.

Philip then arofe from his knees, and after returning thanks to his father, with a low and fubmiffive voice, for the royal gift which his unexampled bounty had beftowed upon him, he addreffed the affembly of the States, and regretting his inability to fpeak the Flemifh language with fuch facility as to exprefs what he felt on this interefting occafion, as well as what he owed to his good fubjects in the Netherlands, he begged that they would permit Granvelle bifhop of Arras, to deliver what he had given him in charge to fpeak in his name. Granvelle, in a long difcourfe, expatiated on the zeal with which Philip was animated for the good of his fubjects, on his refolution to devote all his time and talents to the promoting of their happinefs, and on his intention to imitate his father's example in diftinguifhing the Netherlands with peculiar marks of his regard. Maës, a lawyer of great eloquence, replied, in the name of the States, with large profeffions of their fidelity and affection to their new fovereign.

Then

EMPEROR CHARLES V.

THEN Mary, Queen-dowager of Hungary, resigned the regency with which she had been entrusted by her brother during the space of twenty-five years. Next day Philip, in presence of the States, took the usual oaths to maintain the rights and privileges of his subjects; and all the members, in their own name, and in that of their constituents, swore allegiance to him [t].

A FEW weeks after this transaction, Charles, in an assembly no less splendid, and with a ceremonial equally pompous, resigned to his son the crowns of Spain, with all the territories depending on them, both in the old and in the new world. Of all these vast possessions, he reserved nothing for himself but an annual pension of an hundred thousand crowns, to defray the charges of his family, and to afford him a small sum for acts of beneficence and charity [u].

As

---

[t] Godleveus Relatio Abdicationis Car. V. ap. Goldast. Polit. Imper. p. 377. Strada de Bello Belgico, lib. i. p. 5.

[u] The Emperor's resignation is an event not only of such importance, but of such a nature, that the precise date of it, one would expect, should have been ascertained by historians with the greatest accuracy. There is, however, an amazing and unaccountable diversity among them with regard to this point. All agree, that the deed by which Charles transferred to his son his dominions in the Netherlands, bears date at Brussels the 25th of October. Sandoval fixes on the 28th of October as the day on which the ceremony of resignation happened, and he was present at the transaction, vol. ii. p. 592. Godleveus, who published a treatise de Abdicatione Caroli V. fixes the public ceremony, as well as the date of the

As he had fixed on a place of retreat in Spain, hoping that the dryness and the warmth of the climate in that country might mitigate the violence of his disease, which had been much increased by the moisture of the air and the rigour of the

the instrument of resignation, on the 25th. Pere Barre, I know not on what authority, fixes it on the 24th of November, Hist. d'Alem. viii. 976. Herrera agrees with Godleveus in his account of this matter, tom. i. 155. as likewise does Pallavicini, whose authority with respect to dates, and every thing where a minute accuracy is requisite, is of great weight, Hist. lib. xvi. p. 168. Historians differ no less with regard to the day on which Charles resigned the crown of Spain to his son. According to M. de Thou, it was a month after his having resigned his dominions in the Netherlands, i. e. about the 25th of November, Thuan. lib. xvi. p. 571. According to Sandoval, it was on the 16th of January 1556, Sand. ii. 603. Antonio de Vera agrees with him, Epitome del Vida del Car. V. p. 110. According to Pallavicini, it was on the 17th, Pal. lib. xvi. p. 168. and with him Herrera agrees, Vida del D. Felipe, tom. i. p. 233. But Ferreras fixes it on the first day of January, Hist. Gener. tom. ix. p. 371. M. de Beaucaire supposes the resignation of the crown of Spain to have been executed a few days after the resignation of the Netherlands, Com. de Reb. Gall. p. 879. It is remarkable, that in the treaty of truce at Vaucelles, though Charles had made over all his dominions to his son some weeks previous to the conclusion of it, all the stipulations are in the Emperor's name, and Philip is only styled King of England and Naples. It is certain Philip was not proclaimed King of Castile, &c. at Valladolid sooner than the 24th of March, Sandov. ii. p. 606; and previous to that ceremony, he did not chuse, it should seem, to assume the title of King of any of his Spanish kingdoms, or to perform any act of royal jurisdiction. In a deed annexed to the treaty of truce, dated April 19, he assumes the title of King of Castile, &c. in the usual style of the Spanish monarchs in that age. Corps Dipl. tom. iv. Append. p. 85.

winters

winters in the Netherlands, he was extremely impatient to embark for that kingdom, and to difengage himfelf entirely from bufinefs, which he found to be impoffible while he remained in Bruffels. But his phyficians remonftrated fo ftrongly againft his venturing to fea at that cold and boifterous feafon of the year, that he confented, though with reluctance, to put off his voyage for fome months.

<small>BOOK XI.

1556.

Obliged to remain for fome time in the Netherlands.</small>

By yielding to their intreaties, he had the fatisfaction, before he left the Low-Countries, of taking a confiderable ftep towards a peace with France, which he ardently wifhed for, not only on his fon's account, but that he might have the merit, when quitting the world, of re-eftablifhing that tranquillity in Europe, which he had banifhed out of it almoft from the time that he affumed the adminiftration of affairs. Previous to his refignation, commiffioners had been appointed by him and by the French King, in order to treat of an exchange of prifoners. In their conferences at the abbey of Vaucelles, near Cambray, an expedient was accidentally propofed for terminating hoftilities between the contending monarchs, by a long truce, during the fubfiftence of which, and without difcuffing their refpective claims, each fhould retain what was now in his poffeffion. Charles, fenfible how much his kingdoms were exhaufted by the expenfive and almoft continual wars in which his ambition had engaged him, and eager to gain for his fon a fhort interval

<small>Promotes the negociation for peace.</small>

of peace, that he might establish himself firmly on his throne, declared warmly for closing with the overture, though manifestly dishonourable as well as disadvantageous; and such was the respect due to his wisdom and experience, that Philip, notwithstanding his unwillingness to purchase peace by such concessions, did not presume to urge his opinion in opposition to that of his father.

A truce concluded.

Henry could not have hesitated one moment about giving his consent to a truce on such conditions, as would leave him in quiet possession of the greater part of the Duke of Savoy's dominions, together with the important conquests which he had made on the German frontier. But it was no easy matter to reconcile such a step with the engagements which he had come under to the Pope, in his late treaty with him. The Constable Montmorency, however, represented in such a striking light the imprudence of sacrificing the true interests of his kingdom to these rash obligations, and took such advantage of the absence of the Cardinal of Lorrain, who had seduced the King into his alliance with the Caraffas, that Henry, who was naturally fluctuating and unsteady, and apt to be influenced by the advice last given him, authorised his ambassadors to sign a treaty of truce with the Emperor for five years, on the terms which had been proposed. But that he might not seem to have altogether forgotten his ally the Pope, who, he foresaw, would be highly

5th Feb.

EMPEROR CHARLES V. 217

exasperated, he, in order to soothe him, took care that he should be expressly included in the truce[x].

The Count of Lalain repaired to Blois, and the Admiral Coligny to Brussels, the former to be present when the King of France, and the latter, when the Emperor and his son ratified the treaty and bound themselves by oath to observe it[y]. When an account of the conferences at Vaucelles, and of the conditions of truce which had been proposed there, were first carried to Rome, it gave the Pope no manner of disquiet. He trusted so much to the honour of the French monarch, that he would not allow himself to think that Henry could forget so soon, or violate so shamefully, all the stipulations in his league with him. He had such an high opinion of the Emperor's wisdom, that he made no doubt of his refusing his consent to a truce on such unequal terms; and on both these accounts he confidently pronounced that this, like many pre-

Ratified by both monarchs.

The Pope's astonishment and distress.

---

[x] Mem. de Ribier, ii. 626. Corps Diplom. tom. iv. App. 81.
[y] One of Admiral de Coligny's attendants, who wrote to the court of France an account of what happened while they resided at Brussels, takes notice, as an instance of Philip's unpoliteness, that he received the French ambassador in an apartment hung with tapestry, which represented the battle of Pavia, the manner in which Francis I. was taken prisoner, his voyage to Spain, with all the mortifying circumstances of his captivity and imprisonment at Madrid. Mem. de Ribier, ii. 634.

ceding

ceding negociations, would terminate in nothing. But later and more certain intelligence soon convinced him that no reasoning in political affairs is more fallacious, than, because an event is improbable, to conclude that it will not happen. The sudden and unexpected conclusion of the truce filled Paul with astonishment and terror. The Cardinal of Lorrain durst not encounter that storm of indignation, to which he knew that he should be exposed from the haughty Pontiff, who had so good reason to be incensed; but departing abruptly from Rome, he left to the Cardinal Tournon the difficult task of attempting to soothe Paul and his nephews. They were fully sensible of the perilous situation in which they now stood. By their engagements with France, which were no longer secret, they had highly irritated Philip. They dreaded the violence of his implacable temper. The duke of Alva, a minister fitted, as well by his abilities as by the severity of his nature, for executing all Philip's rigorous schemes, had advanced from Milan to Naples, and began to assemble troops on the frontiers of the Ecclesiastical State. While they, if deserted by France, must not only relinquish all the hopes of dominion and sovereignty to which their ambition aspired, but remain exposed to the resentment of the Spanish monarch, without one ally to protect them against an enemy with whom they were so little able to contend.

UNDER

Under these circumstances, Paul had recourse to the arts of negociation and intrigue, of which the Papal court knows well how to avail itself in order to ward off any calamity threatened by an enemy superior in power. He affected to approve highly of the truce, as an happy expedient for putting a stop to the effusion of Christian blood. He expressed his warmest wishes that it might prove the forerunner of a definitive peace. He exhorted the rival Princes to embrace this favourable opportunity of setting on foot a negociation for that purpose, and offered, as their common father, to be mediator between them. Under this pretext, he appointed Cardinal Rebiba his nuncio to the court of Brussels, and his nephew Cardinal Caraffa to that of Paris. The public instructions given to both were the same; that they should use their utmost endeavours to prevail with the two monarchs to accept of the Pope's mediation, that, by means of it, peace might be re-established, and measures might be taken for assembling a general council. But under this specious appearance of zeal for attaining objects so desirable in themselves, and so becoming his sacred character to pursue, Paul concealed very different intentions. Caraffa, besides his public instructions, received a private commission to solicit the French King to renounce the treaty of truce, and to renew his engagements with the Holy See; and he was empowered to spare neither entreaties, nor promises, nor bribes, in order to gain that point. This, both

1556.
He attempts to rekindle the war.

both the uncle and the nephew confidered as the real end of the embaffy; while the other ferved to amufe the vulgar, or to deceive the Emperor and his fon. The Cardinal, accordingly, fet out inftantly for Paris, and travelled with the greateft expedition, while Rebiba was detained fome weeks at Rome; and when it became neceffary for him to begin his journey, he received fecret orders to protract it as much as poffible, that the iffue of Caraffa's negociation might be known before he fhould reach Bruffels, and according to that, proper directions might be given to him with regard to the tone which he fhould affume, in treating with the Emperor and his fon [z].

His negociations for that purpofe.

CARAFFA made his entry into Paris with extraordinary pomp; and having prefented a confecrated fword to Henry, as the Protector, on whofe aid the Pope relied in the prefent exigency, he befought him not to difregard the entreaties of a parent in diftrefs, but to employ that weapon which he gave him in his defence. This he reprefented not only as a duty of filial piety, but as an act of juftice. As the Pope, from confidence in the affiftance and fupport which his late treaty with France entitled him to expect, had taken fuch fteps as had irritated the King of Spain, he conjured Henry not to fuffer Paul and his family to be crufhed under the weight of that

[z] Pallav. lib. xiii. p. 169. Burnet Hift. of Reform. ii. App. 309.

resentment which they had drawn on themselves merely by their attachment to France. Together with this argument addressed to his generosity, he employed another which he hoped would work on his ambition. He affirmed that now was the time, when, with the most certain prospect of success, he might attack Philip's dominions in Italy; that the flower of the veteran Spanish bands had perished in the wars of Hungary, Germany, and the Low Countries; that the Emperor had left his son an exhausted treasury, and kingdoms drained of men; that he had no longer to contend with the abilities, the experience, and good fortune of Charles, but with a monarch scarcely seated on his throne, unpractised in command, odious to many of the Italian states, and dreaded by all. He promised that the Pope, who had already levied soldiers, would bring a considerable army into the field, which, when joined by a sufficient number of French troops, might, by one brisk and sudden effort, drive the Spaniards out of Naples, and add to the crown of France a kingdom, the conquest of which had been the great object of all his predecessors during half a century, and the chief motive of all their expeditions into Italy.

EVERY word Caraffa spoke made a deep impression on Henry; conscious, on the one hand, that the Pope had just cause to reproach him with having violated the laws not only of generosity

Their effect.
July 31.

rosity but of decency, when he renounced his league with him, and had agreed to the truce of Vaucelles; and eager, on the other hand, not only to distinguish his reign by a conquest, which three former monarchs had attempted without success, but likewise to acquire an establishment of such dignity and value for one of his sons. Reverence, however, for the oath, by which he had so lately confirmed the truce of Vaucelles; the extreme old age of the Pope, whose death might occasion an entire revolution in the political system of Italy; together with the representations of Montmorency, who repeated all the arguments he had used against the first league with Paul, and pointed out the great and immediate advantages which France derived from the truce; kept Henry for some time in suspense, and might possibly have outweighed all Caraffa's arguments. But the Cardinal was not such a novice in the arts of intrigue and negociation, as not to have expedients ready for removing or surmounting all these obstacles. To obviate the king's scruple with regard to his oath, he produced powers from the Pope to absolve him from the obligation of it. By way of security against any danger which he might apprehend from the Pope's death, he engaged that his uncle would make such a nomination of Cardinals, as should give Henry the absolute command of the next election, and enable him to place in the papal chair a person entirely devoted to his interest.

In order to counterbalance the effect of the Conſtable's opinion and influence, he employed not only the active talents of the Duke of Guiſe, and the eloquence of his brother the Cardinal of Lorrain, but the addreſs of the Queen, aided by the more powerful arts of Diana of Poitiers, who, unfortunately for France, co-operated with Catharine in this point, though ſhe took pleaſure, on almoſt every other occaſion, to thwart and mortify her. They, by their united ſolicitations, eaſily ſwayed the King, who leaned, of his own accord, to that ſide towards which they wiſhed him to incline. All Montmorency's prudent remonſtrances were diſregarded; the nuncio abſolved Henry from his oath; and he ſigned a new league with the Pope, which rekindled the flames of war both in Italy and in the Low-Countries.

As ſoon as Paul was informed by his nephew that there was a fair proſpect of his ſucceeding in this negociation, he diſpatched a meſſenger after the nuncio Rebiba, with orders to return to Rome, without proceeding to Bruſſels. As it was now no longer neceſſary to preſerve that tone of moderation, which ſuited the character of a mediator, and which he had affected to aſſume, or to put any farther reſtraint upon his reſentment againſt Philip, he boldly threw off the maſk, and took ſuch violent ſteps as rendered a rupture unavoidable. He ſeized and impriſoned the Spaniſh envoy at his court. He excommunicated

July 31. The Pope's violent proceedings againſt Philip.

cated the Colonnas; and having deprived Mark Antonio, the head of that family, of the dukedom of Paliano, he granted that dignity, together with the territory annexed to it, to his nephew the Count of Montorio. He ordered a legal information to be presented in the consistory of Cardinals against Philip, setting forth that he, notwithstanding the fidelity and allegiance due by him to the Holy See, of which he held the kingdom of Naples, had not only afforded a retreat in his dominions to the Colonnas, whom the Pope had excommunicated and declared rebels, but had furnished them with arms, and was ready, in conjunction with them, to invade the Ecclesiastical State in an hostile manner; that such conduct in a vassal was to be deemed treason against his liege lord, the punishment of which was the forfeiture of his fief. Upon this, the consistorial advocate requested the Pope to take cognizance of the cause, and to appoint a day for hearing of it, when he would make good every article of the charge, and expect from his justice that sentence which the heinousness of Philip's crimes merited. Paul, whose pride was highly flattered with the idea of trying and passing judgment on so great a king, assented to his request, and as if it had been no less easy to execute than to pronounce such a sentence, declared that he would consult with the Cardinals concerning the formalities requisite in conducting the trial [a].

[a] Pallav. lib. xiii. 171.

But while Paul allowed his pride and resentment to drive him on with such headlong impetuosity, Philip discovered an amazing moderation on his part. He had been taught by the Spanish ecclesiastics, who had the charge of his education, a profound veneration for the Holy See. This sentiment, which had been early infused, grew up with him as he advanced in years, and took full possession of his mind, which was naturally thoughtful, serious, and prone to superstition. When he foresaw a rupture with the Pope approaching, he had such violent scruples with respect to the lawfulness of taking arms against the Vicegerent of Christ, and the common father of all Christians, that he consulted some Spanish divines upon that point. They, with the usual dexterity of casuists in accommodating their responses to the circumstances of those who apply to them for direction, assured him that, after employing prayers and remonstrances in order to bring the Pope to reason, he had full right, both by the laws of nature and of Christianity, not only to defend himself when attacked, but to begin hostilities, if that were judged the most proper expedient for preventing the effects of Paul's violence and injustice. Philip nevertheless continued to deliberate and delay, considering it as a most cruel misfortune, that his administration should open with an attack on a person, whose sacred function and character he so highly respected [b].

[b] Ferrer. Hist. de Espagne, ix. 373. Herrera, i. 308.

1556.
The Duke of Alva takes the field againſt the Pope.

Sept. 5.

At laſt the Duke of Alva, who, in compliance with his maſter's ſcruples, had continued to negociate long after he ſhould have begun to act, finding Paul inexorable, and that every overture of peace, and every appearance of heſitation on his part, increaſed the Pontiff's natural arrogance, took the field and entered the eccleſiaſtical territories. His army did not exceed twelve thouſand men, but it was compoſed of veteran ſoldiers, and commanded chiefly by thoſe Roman barons, whom Paul's violence had driven into exile. The valour of the troops, together with the animoſity of their leaders, who fought in their own quarrel, and to recover their own eſtates, ſupplied the want of numbers. As none of the French forces were yet arrived, Alva ſoon became maſter of the Campagna Romana; ſome cities being ſurrendered through the cowardice of the garriſons, which conſiſted of raw ſoldiers, ill diſciplined, and worſe commanded; the gates of others being opened by the inhabitants, who were eager to receive back their ancient maſters. Alva, that he might not be taxed with impiety in ſeizing the patrimony of the church, took poſſeſſion of the towns which capitulated, in the name of the college of cardinals, to which, or to the Pope that ſhould be choſen to ſucceed Paul, he declared that he would immediately reſtore them.

A truce between the Pope and Philip.

The rapid progreſs of the Spaniards, whoſe light troops made excurſions even to the gates of Rome, filled that city with conſternation. Paul, though

though inflexible and undaunted himself, was obliged to give way so far to the fears and solicitations of the Cardinals, as to send deputies to Alva in order to propose a cessation of arms. The Pope yielded the more readily, as he was sensible of a double advantage which might be derived from obtaining that point. It would deliver the inhabitants of Rome from their present terror, and would afford time for the arrival of the succours which he expected from France. Nor was Alva unwilling to close with the overture, both as he knew how desirous his master was to terminate a war, which he had undertaken with reluctance, and as his army was so much weakened by garrisoning the great number of towns which he had reduced, that it was hardly in a condition to keep the field without fresh recruits. A truce was accordingly concluded first for ten, and afterwards for forty days, during which, various schemes of peace were proposed, and perpetual negociations were carried on, but with no sincerity on the part of the Pope. The return of his nephew the Cardinal to Rome, the receipt of a considerable sum remitted by the King of France, the arrival of one body of French troops, together with the expectation of others which had begun their march, rendered him more arrogant than ever, and banished all thoughts from his mind, but those of war and revenge [c].

[c] Pallav. lib. xiii. 177. Thuan. lib. xvii. 588. Mem. de Ribier, ii. 664.

THE HISTORY

OF THE

REIGN

OF THE

EMPEROR CHARLES V.

BOOK XII.

WHILE these operations or intrigues kept the Pope and Philip busy and attentive, the Emperor disentangled himself finally from all the affairs of this world, and set out for the place of his retreat. He had hitherto retained the Imperial dignity, not from any unwillingness to relinquish it, for, after having resigned the real and extensive authority that he enjoyed in his hereditary dominions, to part with the limited and often ideal jurisdiction which belongs to an elective crown, was no great sacrifice. His sole motive for delay was to gain a few months, for making one trial more, in order to accomplish his favourite scheme in behalf of his son. At the very time Charles seemed to be most sensible of the

1556. Charles's new attempt to alter the succession of the empire.

the vanity of worldly grandeur, and when he appeared to be quitting it not only with indifference, but with contempt, the vast schemes of ambition, which had so long occupied and engrossed his mind, still kept possession of it. He could not think of leaving his son in a rank inferior to that which he himself had held among the Princes of Europe. As he had, some years before, made a fruitless attempt to secure the Imperial crown to Philip, that by uniting it to the kingdoms of Spain, and the dominions of the house of Burgundy, he might put it in his power to prosecute, with a better prospect of success, those great plans, which his own infirmities had obliged him to abandon, he was still unwilling to relinquish this flattering project as chimerical or unattainable.

Which proves unsuccessful.

Notwithstanding the repulse which he had formerly met with from his brother Ferdinand, he renewed his solicitations with fresh importunity; and during the summer, had tried every art, and employed every argument, which he thought could induce him to quit the Imperial throne to Philip, and to accept of the investiture of some province, either in Italy, or in the Low Countries, as an equivalent[a]. But Ferdinand, who was so firm and inflexible with regard to this point, that he had paid no regard to the solicitations of the Emperor, even when they were en-

[a] Ambassades des Noailles, tom. v. 356.

forced

forced with all the weight of authority which accompanies supreme power, received the overture, that now came from him in the situation to which he had descended, with greater indifference, and would hardly deign to listen to it. Charles, ashamed of his own credulity in having imagined that he might accomplish that now, which he had attempted formerly without success, desisted finally from his scheme. He then resigned the government of the Empire, and having transferred all his claims of obedience and allegiance from the Germanic body, to his brother the King of the Romans, he executed a deed to that effect, with all the formalities requisite in such an important transaction. The instrument of resignation he commited to William Prince of Orange, and empowered him to lay it before the college of electors [b].

Nothing now remained to detain Charles from that retreat for which he languished. The preparations for his voyage having been made for some time, he set out for Zuitburg in Zealand, where the fleet which was to convoy him had orders to assemble. In his way thither he passed through Ghent, and after stopping there a few days, to indulge that tender and pleasing melancholy, which arises in the mind of every man in the decline of life, on visiting the place of his nativity, and viewing the scenes and objects familiar to him in his

[b] Goldast. Constit. Imper. pars i. 576.

early

BOOK XII.
1556.

early youth, he pursued his journey, accompanied by his son Philip, his daughter the archduchess, his sisters the dowager Queens of France and Hungary, Maximilian his son-in-law, and a numerous retinue of the Flemish nobility. Before he went on board, he dismissed them, with marks of his attention or regard, and taking leave of Philip with all the tenderness of a father who embraced his son for the last time, he set sail on the seventeenth of September, under convoy of a large fleet of Spanish, Flemish, and English ships. He declined a pressing invitation, from the Queen of England, to land in some part of her dominions, in order to refresh himself, and that she might have the comfort of seeing him once more. "It cannot surely," said he, "be agreeable to a Queen to receive a visit from a father-in-law, who is now nothing more than a private gentleman."

His arrival and reception there.

His voyage was prosperous, and he arrived at Laredo in Biscay on the eleventh day after he left Zealand. As soon as he landed, he fell prostrate on the ground; and considering himself now as dead to the world, he kissed the earth, and said, "Naked came I out of my mother's womb, and naked I now return to thee, thou common mother of mankind." From Laredo he pursued his journey to Burgos, carried sometimes in a chair and sometimes in a horse litter, suffering exquisite pain at every step, and advancing with the greatest difficulty. Some of the Spanish nobility repaired to Burgos, in order to pay court

court to him, but they were so few in number, and their attendance was so negligent, that Charles observed it, and felt, for the first time, that he was no longer a Monarch. Accustomed from his early youth to the dutiful and officious respect with which those who possess sovereign power are attended, he had received it with the credulity common to Princes, and was sensibly mortified, when he now discovered, that he had been indebted to his rank and power for much of that obsequious regard which he had fondly thought was paid to his personal qualities. But though he might have soon learned to view with unconcern the levity of his subjects, or to have despised their neglect, he was more deeply afflicted with the ingratitude of his son, who, forgetting already how much he owed to his father's bounty, obliged him to remain some weeks at Burgos, before he paid him the first moiety of that small pension, which was all that he had reserved of so many kingdoms. As without this sum, Charles could not dismiss his domestics with such rewards as their services merited, or his generosity had destined for them, he could not help expressing both surprize and dissatisfaction[c]. At last the money was paid, and Charles having dismissed a great number of his domestics, whose attendance he thought would be superfluous or cumbersome in his retirement, he proceeded to Valladolid. There he took a last and tender leave of his two

[c] Strada de Bello Belg. lib. i. 9.

sisters, whom he would not permit to accompany him to his solitude, though they requested him with tears, not only that they might have the consolation of contributing by their attendance and care to mitigate or to sooth his sufferings, but that they might reap instruction and benefit by joining with him in those pious exercises, to which he had consecrated the remainder of his days.

The place of his retreat.

From Valladolid he continued his journey to Plazencia in Estremadura. He had passed through this place a great many years before, and having been struck at that time with the delightful situation of the monastery of St. Justus, belonging to the order of St. Jerome, not many miles distant from the town, he had then observed to some of his attendants, that this was a spot to which Dioclesian might have retired with pleasure. The impression had remained so strong on his mind, that he pitched upon it as the place of his own retreat. It was seated in a vale of no great extent, watered by a small brook, and surrounded by rising grounds, covered with lofty trees; from the nature of the soil, as well as the temperature of the climate, it was esteemed the most healthful and delicious situation in Spain. Some months before his resignation he had sent an architect thither, to add a new apartment to the monastery, for his accommodation; but he gave strict orders that the style of the building should be such as suited his present station, rather than his former dignity.

dignity. It consisted only of six rooms, four of them in the form of Friars cells, with naked walls; the other two, each twenty feet square, were hung with brown cloth, and furnished in the most simple manner. They were all on a level with the ground; with a door on one side into a garden, of which Charles himself had given the plan, and had filled it with various plants, which he intended to cultivate with his own hands. On the other side they communicated with the chapel of the monastery, in which he was to perform his devotions. Into this humble retreat, hardly sufficient for the comfortable accommodation of a private gentleman, did Charles enter, with twelve domestics only. He buried there, in solitude and silence, his grandeur, his ambition, together with all those vast projects, which, during almost half a century, had alarmed and agitated Europe, filling every kingdom in it, by turns, with the terror of his arms, and the dread of being subdued by his power [d].

THE contrast between Charles's conduct and that of the Pope at this juncture, was so obvious, that it struck even the most careless observers; nor was the comparison which they made to the advantage of Paul. The former, a conqueror, born to reign, long accustomed to the splendour which accompanies supreme power, and to those busy and interesting scenes in which an active

[d] Sandov. ii. 607. & Zuniga, 100. Thuan. lib. xvii. 609.

ambition had engaged him, quitted the world at a period of life not far advanced, that he might close the evening of his days in tranquillity, and secure some interval for sober thought and serious recollection. The latter, a priest, who had passed the early part of his life in the shade of the schools, and in the study of the speculative sciences, who was seemingly so detached from the world, that he had shut himself up for many years in the solitude of a cloyster, and who was not raised to the papal throne until he had reached the extremity of old age, discovered at once all the impetuosity of youthful ambition, and formed extensive schemes, in order to accomplish which, he scrupled not to scatter the seeds of discord, and to kindle the flames of war, in every corner of Europe. But Paul, regardless of the opinion or censures of mankind, held on his own course with his wonted arrogance and violence. These, although they seemed already to have exceeded all bounds, rose to still a greater height, upon the arrival of the Duke of Guise in Italy.

The Duke of Guise leads the French army into Italy.

THAT which the two Princes of Lorrain foresaw and desired, had happened. The Duke of Guise was entrusted with the command of the army appointed to march to the Pope's assistance. It consisted of twenty thousand men, of the best troops in the service of France. So high was the Duke's reputation, and such the general expectation of beholding some extraordinary exertion of his

his courage and abilities in a war into which he had precipitated his country, chiefly with the defign of obtaining a field where he might difplay his own talents, that many of the French nobility who had no command in the troops employed, accompanied him as volunteers. This army paffed the Alps in an inclement feafon, and advanced towards Rome, without any oppofition from the Spaniards, who, as they were not ftrong enough to act in different parts, had collected all their forces in one body on the frontiers of Naples, for the defence of that kingdom.

The Pope renews hoftilities againft Philip.

EMBOLDENED by the approach of the French, the Pope let loofe all the fury of his refentment againft Philip, which, notwithftanding the natural violence of his temper, prudential confiderations had hitherto obliged him to keep under fome reftraint. He named commiffioners, whom he empowered to pafs judgment in the fuit, which the confiftorial advocate had commenced againft Philip, in order to prove that he had forfeited the crown of Naples, by taking arms *Feb. 12.* againft the Holy See, of which he was a vaffal. He recalled all the nuncios refident in the courts of Charles V. of Philip, or of any of their allies. This was levelled chiefly againft Cardinal Pole, *April 9.* the papal legate in the court of England, whofe great merit, in having contributed fo fuccefsfully to reconcile that kingdom to the church of Rome, together with the expectation of farther fervices, which he might perform, was not fufficient to

screen

screen him from the resentment that he had incurred by his zealous endeavours to establish peace between the house of Austria and France. He commanded an addition to be made to the anathemas annually denounced against the enemies of the church on Maundy-Thursday, whereby he inflicted the censure of excommunication on the authors of the late invasion of the ecclesiastical territories, whatever their rank or dignity might be; and, in consequence of this, the usual prayers for the Emperor were omitted next day in the Pope's chapel [e].

<small>His military preparations inadequate.</small>

But while the Pope indulged himself in those wild and childish sallies of rage, either he neglected, or found that it exceeded his power, to take such measures as would have rendered his resentment really formidable, and fatal to his enemies. For when the Duke of Guise entered Rome, where he was received with a triumphal pomp, which would have been more suitable if he had been returning after having terminated the war with glory, than when he was going to begin it with a doubtful chance of success, he found none of the preparations for war in such forwardness as Cardinal Caraffa had promised, or he had expected. The papal troops were far inferior in number to the quota stipulated; no magazines sufficient for their subsistence were formed; nor was money for paying them provided. The Vene-

[e] Pal. lib. xiii. 180. Mem. de Ribier, ii. 678.

tians, agreeably to that cautious maxim which the misfortunes of their state had first led them to adopt, and which was now become a fundamental principle in their policy, declared their resolution to preserve an exact neutrality, without taking any part in the quarrels of Princes, so far superior to themselves in power. The other Italian states were either openly united in league with Philip, or secretly wished success to his arms against a Pontiff, whose inconsiderate ambition had rendered Italy once more the seat of war.

BOOK XII.

1557.

THE Duke of Guise perceived that the whole weight of the war would devolve on the French troops under his command; and became sensible, though too late, how imprudent it is to rely, in the execution of great enterprizes, on the aid of feeble allies. Pushed on, however, by the Pope's impatience for action, as well as by his own desire of performing some part of what he had so confidently undertaken, he marched towards Naples, and began his operations. But the success of these fell far short of his former reputation, of what the world expected, and of what he himself had promised. He opened the campaign with the siege of Civitella, a town of some importance on the Neapolitan frontier. But the obstinacy with which the Spanish governor defended it, baffled all the impetuous efforts of the French valour, and obliged the Duke of Guise, after a siege of three weeks, to retire from the town with disgrace. He endeavoured to wipe off that stain, by advancing

Duke of Guise's operations.

April 13.

vancing boldly towards the Duke of Alva's camp, and offering him battle. But that prudent commander, sensible of all the advantages of standing on the defensive before an invading enemy, declined an engagement, and kept within his intrenchments; and adhering to his plan with the steadiness of a Castilian, eluded, with great address, all the Duke of Guise's stratagems to draw him into action [f]. By this time sickness began to waste the French army; violent dissensions had arisen between the Duke of Guise and the commander of the Pope's forces; the Spaniards renewed their incursions into the ecclesiastical state; the Pope, when he found, instead of the conquests and triumphs which he had fondly expected, that he could not secure his own territories from depredation, murmured, complained, and began to talk of peace. The Duke of Guise, mortified to the last degree with having acted such an inglorious part, not only solicited his court either to reinforce his army, or to recal him, but urged Paul to fulfil his engagements; and called on Cardinal Caraffa, sometimes with reproaches, sometimes with threats, to make good those magnificent promises, from a rash confidence in which he had advised his master to renounce the truce of Vaucelles, and to join in league with the Pope [g].

Hostilities in the Low Countries.

BUT while the French affairs in Italy were in this wretched situation, an unexpected event hap-

[f] Herrera Vida de Felipe, 181. [g] Thuan. lib. xxviii. 614. Pallav. lib. xiii. 181. Burn. ii. app. 317.

pened in the Low Countries, which called the Duke of Guife from a ftation wherein he could acquire no honour, to the moſt dignified and important charge which could be committed to a fubject. As foon as the French had difcovered their purpofe of violating the truce of Vaucelles, not only by fending an army into Italy, but by attempting to furprize fome of the frontier towns in Flanders, Philip, though willing to have avoided a rupture, determined to profecute the war with fuch fpirit, as fhould make his enemies fenfible, that his father had not erred, when he judged him to be fo capable of government, that he had given up the reins into his hands. As he knew that Henry had been at great expence in fitting out the army under the Duke of Guife, and that his treafury was hardly able to anfwer the exorbitant and endlefs demands of a diftant war, he forefaw that all his operations in the Low Countries muft, of confequence, prove feeble, and be confidered only as fecondary to thofe in Italy. For that reafon, he prudently refolved to make his principal effort in that place where he expected the French to be weakeft, and to bend his chief force againft that quarter where they would feel a blow moft fenfibly. With this view, he affembled in the Low Countries an army of about fifty thoufand men, the Flemings ferving him on this occafion with that active zeal which fubjects are wont to exert in obeying the firſt commands of a new fovereign. But Philip, cautious and provident, even at this early period of life, did

did not reſt all his hopes of ſucceſs on that formidable force alone.

Philip endeavours to engage England in the war.

He had been labouring for ſome time to engage the Engliſh to eſpouſe his quarrel; and though it was manifeſtly the intereſt of that kingdom to maintain a ſtrict neutrality, and the people themſelves were ſenſible of the advantages which they derived from it; though he knew how odious his name was to the Engliſh, and how averſe they would be to co-operate with him in any meaſure, he nevertheleſs did not deſpair of accompliſhing his point. He relied on the affection with which the Queen doated on him, which was ſo violent, that even his coldneſs and neglect had not extinguiſhed it; he knew her implicit reverence for his opinion, and her fond deſire of gratifying him in every particular. That he might work on theſe with greater facility and more certain ſucceſs, he ſet out for England. The Queen, who, during her huſband's abſence, had languiſhed in perpetual dejection, reſumed freſh ſpirits on his arrival; and, without paying the leaſt attention either to the intereſt or to the inclinations of her people, entered warmly into all his ſchemes. In vain did her privy-council remonſtrate againſt the imprudence as well as danger of involving the nation in an unneceſſary war; in vain did they put her in mind of the ſolemn treaties of peace ſubſiſting between England and France, which the conduct of that nation had

had afforded her no pretext to violate. Mary, soothed by Philip's careffes, or intimidated by the threats which his afcendant over her emboldened him at fome times to throw out, was deaf to every thing that could be urged in oppofition to his fentiments, and infifted with the greateft vehemence on an immediate declaration of war againft France. The council, though all Philip's addrefs and Mary's authority were employed to gain or overawe them, after ftruggling long, yielded at laft, not from conviction, but merely from deference to the will of their fovereign. War was declared againft France, the only one perhaps againft that kingdom into which the Englifh ever entered with reluctance. As Mary knew the averfion of the nation to this meafure, fhe durft not call a parliament in order to raife money for carrying on the war. She fupplied this want, however, by a ftretch of royal prerogative, not unufual in that age; and levied large fums on her fubjects by her own authority. This enabled her to affemble a fufficient body of troops, and to fend eight thoufand men under the conduct of the earl of Pembroke to join Philip's army [h].

PHILIP, who was not ambitious of military glory, gave the command of his army to Emanuel Philibert, Duke of Savoy, and fixed his own refidence at Cambray, that he might be at hand to receive the earlieft intelligence of his motions,

[h] Carte, iii. 337.

BOOK XII.
1557.

and to aid him with his counſels. The Duke opened the campaign with a maſterly ſtroke of addreſs, which juſtified Philip's choice, and diſcovered ſuch a ſuperiority of genius over the French generals, as almoſt enſured ſucceſs in his ſubſequent operations. He appointed the general rendezvous of his troops at a place conſiderably diſtant from the country which he deſtined to be the ſcene of action; and having kept the enemy in ſuſpenſe for a good time with regard to his intentions, he at laſt deceived them ſo effectually by the variety of his marches and countermarches, as led them to conclude that he meant to bend all his force againſt the province of Champagne, and would attempt to penetrate into the kingdom on that ſide. In conſequence of this opinion, they drew all their ſtrength towards that quarter, and reinforcing the garriſon there, left the towns on other parts of the frontier deſtitute of troops ſufficient to defend them.

Inveſts St. Quintin.

THE Duke of Savoy, as ſoon as he perceived that this feint had its full effect, turned ſuddenly to the right, advanced by rapid marches into Picardy, and ſending his cavalry, in which he was extremely ſtrong, before him, inveſted St. Quintin. This was a town deemed in that age of conſiderable ſtrength, and of great importance, as there were few fortified cities between it and Paris. The fortifications, however, had been much neglected; the garriſon, weakened by draughts ſent towards Champagne, did not amount to a

fifth

fifth part of the number requisite for its defence; and the governor, though a brave officer, was neither of rank, nor authority, equal to the command in a place of so much consequence, besieged by such a formidable army. A few days must have put the Duke of Savoy in possession of the town, if the Admiral de Coligny, who thought it concerned his honour to attempt saving a place of such importance to his country, and which lay within his jurisdiction as governor of Picardy, had not taken the gallant resolution of throwing himself into it, with such a body of men as he could collect on a sudden. This resolution he executed with great intrepidity, and, if the nature of the enterprize be considered, with no contemptible success; for though one half of his small body of troops was cut off, he, with the other, broke through the enemy, and entered the town. The unexpected arrival of an officer of such high rank and reputation, and who had exposed himself to such danger in order to join them, inspired the desponding garrison with courage. Every thing that the Admiral's great skill and experience in the art of war could suggest, for annoying the enemy, or defending the town, was attempted; and the citizens, as well as the garrison, seconding his zeal with equal ardour, seemed to be determined that they would hold out to the last, and sacrifice themselves in order to save their country[1].

[1] Thuan. lib. xix. 647.

BOOK XII.

1557.
The French endeavour to relieve the town.

The Duke of Savoy, whom the English, under the Earl of Pembroke, joined about this time, pushed on the siege with the greatest vigour. An army so numerous, and so well supplied with every thing requisite, carried on its approaches with great advantage against a garrison which was still so feeble that it durst seldom venture to disturb or retard the enemy's operations by sallies. The Admiral, sensible of the approaching danger, and unable to avert it, acquainted his uncle the Constable Montmorency, who had the command of the French army, with his situation, and pointed out to him a method by which he might throw relief into the town. The Constable, solicitous to save a town, the loss of which would open a passage for the enemy into the heart of France; and eager to extricate his nephew out of that perilous situation, in which zeal for the public had engaged him; resolved, though aware of the danger, to attempt what he desired. With this view, he marched from La Fere towards St. Quintin at the head of his army, which was not by one half so numerous as that of the enemy, and having given the command of a body of chosen men to Coligny's brother Dandelot, who was colonel general of the French infantry, he ordered him to force his way into the town by that avenue which the Admiral had represented as most practicable, while he himself, with the main army, would give the alarm to the enemy's camp on the opposite side, and endeavour to draw all their attention towards that quarter. Dandelot
executed

executed his orders with greater intrepidity than conduct. He rushed on with such headlong impetuosity, that, though it broke the first body of the enemy which stood in his way, it threw his own soldiers into the utmost confusion; and as they were attacked in that situation by fresh troops which closed in upon them on every side, the greater part of them were cut in pieces, Dandelot, with about five hundred of the most adventurous and most fortunate, making good his entrance into the town.

MEANWHILE the Constable, in executing his part of the plan, advanced so near the camp of the besiegers, as rendered it impossible to retreat with safety in the face of an enemy so much superior in number. The Duke of Savoy instantly perceived Montmorency's error, and prepared, with the presence of mind and abilities of a great general, to avail himself of it. He drew up his army in order of battle, with the greatest expedition, and watching the moment when the French began to file off towards La Fere, he detached all his cavalry, under the command of the Count of Egmont, to fall on their rear, while he himself, at the head of his infantry, advanced to support him. The French retired at first in perfect order, and with a good countenance; but when they saw Egmont draw near with his formidable body of cavalry, the shock of which they were conscious that they could not withstand, the prospect of imminent danger, added to distrust of

The battle of St. Quintin.

BOOK XII.
1557.

Total defeat of the French.

their general, whose imprudence every soldier now perceived, struck them with general consternation. They began insensibly to quicken their pace, and those in the rear pressed so violently on such as were before them, that in a short time their march resembled a flight rather than a retreat. Egmont, observing their confusion, charged them with the greatest fury, and in a moment all their men at arms, the pride and strength of the French troops in that age, gave way and fled with precipitation. The infantry, however, whom the Constable, by his presence and authority, kept to their colours, still continued to retreat in good order, until the enemy brought some pieces of cannon to bear upon their centre, which threw them into such confusion, that the Flemish cavalry, renewing their attack, broke in, and the rout became universal. About four thousand of the French fell in the field, and among these the Duke of Anguien, a Prince of the blood, together with six hundred gentlemen. The Constable, as soon as he perceived the fortune of the day to be irretrievable, rushed into the thickest of the enemy, with a resolution not to survive the calamity which his ill-conduct had brought upon his country; but having received a dangerous wound, and being wasted with the loss of blood, he was surrounded by some Flemish officers, to whom he was known, who protected him from the violence of the soldiers, and obliged him to surrender. Besides the Constable, the Dukes of Montpensier and Longueville, the Marechal St Andrè, many

officers

officers of diftinction, three hundred gentlemen, and near four thoufand private foldiers, were taken prifoners. All the colours belonging to the infantry, all the ammunition, and all the cannon, two pieces excepted, fell into the enemy's hands. The victorious army did not lofe above fourfcore men [k].

The firft effects of it.

THIS battle, no lefs fatal to France than the ancient victories of Crecy and Agincourt, gained by the Englifh on the fame frontier, bore a near refemblance to thofe difaftrous events, in the fuddennefs of the rout; in the ill-conduct of the commander in chief; in the number of perfons of note flain or taken; and in the fmall lofs fuftained by the enemy. It filled France with equal confternation. Many inhabitants of Paris, with the fame precipitancy and trepidation as if the enemy had been already at their gates, quitted the city, and retired into the interior provinces. The King, by his prefence and exhortations, endeavoured to confole and to animate fuch as remained, and applying himfelf with the greateft diligence to repair the ruinous fortifications of the city, prepared to defend it againft the attack which he inftantly expected. But happily for France, Philip's caution, together with the intrepid firmnefs of the Admiral de Coligny, not only faved the capital from the danger to which it was expofed, but gained the nation a fhort in-

[k] Thuan. 650. Hærei Annal. Brabant. ii. 692. Herrera, 291.

terval,

terval, during which the people recovered from the terror and dejection occasioned by a blow no less severe than unexpected, and Henry had leisure to take measures for the public security, with the spirit which became the sovereign of a powerful and martial people.

Philip repairs to his army.

Philip, immediately after the battle, visited the camp at St. Quintin, where he was received with all the exultation of military triumph; and such were his transports of joy on account of an event which threw so much lustre on the beginning of his reign, that they softened his severe and haughty temper into an unusual flow of courtesy. When the Duke of Savoy approached, and was kneeling to kiss his hands, he caught him in his arms, and embracing him with warmth, "It becomes me, says he, rather to kiss your hands, which have gained me such a glorious and almost bloodless victory."

His deliberations concerning the prosecution of the war.

As soon as the rejoicings and congratulations on Philip's arrival were over, a council of war was held, in order to determine how they might improve their victory to the best advantage. The Duke of Savoy, seconded by several of the ablest officers formed under Charles V. insisted that they should immediately relinquish the siege of St. Quintin, the reduction of which was now an object below their attention, and advance directly towards Paris; that as there were neither troops to oppose, nor any town of strength to retard their

their march, they might reach that capital while under the full impression of the astonishment and terror occasioned by the rout of the army, and take possession of it without resistance. But Philip, less adventurous or more prudent than his generals, preferred a moderate but certain advantage, to an enterprize of greater splendour, but of more doubtful success. He represented to the council the infinite resources of a kingdom so powerful as France; the great number as well as martial spirit of its nobles; their attachment to their sovereign; the manifold advantages with which they could carry on war in their own territories; and the unavoidable destruction which must be the consequence of their penetrating too rashly into the enemy's country, before they had secured such a communication with their own as might render a retreat safe, if, upon any disastrous event, that measure should become necessary. On all these accounts, he advised the continuance of the siege, and his generals acquiesced the more readily in his opinion, as they made no doubt of being masters of the town in a few days, a loss of time of so little consequence in the execution of their plan, that they might easily repair it by their subsequent activity [1].

St. Quintin defended by Admiral Coligny;

THE weakness of the fortifications, and the small number of the garrison, which could no longer hope either for reinforcement or relief, seemed to authorize this calculation of Philip's generals.

[1] Belcar. Commentar. de Reb. Gallic. 901.

generals. But, in making it, they did not attend sufficiently to the character of Admiral de Coligny, who commanded in the town. A courage undismayed, and tranquil amidst the greatest dangers, an invention fruitful in resources, a genius which roused and seemed to acquire new force upon every disaster, a talent of governing the minds of men, together with a capacity of maintaining his ascendant over them even under circumstances the most adverse and distressful, were qualities which Coligny possessed in a degree superior to any general of that age. These qualities were peculiarly adapted to the station in which he was now placed; and as he knew the infinite importance to his country of every hour which he could gain at this juncture, he exerted himself to the utmost in contriving how to protract the siege, and to detain the enemy from attempting any enterprize more dangerous to France. Such were the perseverance and skill with which he conducted the defence, and such the fortitude as well as patience with which he animated the garrison, that though the Spaniards, the Flemings, and the English, carried on the attack with all the ardour which national emulation inspires, he held out the town seventeen days. He was taken prisoner, at last, on the breach, overpowered by the superior number of the enemy.

HENRY availed himself, with the utmost activity, of the interval which the Admiral's well-timed

timed obstinacy had afforded him. He appointed officers to collect the scattered remains of the Constable's army; he issued orders for levying soldiers in every part of the kingdom; he commanded the ban and arriere ban of the frontier provinces instantly to take the field, and to join the Duke of Nevers at Laon in Picardy; he recalled the greater part of the veteran troops which served under the Marechal Brissac in Piedmont; he sent courier after courier to the Duke of Guise, requiring him, together with all his army, to return instantly for the defence of their country; he dispatched one envoy to the Grand Signior, to solicit the assistance of his fleet, and the loan of a sum of money; he sent another into Scotland, to incite the Scots to invade the north of England, that, by drawing Mary's attention to that quarter, he might prevent her from reinforcing her troops which served under Philip. These efforts of the King were warmly seconded by the zeal of his subjects. The city of Paris granted him a free gift of three hundred thousand livres. The other great towns imitated the liberality of the capital, and contributed in proportion. Several noblemen of distinction engaged, at their own expence, to garrison and defend the towns which lay most exposed to the enemy. Nor was the general concern for the public confined to corporate bodies alone, or to those in the higher sphere of life, but diffusing itself among persons of every rank, each individual seemed disposed to act with as much vigour as as if the honour of the King, and the safety of the state, had depended solely on his single efforts[m].

The victory of St. Quintin productive of few beneficial consequences.

PHILIP, who was no stranger either to the prudent measures taken by the French monarch for the security of his dominions, or to the spirit with which his subjects prepared to defend themselves, perceived, when it was too late, that he had lost an opportunity which could never be recalled, and that it was now vain to think of penetrating into the heart of France. He abandoned, therefore, without much reluctance, a scheme which was too bold and hazardous to be perfectly agreeable to his cautious temper; and employed his army, during the remainder of the campaign, in the sieges of Ham and Catelet. Of these, he soon became master; and the reduction of two such petty towns, together with the acquisition of St. Quintin, were all the advantages which he derived from one of the most decisive victories gained in that century. Philip himself, however, continued in high exultation on account of his success; and as all his passions were tinged with superstition, he, in memory of the battle of St. Quintin, which had been fought on the day consecrated to St. Laurence, vowed to build a church, a monastery, and a palace, in honour of that saint and martyr. Before the expiration of the year, he laid the foundation of an edifice, in which all these were united, at the Escurial in the

[m] Mem. de Ribier, ii. 701. 703.

neighbourhood of Madrid; and the same principle which dictated the vow, directed the building. For the plan of the work was so formed as to resemble a gridiron, which, according to the legendary tale, had been the instrument of St. Laurence's martyrdom. Notwithstanding the great and expensive schemes in which his restless ambition involved him, Philip continued the building with such perseverance for twenty-two years, and reserved such large sums for this monument of his devotion and vanity, that the monarchs of Spain are indebted to him for a royal residence, which, though not the most elegant, is certainly the most sumptuous and magnificent of any in Europe[n].

The French army recalled out of Italy.

THE first account of that fatal blow which the French had received at St. Quintin was carried to Rome by the courier whom Henry had sent to recal the Duke of Guise. As Paul, even with the assistance of his French auxiliaries, had hardly been able to check the progress of the Spanish arms, he foresaw that, as soon as he was deprived of their protection, his territories must be over-run in a moment. He remonstrated therefore with the greatest violence against the departure of the French army, reproaching the Duke of Guise for his ill-conduct, which had brought him into such an unhappy situation; and complaining of the King for deserting him so unge-

---

[n] Colmenar Annales d'Espagne, tom. ii. p. 136.

neroufly

neroufly under fuch circumftances. The Duke of Guife's orders, however, were peremptory. Paul, inflexible as he was, found it neceffary to accommodate his conduct to the exigency of his affairs, and to employ the mediation of the Venetians, and of Cofmo di Medici, in order to obtain peace. Philip, who had been forced unwillingly to a rupture with the Pope, and who, even while fuccefs crowned his arms, doubted fo much the juftice of his own caufe, that he had made frequent overtures of pacification, liftened eagerly to the firft propofals of this nature from Paul, and difcovered fuch moderation in his demands, as could hardly have been expected from a Prince elated with victory.

A treaty of peace between the Pope and Philip.

The Duke of Alva on the part of Philip, and the Cardinal Caraffa in the name of his uncle, met at Cavi, and both being equally difpofed to peace, they, after a fhort conference, terminated the war by a treaty on the following terms: That Paul fhould renounce his league with France, and maintain for the future fuch a neutrality as became the common father of Chriftendom; That Philip fhould inftantly reftore all the towns of the ecclefiaftical territory of which he had taken poffeffion; That the claims of the Caraffas to the dutchy of Paliano, and other demefnes of the Colonnas, fhould be referred to the decifion of the republic of Venice; That the Duke of Alva fhould repair in perfon to Rome, and after afking pardon of Paul in his own name, and in that of his

his master, for having invaded the patrimony of the church, should receive the Pope's absolution from that crime. Thus Paul, through Philip's scrupulous timidity, finished an unprosperous war without any detriment to the Papal See. The conqueror appeared humble, and acknowledged his error; while he who had been vanquished retained his usual haughtiness, and was treated with every mark of superiority °. The Duke of Alva, in terms of the treaty, repaired to Rome, and, in the posture of a supplicant, kissed the feet, and implored the forgiveness of that very person whom his arms had reduced to the last extremity. Such was the superstitious veneration of the Spaniards for the Papal character, that Alva, though perhaps the proudest man of the age, and accustomed from his infancy to a familiar intercourse with Princes, acknowledged that when he approached the Pope, he was so much overawed, that his voice failed, and his presence of mind forsook him ᵖ.

Philip restores Placentia to Octavio Farnese.

But though this war, which at its commencement threatened mighty revolutions, was brought to an end without occasioning any alteration in those States which were its immediate object, it had produced during its progress effects of considerable consequence in other parts of Italy. As Philip was extremely solicitous to terminate his

° Pallav. lib. xiii. 183. F. Paul, 380. Herrera, vol. I. 310. ᵖ Pallav. lib. xiii. 185. Summonte Istoria di Napoli, iv. 286.

quarrel with Paul as speedily as possible, he was willing to make any sacrifice in order to gain those Princes, who, by joining their troops to the Papal and French army, might have prolonged the war. With this view, he entered into a negociation with Octavio Farnese, Duke of Parma, and, in order to seduce him from his alliance with France, he restored to him the city of Placentia, with the territory depending on it, which Charles V. had seized in the year one thousand five hundred and forty-seven, had kept from that time in his possession, and had transmitted, together with his other dominions, to Philip.

Cosmo di Medici's measures for obtaining Siena.

This step made such a discovery of Philip's character and views to Cosmo di Medici, the most sagacious as well as provident of all the Italian Princes, that he conceived hopes of accomplishing his favourite scheme of adding Siena and its territories to his dominions in Tuscany. As his success in this attempt depended entirely on the delicacy of address with which it should be conducted, he employed all the refinements of policy in the negociation which he set on foot for this purpose. He began with soliciting Philip, whose treasury he knew to be entirely drained by the expence of the war, to repay the great sums which he had advanced to the Emperor during the siege of Siena. When Philip endeavoured to elude a demand which he was unable to satisfy, Cosmo affected to be extremely disquieted, and making no secret of his disgust, instructed his ambassador at Rome to open a negociation with the Pope, which seemed to be the effect of it. The ambassador executed his commission with such dexterity, that Paul, imagining Cosmo to be entirely alienated from the Spanish interest, proposed to him an alliance with France which should be cemented by the marriage of his eldest son to one of Henry's daughters. Cosmo received the overture with such apparent satisfaction, and with so many professions of gratitude for the high honour of which he had the prospect, that not only the Pope's ministers, but the French envoy at Rome, talked confidently, and with little reserve, of the accession of that important ally, as a matter certain and decided. The account of this was quickly carried to Philip; and Cosmo, who foresaw how much it would alarm him, had dispatched his nephew Ludovico de Toledo into the Netherlands, that he might be at hand to observe and take advantage of his consternation, before the first impression which it made should in any degree abate. Cosmo was extremely fortunate in the choice of the instrument whom he employed. Toledo waited, with patience, until he discovered with certainty, that Philip had received such intelligence of his uncle's negociations at Rome, as must have filled his suspicious mind with fear and jealousy; and then craving an audience, he required payment of the money which had been borrowed by the Emperor, in the most earnest and peremptory terms. In urging that point, he artfully threw out several dark hints

hints and ambiguous declarations, concerning the extremities to which Cosmo might be driven by a refusal of this just demand, as well as by other grievances of which he had good reason to complain.

Their success.

PHILIP, astonished at an address in such a strain, from a Prince so far his inferior as the Duke of Tuscany, and comparing what he now heard with the information which he had received from Italy, immediately concluded that Cosmo had ventured to assume this bold and unusual tone on the prospect of his union with France. In order to prevent the Pope and Henry from acquiring an ally, who, by his abilities, as well as the situation of his dominions, would have added both reputation and strength to their confederacy, he offered to grant Cosmo the investiture of Siena, if he would consent to accept of it as an equivalent for the sums due to him, and engage to furnish a body of troops towards the defence of Philip's territories in Italy, against any power who should attack them. As soon as Cosmo had brought Philip to make this concession, which was the object of all his artifices and intrigues, he did not protract the negociation by any unnecessary delay, or any excess of refinement, but closed eagerly with the proposal, and Philip, in spite of the remonstrances of his ablest counsellors, signed a treaty with him to that effect [q].

[q] Thuan. lib. xviii. 624. Herrera, i. 263. 275. Pallav. lib. xiii. 180.

As no Prince was ever more tenacious of his rights than Philip, or less willing to relinquish any territory which he possessed, by what tenure soever he held it, these unusual concessions to the Dukes of Parma and Tuscany, by which he wantonly gave up countries, in acquiring or defending which his father had employed many years, and wasted much blood and treasure, cannot be accounted for from any motive, but his superstitious desire of extricating himself out of the war which he had been forced to wage against the Pope. By these treaties, however, the balance of power among the Italian States was poised with greater equality, and rendered less variable than it had been since it received the first violent shock from the invasion of Charles VIII. of France. From this period Italy ceased to be the great theatre, on which the monarchs of Spain, France, and Germany, contended for power or for fame. Their dissensions and hostilities, though as frequent and violent as ever, being excited by new objects, stained other regions of Europe with blood, and rendered them miserable, in their turn, by the devastations of war.

The Duke of Guise left Rome on the same day that his adversary the Duke of Alva made his humiliating submission to the Pope. He was received in France as the guardian angel of the kingdom. His late ill success in Italy seemed to be forgotten, while his former services, particularly his defence of Metz, were recounted with exagge-

Sept. 29.
The Duke of Guise's reception in France.

exaggerated praise; and he was welcomed in every city through which he passed, as the restorer of public security, who, after having set bounds by his conduct and valour to the victorious arms of Charles V. returned now, at the call of his country, to check the formidable progress of Philip's power. The reception which he met with from Henry was no less cordial and honourable. New titles were invented, and new dignities created, in order to distinguish him. He was appointed lieutenant-general in chief both within and without the kingdom, with a jurisdiction almost unlimited, and hardly inferior to that which was possessed by the King himself. Thus, through the singular felicity which attended the Princes of Lorrain, the miscarriage of their own schemes contributed to aggrandize them. The calamities of his country, and the ill-conduct of his rival the constable, exalted the Duke of Guise to a height of dignity and power, which he could not have expected to attain by the most fortunate and most complete success of his own ambitious projects.

Takes the command of the army. The Duke of Guise, eager to perform something suitable to the high expectations of his countrymen, and that he might justify the extraordinary confidence which the King had reposed in him, ordered all the troops, which could be got together, to assemble at Compeigne. Though the winter was well advanced, and had set in with extreme severity, he placed himself at their head, and

and took the field. By Henry's activity and the zeal of his subjects, so many soldiers had been raised in the kingdom, and such considerable reinforcements had been drawn from Germany and Swisserland, as formed an army respectable even in the eyes of a victorious enemy. Philip, alarmed at seeing it put in motion at such an uncommon season, began to tremble for his new conquests, particularly St. Quintin, the fortifications of which were hitherto but imperfectly repaired.

But the Duke of Guise meditated a more important enterprize; and after amusing the enemy with threatening successively different towns on the frontiers of Flanders, he turned suddenly to the left, and invested Calais with his whole army. Calais had been taken by the English under Edward III. and was the fruit of that monarch's glorious victory at Crecy. Being the only place that they retained of their ancient and extensive territories in France, and which opened to them, at all times, an easy and secure passage into the heart of that kingdom, their keeping possession of it soothed the pride of the one nation as much as it mortified the vanity of the other. Its situation was naturally so strong, and its fortifications deemed so impregnable, that no monarch of France, how adventurous soever, had been bold enough to attack it. Even when the domestic strength of England was broken and exhausted by the bloody wars between the houses of York and Lancaster, and its attention entirely diverted from foreign objects, Calais had remained undisturbed and unthreatened. Mary and her council, composed chiefly of ecclesiastics, unacquainted with military affairs, and whose whole attention was turned towards extirpating heresy out of the kingdom, had not only neglected to take any precautions for the safety of this important place, but seemed to think that the reputation of its strength was alone sufficient for its security. Full of this opinion, they ventured, even after the declaration of war, to continue a practice which the low state of the Queen's finances had introduced in times of peace. As the country adjacent to Calais was overflowed during the winter, and the marshes around it became impassable, except by one avenue, which the forts of St. Agatha and Newnham-bridge commanded, it had been the custom of the English to dismiss the greater part of the garrison towards the end of autumn, and to replace it in the spring. In vain did Lord Wentworth, the Governor of Calais, remonstrate against this ill-timed parsimony, and represent the possibility of his being attacked suddenly, while he had not troops sufficient to man the works. The privy-council treated these remonstrances with scorn, as if they had flowed from the timidity or the rapaciousness of the governor; and some of them, with that confidence which is the companion of ignorance, boasted that they would defend Calais with their white rods against any enemy who should

should approach it during winter[r]. In vain did Philip, who had passed through Calais as he returned from England to the Netherlands, warn the Queen of the danger to which it was exposed; and acquainting her with what was necessary for its security, in vain did he offer to reinforce the garrison during winter with a detachment of his own troops. Mary's counsellors, though obsequious to her in all points wherein religion was concerned, distrusted, as much as the rest of their countrymen, every proposition that came from her husband; and suspecting this to be an artifice of Philip's in order to gain the command of the town, they neglected his intelligence, declined his offer, and left Calais with less than a fourth part of the garrison requisite for its defence.

His knowledge of this encouraged the Duke of Guise to venture on an enterprize, that surprized his own countrymen no less than his enemies. As he knew that its success depended on conducting his operations with such rapidity as would afford the English no time for throwing relief into the town by sea, and prevent Philip from giving him any interruption by land, he pushed the attack with a degree of vigour little known in carrying on sieges during that age. He drove the English from fort St. Agatha at the first assault. He obliged them to abandon the fort of Newnham-bridge after defending it only three days.

Guise pushes the siege with vigour.

[r] Carte, iii. 345.

days. He took the castle which commanded the harbour by storm; and on the eighth day after he appeared before Calais, compelled the governor to surrender, as his feeble garrison, which did not exceed five hundred men, was worn out with the fatigue of sustaining so many attacks, and defending such extensive works.

THE Duke of Guise, without allowing the English time to recover from the consternation occasioned by this blow, immediately invested Guisnes, the garrison of which, though more numerous, defended itself with less vigour, and after standing one brisk assault, gave up the town. The castle of Hames was abandoned by the troops posted there, without waiting the approach of the enemy.

THUS, in a few days, during the depth of winter, and at a time when the fatal battle of St. Quintin had so depressed the sanguine spirit of the French, that their utmost aim was to protect their own country, without dreaming of making conquests on the enemy, the enterprizing valour of one man drove the English out of Calais, after they had held it two hundred and ten years, and deprived them of every foot of land in a kingdom, where their dominions had been once very extensive. This exploit, at the same time that it gave an high idea of the power and resources of France to all Europe, set the Duke of Guise, in the opinion of his countrymen, far above

above all the generals of the age. They celebrated his conquests with immoderate transports of joy; while the English gave vent to all the passions which animate a high-spirited people, when any great national calamity is manifestly owing to the ill conduct of their rulers. Mary and her ministers, formerly odious, were now contemptible in their eyes. All the terrors of her severe and arbitrary administration could not restrain them from uttering execrations and threats against those, who having wantonly involved the nation in a quarrel wherein it was nowise interested, had by their negligence or incapacity brought irreparable disgrace on their country, and lost the most valuable possession belonging to the English crown.

The King of France imitated the conduct of its former conqueror, Edward III. with regard to Calais. He commanded all the English inhabitants to quit the town, and giving their houses to his own subjects, whom he allured to settle there by granting them various immunities, he left a numerous garrison, under an experienced governor, for their defence. After this, his victorious army was conducted into quarters of refreshment, and the usual inaction of winter returned.

During these various operations, Ferdinand assembled the college of Electors at Frankfort, in order to lay before them the instrument whereby Charles V. had resigned the Imperial crown, and

Feb. 24. Charles's resignation of the Imperial crown.

transferred it to him. This he had hitherto delayed on account of some difficulties which had occurred concerning the formalities requisite in supplying a vacancy occasioned by an event, to which there was no parallel in the annals of the Empire. These being at length adjusted, the Prince of Orange executed the commission with which he had been entrusted by Charles; the Electors accepted of his resignation; declared Ferdinand his lawful successor; and put him in possession of all the ensigns of the Imperial dignity.

The Pope refuses to acknowledge Ferdinand as Emperor.

But when the new Emperor sent Gusman his chancellor to acquaint the Pope with this transaction, to testify his reverence towards the Holy See, and to signify that, according to form, he would soon dispatch an ambassador extraordinary to treat with his Holiness concerning his coronation; Paul, whom neither experience nor disappointments could teach to bring down his lofty ideas of the papal prerogative to such a moderate standard as suited the genius of the times, refused to admit the envoy into his presence, and declared all the proceedings at Frankfort irregular and invalid. He contended that the Pope, as the vicegerent of Christ, was entrusted with the keys both of spiritual and of civil government; that from him the Imperial jurisdiction was derived; that though his predecessors had authorised the Electors to chuse an Emperor whom the Holy See confirmed, this privilege was confined to those

those cases when a vacancy was occasioned by death; that the instrument of Charles's resignation had been presented in an improper court, as it belonged to the Pope alone to reject or to accept of it, and to nominate a person to fill the Imperial throne; that, setting aside all these objections, Ferdinand's election laboured under two defects which alone were sufficient to render it void, for the Protestant Electors had been admitted to vote, though by their apostacy from the Catholic faith, they had forfeited that and every other privilege of the electoral office; and Ferdinand, by ratifying the concessions of several Diets in favour of heretics, had rendered himself unworthy of the Imperial dignity, which was instituted for the protection, not for the destruction, of the church. But after thundering out these extravagant maxims, he added, with an appearance of condescension, that if Ferdinand would renounce all title to the Imperial crown, founded on the election at Frankfort, make professions of repentance for his past conduct, and supplicate him, with due humility, to confirm Charles's resignation, as well as his own assumption to the Empire, he might expect every mark of favour from his paternal clemency and goodness. Gusman, though he had foreseen considerable difficulties in his negociation with the Pope, little expected that he would have revived those antiquated and wild pretensions, which astonished him so much, that he hardly knew in what tone he ought to reply. He prudently declined entering

ing into any controversy concerning the nature or extent of the papal jurisdiction, and confining himself to the political considerations, which should determine the Pope to recognize an Emperor already in possession, he endeavoured to place them in such a light, as he imagined could scarcely fail to strike Paul, if he were not altogether blind to his own interest. Philip seconded Gusman's arguments with great earnestness, by an ambassador whom he sent to Rome on purpose, and besought the Pope to desist from claims so unseasonable, as might not only irritate and alarm Ferdinand and the Princes of the Empire, but furnish the enemies of the Holy See with a new reason for representing its jurisdiction as incompatible with the rights of Princes, and subversive of all civil authority. But Paul, who deemed it a crime to attend to any consideration suggested by human prudence or policy, when he thought himself called upon to assert the prerogatives of the Papal See, remained inflexible; and, during his pontificate, Ferdinand was not acknowledged as Emperor by the court of Rome[s].

Henry endeavours to excite the Scots against England.

WHILE Henry was intent upon his preparations for the approaching campaign, he received accounts of the issue of his negociations in Scotland. Long experience having at last taught the Scots the imprudence of involving their country in every quarrel between France and England,

---

[s] Godleveus de Abdicat. Car. V. ap. Gold. Polit. Imper. 392. Pallav. lib. xii. 189. Ribier, ii. 746. 759.

neither the folicitations of the French ambaffador, nor the addrefs and authority of the Queen-regent, could prevail on them to take arms againft a kingdom with which they were at peace. On this occafion the ardour of a martial nobility and of a turbulent people was reftrained by regard for the public intereft and tranquillity, which in former deliberations of this kind had been feldom attended to by a nation always prone to rufh into every new war. But though the Scots adhered with fteadinefs to their pacific fyftem, they were extremely ready to gratify the French King in another particular, which he had given in charge to his ambaffador.

Marriage of the Dauphin with the Queen of Scots.

The young Queen of Scots had been affianced to the Dauphin in the year one thoufand five hundred and forty-eight, and having been educated fince that time in the court of France, fhe had grown up to be the moft amiable, and one of the moft accomplifhed Princeffes of that age. Henry demanded the confent of her fubjects to the celebration of the marriage, and a parliament, which was held for that purpofe, appointed eight commiffioners to reprefent the whole body of the nation at that folemnity, with power to fign fuch deeds as might be requifite before it was concluded. In fettling the articles of the marriage, the Scots took every precaution that prudence could dictate, in order to preferve the liberty and independence of their country; while the French ufed every art to fecure to the Dauphin the conduct

duct of affairs during the Queen's life, and the succession of the crown on the event of her demise. The marriage was celebrated with pomp suitable to the dignity of the parties, and the magnificence of a court at that time the most splendid in Europe[t]. Thus Henry, in the course of a few months, had the glory of recovering an important possession which had anciently belonged to the crown of France, and of adding to it the acquisition of a new kingdom. By this event, too, the Duke of Guise acquired new consideration and importance; the marriage of his niece to the apparent heir of the crown, raising him so far above the condition of other subjects, that the credit which he had gained by his great actions, seemed thereby to be rendered no less permanent than it was extensive.

The campaign opened.

WHEN the campaign opened, soon after the Dauphin's marriage, the Duke of Guise was placed at the head of the army, with the same unlimited powers as formerly. Henry had received such liberal supplies from his subjects, that the troops under his command were both numerous and well appointed; while Philip, exhausted by the extraordinary efforts of the preceding year, had been obliged to dismiss so many of his forces during the winter, that he could not bring an army into the field capable of making head against the enemy. The Duke of

[t] Keith's History of Scotland, p. 73. Append. 13. Corps Diplom. v. 21.

Guise did not lose the favourable opportunity which his superiority afforded him. He invested Thionville in the dutchy of Luxemburg, one of the strongest towns on the frontier of the Netherlands, and of great importance to France by its neighbourhood to Metz; and, notwithstanding the obstinate valour with which it was defended, he forced it to capitulate after a siege of three weeks[u].

June 22.

The French army defeated at Gravelines.

But the success of this enterprize, which it was expected would lead to other conquests, was more than counterbalanced by an event that happened in another part of the Low-Countries. The Marechal de Termes, governor of Calais, having penetrated into Flanders without opposition, invested Dunkirk with an army of fourteen thousand men, and took it by storm on the fifth day of the siege. Hence he advanced towards Nieuport, which must have soon fallen into his hands, if the approach of the Count of Egmont with a superior army had not made it prudent to retreat. The French troops were so much encumbered with the booty which they had got at Dunkirk, or by ravaging the open country, that they moved slowly; and Egmont, who had left his heavy baggage and artillery behind him, marched with such rapidity, that he came up with them near Gravelines, and attacked them with

[u] Thuan. lib. xx. 690.

the utmoft impetuofity. De Termes, who had the choice of the ground, having pofted his troops to advantage in the angle formed by the mouth of the river Aa and the fea, received him with great firmnefs. Victory remained for fome time in fufpenfe, the defperate valour of the French, who forefaw the unavoidable deftruction that muft follow upon a rout in an enemy's country, counterbalancing the fuperior number of the Flemings, when one of thofe accidents to which human prudence does not extend, decided the conteft in favour of the latter. A fquadron of Englifh fhips of war, which was cruizing on the coaft, being drawn by the noife of the firing towards the place of the engagement, entered the river Aa, and turned its great guns againft the right wing of the French, with fuch effect, as immediately broke that body, and fpread terror and confufion through the whole army. The Flemings, to whom affiftance, fo unexpected and fo feafonable, gave frefh fpirit, redoubled their efforts, that they might not lofe the advantage which fortune had prefented them, or give the enemy time to recover from their confternation, and the rout of the French foon became univerfal. Near two thoufand were killed on the fpot; a greater number fell by the hands of the peafants, who, in revenge for the cruelty with which their country had been plundered, purfued the fugitives, and maffacred them without mercy; the reft were taken prifoners, together with

De

De Termes their general, and many officers of diſtinction [x].

BOOK XII.
1558.
The Duke of Guiſe oppoſed to the victorious army.

THIS ſignal victory, for which the Count of Egmont was afterwards ſo ill requited by Philip, obliged the Duke of Guiſe to relinquiſh all other ſchemes, and to haſten towards the frontier of Picardy, that he might oppoſe the progreſs of the enemy in that province. This diſaſter, however, reflected new luſtre on his reputation, and once more turned the eyes of his countrymen towards him, as the only general on whoſe arms victory always attended, and in whoſe conduct, as well as good fortune, they could confide in every danger. Henry reinforced the Duke of Guiſe's army with ſo many troops drawn from the adjacent garriſons, that it ſoon amounted to forty thouſand men. That of the enemy, after the junction of Egmont with the Duke of Savoy, was not inferior in number. They encamped at the diſtance of a few leagues from one another; and each monarch having joined his reſpective army, it was expected, after the viciſſitudes of good and bad ſucceſs during this and the former campaign, that a deciſive battle would at laſt determine, which of the rivals ſhould take the aſcendant for the future, and give law to Europe. But though both had it in their power, neither of them diſcovered any inclination to bring the determination of ſuch an important point to depend upon the uncertain

[x] Thuan. lib. xx. 694.

issue of a single battle. The fatal engagements at St. Quintin and Gravelines were too recent to be so soon forgotten, and the prospect of encountering the same troops, commanded by the same generals who had twice triumphed over his arms, inspired Henry with a degree of caution which was not common to him. Philip, of a genius averse to bold operations in war, naturally leaned to cautious measures, and was not disposed to hazard any thing against a general so fortunate and successful as the Duke of Guise. Both monarchs, as if by agreement, stood on the defensive, and fortifying their camps carefully, avoided every skirmish or rencounter that might bring on a general engagement.

Both monarchs begin to desire peace.

WHILE the armies continued in this inaction, peace began to be mentioned in each camp, and both Henry and Philip discovered an inclination to listen to any overture that tended to re-establish it. The kingdoms of France and Spain had been engaged during half a century in almost continual wars, carried on at great expence, and productive of no considerable advantage to either. Exhausted by extraordinary and unceasing efforts, which far exceeded those to which the nations of Europe had been accustomed before the rivalship between Charles V. and Francis I. both nations longed so much for an interval of repose, in order to recruit their strength, that their sovereigns drew from them with difficulty the supplies necessary for carrying on hostilities.

The

EMPEROR CHARLES V.

BOOK XII.
1558.

The private inclinations of both the Kings concurred with those of their people. Philip was prompted to wish for peace by his fond desire of returning to Spain. Accustomed from his infancy to the climate and manners of that country, he was attached to it with such extreme predilection, that he never felt himself at ease in any other part of his dominions. But as he could not quit the Low Countries, either with decency or safety, and venture on a voyage to Spain during the continuance of war, the prospect of a pacification which would put it in his power to execute his favourite scheme, was highly acceptable. Henry was no less desirous of being delivered from the burden and occupations of war, that he might have leisure to turn all his attention, and bend the whole force of his government, towards suppressing the opinions of the Reformers, which were spreading with such rapidity in Paris and other great towns of France, that they began to grow formidable to the established church.

Besides these public and avowed considerations arising from the state of the two hostile kingdoms, or from the wishes of their respective monarchs, there was a secret intrigue carried on in the court of France, which contributed as much as either of the other, to hasten and to facilitate the negociation of a peace. The Constable Montmorency, during his captivity, beheld the rapid success and growing favour of the Duke of Guise with the envy natural to a rival. Every

An intrigue in the court of France facilitates it.

advantage gained by the Princes of Lorrain he considered as a fresh wound to his own reputation, and he knew with what malevolent address it would be improved to diminish his credit with the King, and to augment that of the Duke of Guise. These arts, he was afraid, might, by degrees, work on the easy and ductile mind of Henry, so as to efface all remains of his ancient affection towards himself. But he could not discover any remedy for this, unless he were allowed to return home, that he might try whether by his presence he could defeat the artifices of his enemies, and revive those warm and tender sentiments which had long attached Henry to him, with a confidence so entire, as resembled rather the cordialty of private friendship, than the cold and selfish connexion between a monarch and one of his courtiers. While Montmorency was forming schemes and wishes for his return to France with much anxiety of mind, but with little hope of success, an unexpected incident prepared the way for it. The Cardinal of Lorrain, who had shared with his brother in the King's favour, and participated of the power which that conferred, did not bear prosperity with the same discretion as the Duke of Guise. Intoxicated with their good fortune, he forgot how much they had been indebted for their present elevation to their connexions with the Dutchess of Valentinois, and vainly ascribed all to the extraordinary merit of their family. This led him not only to neglect his benefactress, but to thwart her schemes, and to talk with a sarcastic liberty of her character and person. That singular woman, who, if we may believe contemporary writers, retained the beauty and charms of youth at the age of threescore, and on whom it is certain that Henry still doated with all the fondness of love, felt this injury with sensibility, and set herself with eagerness to inflict the vengeance which it merited. As there was no method of supplanting the Princes of Lorrain so effectually as by a coalition of interests with the Constable, she proposed the marriage of her grand-daughter with one of his sons, as the bond of their future union; and Montmorency readily gave his consent to the match. Having thus cemented their alliance, the Dutchess employed all her influence with the King, in order to confirm his inclinations towards peace, and induce him to take the steps necessary for attaining it. She insinuated that any overture of that kind would come with great propriety from the Constable, and if entrusted to the conduct of his prudence, could hardly fail of success.

Henry, long accustomed to commit all affairs of importance to the management of the Constable, and needing only this encouragement to return to his ancient habits, wrote to him immediately with his usual familiarity and affection, empowering him at the same time to take the first opportunity of sounding Philip and his ministers with regard to peace. Montmorency made his application to Philip by the most proper channel.

Henry commits the negociation to Montmorency.

He opened himself to the Duke of Savoy, who, notwithstanding the high command to which he had been raised, and the military glory which he had acquired in the Spanish service, was weary of remaining in exile, and languished to return into his paternal dominions. As there was no prospect of his recovering possession of them by force of arms, he considered a definitive treaty of peace between France and Spain, as the only event by which he could hope to obtain restitution. Being no stranger to Philip's private wishes with regard to peace, he easily prevailed on him not only to discover a disposition on his part towards accommodation, but to permit Montmorency to return, on his parole, to France, that he might confirm his own sovereign in his pacific sentiments. Henry received the Constable with the most flattering marks of regard; absence, instead of having abated or extinguished the Monarch's friendship, seemed to have given it new ardour. Montmorency, from the moment of his appearance in court, assumed, if possible, a higher place than ever in his affection, and a more perfect ascendant over his mind. The Cardinal of Lorrain and Duke of Guise prudently gave way to a tide of favour too strong for them to oppose, and confining themselves to their proper departments, permitted, without any struggle, the Constable and Dutchess of Valentinois to direct public affairs at their pleasure. They soon prevailed on the King to nominate plenipotentiaries to treat of peace. Philip did the same. The abbey of Cercamp was

fixed

fixed on as the place of congress; and all military operations were immediately terminated by a suspension of arms.

Death of Charles V.

WHILE these preliminary steps were taking towards a treaty which restored tranquillity to Europe, Charles V. whose ambition had so long disturbed it, ended his days in the monastery of St. Justus. When Charles entered this retreat, he formed such a plan of life for himself, as would have suited the condition of a private gentleman of a moderate fortune. His table was neat, but plain; his domestics few; his intercourse with them familiar; all the cumbersome and ceremonious forms of attendance on his person were entirely abolished, as destructive of that social ease and tranquillity which he courted, in order to soothe the remainder of his days. As the mildness of the climate, together with his deliverance from the burdens and cares of government, procured him, at first, a considerable remission from the acute pains with which he had been long tormented; he enjoyed, perhaps, more complete satisfaction in this humble solitude, than all his grandeur had ever yielded him. The ambitious thoughts and projects which had so long engrossed and disquieted him, were quite effaced from his mind; far from taking any part in the political transactions of the Princes of Europe, he restrained his curiosity even from any inquiry concerning them; and he seemed to view the busy scene which he had abandoned with all the contempt

contempt and indifference arising from his thorough experience of its vanity, as well as from the pleasing reflection of having disentangled himself from its cares.

His amusements in his retreat.

OTHER amusements, and other objects now occupied him. Sometimes he cultivated the plants in his garden with his own hands; sometimes he rode out to the neighbouring wood on a little horse, the only one that he kept, attended by a single servant on foot. When his infirmities confined him to his apartment, which often happened, and deprived him of these more active recreations, he either admitted a few gentlemen who resided near the monastery to visit him, and entertained them familiarly at his table; or he employed himself in studying mechanical principles, and in forming curious works of mechanism, of which he had always been remarkably fond, and to which his genius was peculiarly turned. With this view he had engaged Turriano, one of the most ingenious artists of that age, to accompany him in his retreat. He laboured together with him in framing models of the most useful machines, as well as in making experiments with regard to their respective powers, and it was not seldom that the ideas of the monarch assisted or perfected the inventions of the artist. He relieved his mind, at intervals, with slighter and more fantastic works of mechanism, in fashioning puppets, which, by the structure of internal springs, mimicked the gestures and actions of men, to the astonishment of the ignorant monks, who beholding movements which they could not comprehend, sometimes diftrufted their own fenfes, and fometimes fufpected Charles and Turriano of being in compact with invifible powers. He was particularly curious with regard to the conftruction of clocks and watches; and having found, after repeated trials, that he could not bring any two of them to go exactly alike, he reflected, it is faid, with a mixture of furprife as well as regret, on his own folly, in having beftowed fo much time and labour on the more vain attempt of bringing mankind to a precife uniformity of fentiment concerning the profound and myfterious doctrines of religion.

But in what manner foever Charles difpofed of the reft of his time, he conftantly referved a confiderable portion of it for religious exercifes. He regularly attended divine fervice in the chapel of the monaftery, every morning and evening; he took great pleafure in reading books of devotion, particularly the works of St. Auguftine and St. Bernard; and converfed much with his confeffor, and the prior of the monaftery, on pious fubjects. Thus did Charles pafs the firft year of his retreat, in a manner not unbecoming a man perfectly difengaged from the affairs of the prefent life, and ftanding on the confines of a future world; either in innocent amufements, which foothed his pains, and relieved a mind worn out with exceffive application to bufinefs; or in devout occupations,

His more ferious occupations.

which

which he deemed neceſſary in preparing for another ſtate.

The cauſes of his death.

But about ſix months before his death, the gout, after a longer intermiſſion than uſual, returned with a proportional increaſe of violence. His ſhattered conſtitution had not vigour enough remaining to withſtand ſuch a ſhock. It enfeebled his mind as much as his body, and from this period we hardly diſcern any traces of that ſound and maſculine underſtanding, which diſtinguiſhed Charles among his contemporaries. An illiberal and timid ſuperſtition depreſſed his ſpirit. He had no reliſh for amuſements of any kind. He endeavoured to conform, in his manner of living, to all the rigour of monaſtic auſterity. He deſired no other ſociety than that of monks, and was almoſt continually employed with them in chanting the hymns of the Miſſal. As an expiation for his ſins, he gave himſelf the diſcipline in ſecret with ſuch ſeverity, that the whip of cords which he employed as the inſtrument of his puniſhment, was found after his deceaſe tinged with his blood. Nor was he ſatisfied with theſe acts of mortification, which, however ſevere, were not unexampled. The timorous and diſtruſtful ſolicitude which always accompanies ſuperſtition, ſtill continued to diſquiet him, and depreciating all the devout exerciſes in which he had hitherto been engaged, prompted him to aim at ſomething extraordinary, at ſome new and ſingular act of piety that would diſplay his zeal, and merit

merit the favour of Heaven. The act on which he fixed was as wild and uncommon as any that superstition ever suggested to a weak and disordered fancy. He resolved to celebrate his own obsequies before his death. He ordered his tomb to be erected in the chapel of the monastery. His domestics marched thither in funeral procession, with black tapers in their hands. He himself followed in his shroud. He was laid in his coffin, with much solemnity. The service for the dead was chanted, and Charles joined in the prayers which were offered up for the rest of his soul, mingling his tears with those which his attendants shed, as if they had been celebrating a real funeral. The ceremony closed with sprinkling holy water on the coffin in the usual form, and all the assistants retiring, the doors of the chapel were shut. Then Charles rose out of the coffin, and withdrew to his apartment, full of those awful sentiments which such a singular solemnity was calculated to inspire. But either the fatiguing length of the ceremony, or the impression which the image of death left on his mind, affected him so much, that next day he was seized with a fever. His feeble frame could not long resist its violence, and he expired on the twenty-first of September, after a life of fifty-eight years, six months, and twenty-five days [y].

[y] Strada de Bello Belg. lib. i. p. 11. Thuan. 723. Sandov. ii. 609, &c. Miniana Contin. Marianæ, vol. iv. 216. Vera y Zuniga Vida de Carlos, p. 111.

BOOK
XII.

1558.
His character.

As Charles was the first Prince of the age in rank and dignity, the part which he acted, whether we consider the greatness, the variety, or the success of his undertakings, was the most conspicuous. It is from an attentive observation of his conduct, not from the exaggerated praises of the Spanish historians, or the undistinguishing censure of the French, that a just idea of Charles's genius and abilities is to be collected. He possessed qualities so peculiar, that they strongly mark his character, and not only distinguish him from the Princes who were his contemporaries, but account for that superiority over them which he so long maintained. In forming his schemes, he was, by nature, as well as by habit, cautious and considerate. Born with talents which unfolded themselves slowly, and were late in attaining maturity, he was accustomed to ponder every subject that demanded his consideration, with a careful and deliberate attention. He bent the whole force of his mind towards it, and dwelling upon it with a serious application, undiverted by pleasure, and hardly relaxed by any amusement, he revolved it, in silence, in his own breast. He then communicated the matter to his ministers, and after hearing their opinions, took his resolution with a decisive firmness, which seldom follows such slow, and seemingly hesitating consultations. Of consequence, Charles's measures, instead of resembling the desultory and irregular sallies of Henry VIII. or Francis I. had the appearance of a consistent system, in which all the parts were arranged,

ged, all the effects were foreseen, and even every accident was provided for. His promptitude in execution was no less remarkable than his patience in deliberation. He did not discover greater sagacity in his choice of the measures which it was proper to pursue, than fertility of genius in finding out the means for rendering his pursuit of them successful. Though he had naturally so little of the martial turn, that during the most ardent and bustling period of life, he remained in the cabinet inactive, yet when he chose at length to appear at the head of his armies, his mind was so formed for vigorous exertions in every direction, that he acquired such knowledge in the art of war, and such talents for command, as rendered him equal in reputation and success to the most able generals of the age. But Charles possessed, in the most eminent degree, the science which is of greatest importance to a monarch, that of knowing men, and of adapting their talents to the various departments which he allotted to them. From the death of Chievres to the end of his reign, he employed no general in the field, no minister in the cabinet, no ambassador to a foreign court, no governor of a province, whose abilities were inadequate to the trust which he reposed in them. Though destitute of that bewitching affability of manners, which gained Francis the hearts of all who approached his person, he was no stranger to the virtues which secure fidelity and attachment. He placed unbounded confidence in his generals; he rewarded their

their services with munificence; he neither envied their fame, nor discovered any jealousy of their power. Almost all the generals who conducted his armies, may be placed on a level with those illustrious personages who have attained the highest eminence of military glory; and his advantages over his rivals, are to be ascribed so manifestly to the superior abilities of the commanders whom he set in opposition to them, that this might seem to detract, in some degree, from his own merit, if the talent of discovering and steadiness in employing such instruments were not the most undoubted proofs of a capacity for government.

THERE were, nevertheless, defects in his political character which must considerably abate the admiration due to his extraordinary talents. Charles's ambition was insatiable; and though there seems to be no foundation for an opinion prevalent in his own age, that he had formed the chimerical project of establishing an universal monarchy in Europe, it is certain that his desire of being distinguished as a conqueror involved him in continual wars, which not only exhausted and oppressed his subjects, but left him little leisure for giving attention to the interior police and improvement of his kingdoms, the great objects of every Prince who makes the happiness of his people the end of his government. Charles, at a very early period of life, having added the Imperial crown to the kingdoms of Spain, and to the

the hereditary dominions of the houses of Austria and Burgundy, this opened to him such a vast field of enterprize, and engaged him in schemes so complicated as well as arduous, that feeling his power to be unequal to the execution of them, he had often recourse to low artifices, unbecoming his superior talents, and sometimes ventured on such deviations from integrity, as were dishonourable in a great Prince. His insidious and fraudulent policy appeared more conspicuous, and was rendered more odious by a comparison with the open and undesigning character of his contemporaries Francis I. and Henry VIII. This difference, though occasioned chiefly by the diversity of their tempers, must be ascribed, in some degree, to such an opposition in the principles of their political conduct as affords some excuse for this defect in Charles's behaviour, though it cannot serve as a justification of it. Francis and Henry seldom acted but from the impulse of their passions, and rushed headlong towards the object in view. Charles's measures, being the result of cool reflection, were disposed into a regular system, and carried on upon a concerted plan. Persons who act in the former manner, naturally pursue the end in view, without assuming any disguise, or displaying much address. Such as hold the latter course, are apt, in forming, as well as in executing their designs, to employ such refinements as always lead to artifice in conduct, and often degenerate into deceit.

THE circumstances transmitted to us, with respect to Charles's private deportment and character, are fewer and less interesting, than might have been expected from the great number of authors who have undertaken to write an account of his life. These are not the object of this history, which aims more at representing the great transactions of the reign of Charles V. and pointing out the manner in which they affected the political state of Europe, than at delineating his private virtues or defects.

Conference in order to peace.

THE plenipotentiaries of France, Spain, and England, continued their conferences at Cercamp; and though each of them, with the usual art of negociators, made at first very high demands in the name of their respective courts, yet as they were all equally desirous of peace, they would have consented reciprocally to such abatements and restrictions of their claims, as must have removed every obstacle to an accommodation. The death of Charles V. was a new motive with Philip to hasten the conclusion of a treaty; as it increased his impatience for returning into Spain, where there was now no person greater or more illustrious than himself. But, in spite of the concurring wishes of all the parties interested, an event happened which occasioned an unavoidable delay in their negociations. About a month after the opening of the conferences at Cercamp, Mary of England ended her short and inglorious reign, and Elizabeth, her sister, was immediately proclaimed

Nov. 17. Death of Mary of England.

proclaimed Queen with univerſal joy. As the powers of the Engliſh plenipotentiaries expired on the death of their miſtreſs, they could not proceed until they received a commiſſion and inſtructions from their new ſovereign.

<small>BOOK XII.
1558.</small>

Henry and Philip beheld Elizabeth's elevation to the throne with equal ſolicitude. As during Mary's jealous adminiſtration, under the moſt difficult circumſtances, and in a ſituation extremely delicate, that Princeſs had conducted herſelf with prudence and addreſs far exceeding her years, they had conceived an high idea of her abilities, and already formed expectations of a reign very different from that of her ſiſter. Equally ſenſible of the importance of gaining her favour, both monarchs ſet themſelves with emulation to court it, and employed every art in order to inſinuate themſelves into her confidence. Each of them had ſomething meritorious, with regard to Elizabeth, to plead in his own behalf. Henry had offered her a retreat in his dominions, if the dread of her ſiſter's violence ſhould force her to fly for ſafety out of England. Philip, by his powerful interceſſion, had prevented Mary from proceeding to the moſt fatal extremities againſt her ſiſter. Each of them endeavoured now to avail himſelf of the circumſtances in his favour. Henry wrote to Elizabeth ſoon after her acceſſion, with the warmeſt expreſſions of regard and friendſhip. He repreſented the war which had unhappily been kindled between their kingdoms, not as a

<small>Henry and Philip court Elizabeth her ſucceſſor.</small>

U 2 national

national quarrel, but as the effect of Mary's blind partiality to her hufband, and fond compliance with all his wifhes. He entreated her to difengage herfelf from an alliance which had proved fo unfortunate to England, and to confent to a feparate peace with him, without mingling her interefts with thofe of Spain, from which they ought now to be altogether disjoined. Philip, on the other hand, unwilling to lofe his connexion with England, the importance of which, during a rupture with France, he had fo recently experienced, not only vied with Henry in declarations of efteem for Elizabeth, and in profeffions of his refolution to cultivate the ftricteft amity with her, but, in order to confirm and perpetuate their union, he offered himfelf to her in marriage, and undertook to procure a difpenfation from the Pope for that purpofe.

Elizabeth's deliberation concerning her conduct.

ELIZABETH weighed the propofals of the two Monarchs attentively, and with that provident difcernment of her true intereft, which was confpicuous in all her deliberations. She gave fome encouragement to Henry's overture of a feparate negociation, becaufe it opened a channel of correfpondence with France, which fhe might find to be of great advantage, if Philip fhould not difcover fufficient zeal and folicitude for fecuring to her proper terms in the joint treaty. But fhe ventured on this ftep with the moft cautious referve, that fhe might not alarm Philip's fufpicious temper; and lofe an ally in attempting to gain

an

an enemy[z]. Henry himself, by an unpardonable act of indiscretion, prevented her from carrying her intercourse with him, to such a length as might have offended or alienated Philip. At the very time when he was courting Elizabeth's friendship with the greatest assiduity, he yielded with an inconsiderate facility to the solicitations of the Princess of Lorrain, and allowed his daughter-in-law the Queen of Scots to assume the title and arms of Queen of England. This ill-timed pretension, the source of many calamities to the unfortunate Queen of Scots, extinguished at once all the confidence that might have grown between Henry and Elizabeth, and left in its place distrust, resentment, and antipathy. Elizabeth soon found that she must unite her interests closely with Philip's, and expect peace only from negociations carried on in conjunction with him [a].

She empowers her ambassadors to treat of peace.

As she had granted a commission, immediately after her accession, to the same plenipotentiaries whom her sister had employed, she now instructed them to act in every point in concert with the plenipotentiaries of Spain, and to take no step until they had previously consulted with them [b]. But though she deemed it prudent to assume this appearance of confidence in the Spanish Monarch, she knew precisely how far to carry it; and discovered no inclination to accept of that extraor-

[z] Forbes, i. p. 4.   [a] Strype's Annals of the Reformation, i. 11. Carte's Hist. of England, vol. iii. p. 375.
[b] Forbes's full View, i. p. 37. 40.

dinary proposal of marriage which Philip had made to her. The English had expressed so openly their detestation of her sister's choice of him, that it would have been highly imprudent to have exasperated them by renewing that odious alliance. She was too well acquainted with Philip's harsh imperious temper, to think of him for a husband. Nor could she admit a dispensation from the Pope to be sufficient to authorize her marrying him, without condemning her father's divorce from Catharine of Aragon, and acknowledging of consequence that her mother's marriage was null, and her own birth illegitimate. But though she determined not to yield to Philip's addresses, the situation of her affairs rendered it dangerous to reject them; she returned her answer, therefore, in terms which were evasive, but so tempered with respect, that though they gave him no reason to be secure of success, they did not altogether extinguish his hopes.

Negeciations at Cateau-Cambresis.

By this artifice, as well as by the prudence with which she concealed her sentiments and intentions concerning religion, for some time after her accession, she so far gained upon Philip, that he warmly espoused her interest in the conferences which were renewed at Cercamp, and afterwards removed to Cateau-Cambresis. A definitive treaty, which was to adjust the claims and pretensions of so many princes, required the examination of such a variety of intricate points, and led to such infinite and minute details, as

1559. February 6.

drew

drew out the negociations to a great length. But the Conſtable Montmorency exerted himſelf with ſuch indefatigable zeal and induſtry, repairing alternately to the courts of Paris and Bruſſels, in order to obviate or remove every difficulty, that all points in diſpute were adjuſted at length in ſuch a manner, as to give entire ſatisfaction in every particular to Henry and Philip; and the laſt hand was ready to be put to the treaty between them.

Difficulties with regard to the claims of England.

The claims of England remained as the only obſtacle to retard it. Elizabeth demanded the reſtitution of Calais in the moſt peremptory tone, as an eſſential condition of her conſenting to peace; Henry refuſed to give up that important conqueſt; and both ſeemed to have taken their reſolution with unalterable firmneſs. Philip warmly ſupported Elizabeth's pretenſions to Calais, not merely from a principle of equity towards the Engliſh nation, that he might appear to have contributed to their recovering what they had loſt by eſpouſing his cauſe; nor ſolely with a view of ſoothing Elizabeth by this manifeſtation of zeal for her intereſt; but in order to render France leſs formidable, by ſecuring to her ancient enemy this eaſy acceſs into the heart of the kingdom. The earneſtneſs, however, with which he ſeconded the arguments of the Engliſh plenipotentiaries, ſoon began to relax. During the courſe of the negociation, Elizabeth, who now felt herſelf firmly ſeated on her throne, began to take ſuch open and vigorous meaſures

measures not only for overturning all that her sister had done in favour of popery, but for establishing the protestant church on a firm foundation, as convinced Philip that his hopes of an union with her had been from the beginning vain, and were now desperate. From that period, his interpositions in her favour became more cold and formal, flowing merely from a regard to decorum, or from the consideration of remote political interests. Elizabeth, having reason to expect such an alteration in his conduct, quickly perceived it. But as nothing would have been of greater detriment to her people, or more inconsistent with her schemes of domestic administration, than the continuance of war, she saw the necessity of submitting to such conditions as the situation of her affairs imposed, and that she must reckon upon being deserted by an ally who was now united to her by a very feeble tie, if she did not speedily reduce her demands to what was moderate and attainable. She accordingly gave new instructions to her ambassadors; and Philip's plenipotentiaries acting as mediators between the French and them [c], an expedient was fallen upon, which, in some degree, justified Elizabeth's departing from the rigour of her first demand with regard to Calais. All lesser articles were settled without much discussion or delay. Philip, that he might not appear to have abandoned the English, insisted that the treaty between Henry and Elizabeth

[c] Forbes, i. 59.

should be concluded in form, before that between the French monarch and himself. The one was signed on the second day of April, the other on the day following.

Articles of peace between France and England.

THE treaty of peace between France and England contained no articles of real importance, but that which refpected Calais. It was ftipulated, That the King of France fhould retain poffeffion of that town, with all its dependencies, during eight years; That, at the expiration of that term, he fhould reftore it to England; That in cafe of non-performance, he fhould forfeit five hundred thoufand crowns, for the payment of which fum, feven or eight wealthy merchants, who were not his fubjects, fhould grant fecurity; That five perfons of diftinction fhould be given as hoftages until that fecurity were provided; That, although the forfeit of five hundred thoufand crowns fhould be paid, the right of England to Calais fhould ftill remain entire, in the fame manner as if the term of eight years were expired; That the King and Queen of Scotland fhould be included in the treaty; That if they, or the French King, fhould violate the peace by any hoftile action, Henry fhould be obliged inftantly to reftore Calais; That, on the other hand, if any breach of the treaty proceeded from Elizabeth, then Henry and the King and Queen of Scots were abfolved from all the engagements which they had come under by this treaty.

NOTWITH-

BOOK XII.

1559.
The views of both parties with respect to these.

Notwithstanding the studied attention with which so many precautions were taken, it is evident that Henry did not intend the restitution of Calais, nor is it probable that Elizabeth expected it. It was hardly possible that she could maintain, during the course of eight years, such perfect concord both with France and Scotland, as not to afford Henry some pretext for alleging that she had violated the treaty. But even if that term should elapse without any ground for complaint, Henry might then chuse to pay the sum stipulated, and Elizabeth had no method of asserting her right but by force of arms. However, by throwing the articles in the treaty with regard to Calais into this form, Elizabeth satisfied her subjects of every denomination; she gave men of discernment a striking proof of her address, in palliating what she could not prevent; and amused the multitude, to whom the cession of such an important place would have appeared altogether infamous, with the prospect of recovering in a short time that favourite possession.

An expedient which promotes peace between France and Spain.

THE expedient which Montmorency employed, in order to facilitate the conclusion of peace between France and Spain, was the negociating two treaties of marriage, one between Elizabeth, Henry's eldest daughter, and Philip, who supplanted his son, the unfortunate Don Carlos, to whom that Princess had been promised in the former conferences at Cercamp; the other between Margaret,

Margaret, Henry's only fifter, and the Duke of Savoy. For however feeble the ties of blood may often be among Princes, or how little foever they may regard them when pufhed on to act by motives of ambition, they affume on other occafions the appearance of being fo far influenced by thefe domeftic affections, as to employ them to juftify meafures and conceffions which they find to be neceffary, but know to be impolitic or difhonourable. Such was the ufe Henry made of the two marriages to which he gave his confent. Having fecured an honourable eftablifhment for his fifter and his daughter, he, in confideration of thefe, granted terms both to Philip and the Duke of Savoy, of which he would not, on any other account, have ventured to approve.

The principal articles in the treaty between France and Spain were, That fincere and perpetual amity fhould be eftablifhed between the two crowns and their refpective allies; That the two monarchs fhould labour in concert to procure the convocation of a general council, in order to check the progrefs of herefy, and reftore unity and concord to the Chriftian church; That all conquefts made by either party, on this fide of the Alps, fince the commencement of the war in one thoufand five hundred and fifty-one, fhould be mutually reftored; That the dutchy of Savoy, the principality of Piedmont, the country of Breffe, and all the other territories formerly fubject to the dukes of Savoy, fhould be reftored to Emanuel

The terms of pacification.

Emanuel Philibert, immediately after the celebration of his marriage with Margaret of France, the towns of Turin, Quiers, Pignerol, Chivaz, and Villanova excepted, of which Henry should keep possession until his claims to these places, in right of his grandmother, should be tried and decided in course of law; That as long as Henry retained these places in his hands, Philip should be at liberty to keep garrisons in the towns of Vercelli and Asti; That the French King should immediately evacuate all the places which he held in Tuscany and the Sienese, and renounce all future pretensions to them; that he should restore the marquisate of Montferrat to the Duke of Mantua; That he should receive the Genoese into favour, and give up to them the towns which he had conquered in the island of Corsica; That none of the Princes or States, to whom these cessions were made, should call their subjects to account for any part of their conduct while under the dominion of their enemies, but should bury all past transactions in oblivion. The Pope, the Emperor, the Kings of Denmark, Sweden, Poland, Portugal, the King and Queen of Scots, and almost every Prince and State in Christendom, were comprehended in this pacification as the allies either of Henry or of Philip [d].

Which re-establishes tranquillity in Europe.

Thus, by this famous treaty, peace was re-established in Europe. All the causes of discord

[d] Recueil des Traitez, tom. ii. 287.

which had so long embroiled the powerful monarchs of France and Spain, which had transmitted hereditary quarrels and wars from Charles to Philip, and from Francis to Henry, seemed to be wholly removed, or finally terminated. The French alone complained of the unequal conditions of a treaty, into which an ambitious minister, in order to recover his liberty, and an artful mistress, that she might gratify her resentment, had seduced their too easy monarch. They exclaimed loudly against the folly of giving up to the enemies of France an hundred and eighty-nine fortified places, in the Low-countries or in Italy, in return for the three insignificant towns of St. Quintin, Ham, and Catelet. They considered it as an indelible stain upon the glory of the nation, to renounce in one day territories so extensive, and so capable of being defended, that the enemy could not have hoped to wrest them out of its hands, after many years of victory.

BOOK XII.
1559.

But Henry, without regarding the sentiments of his people, or being moved by the remonstrances of his council, ratified the treaty, and executed with great fidelity whatever he had stipulated to perform. The duke of Savoy repaired with a numerous retinue to Paris, in order to celebrate his marriage with Henry's sister. The Duke of Alva was sent to the same capital, at the head of a splendid embassy, to espouse Elizabeth in name of his master. They were received

The peace between France and Spain ratified.

received with extraordinary magnificence by the French court. Amidst the rejoicings and festivities on that occasion, Henry's days were cut short by a singular and tragical accident. His son, Francis II. a prince under age, of a weak constitution, and of a mind still more feeble, succeeded him. Soon after, Paul ended his violent and imperious Pontificate, at enmity with all the world, and disgusted even with his own nephews. They, persecuted by Philip, and deserted by the succeeding Pope, whom they had raised by their influence to the papal throne, were condemned to the punishment which their crimes and ambition had merited, and their death was as infamous as their lives had been criminal. Thus most of the personages, who had long sustained the principal characters on the great theatre of Europe, disappeared about the same time. A more known period of history opens at this æra; other actors enter upon the stage, with different views, as well as different passions; new contests arose, and new schemes of ambition occupied and disquieted mankind.

A general review of the whole period.

Upon reviewing the transactions of any active period, in the history of civilised nations, the changes which are accomplished appear wonderfully disproportioned to the efforts which have been exerted. Conquests are never very extensive or rapid, but among nations whose progress in improvement is extremely unequal. When Alexander the Great, at the head of a gallant people,

people, of simple manners, and formed to war by admirable military institutions, invaded a state sunk in luxury, and enervated by excessive refinement; when Genchizcan and Tamerlane, with their armies of hardy barbarians, poured in upon nations, enfeebled by the climate in which they lived, or by the arts and commerce which they cultivated, these conquerors, like a torrent, swept every thing before them, subduing kingdoms and provinces in as short a space of time as was requisite to march through them. But when nations are in a state similar to each other, and keep equal pace in their advances towards refinement, they are not exposed to the calamity of sudden conquests. Their acquisitions of knowledge, their progress in the art of war, their political sagacity and address, are nearly equal. The fate of states in this situation, depends not on a single battle. Their internal resources are many and various. Nor are they themselves alone interested in their own safety, or active in their own defence. Other states interpose, and balance any temporary advantage which either party may have acquired. After the fiercest and most lengthened contest, all the rival nations are exhausted, none are conquered. At length they find it necessary to conclude a peace, which restores to each almost the same power and the same territories of which they were formerly in possession.

Such was the state of Europe during the reign of Charles V. No Prince was so much superior to the rest in power, as to render his efforts irresistible,

The nations of Europe in a similar state during the sixteenth century.

fiftible, and his conquests easy. No nation had made progress in improvement so far beyond its neighbours, as to have acquired a very manifest pre-eminence. Each state derived some advantage, or was subject to some inconvenience from its situation or its climate; each was distinguished by something peculiar in the genius of its people, or the constitution of its government. But the advantages possessed by one state, were counterbalanced by circumstances favourable to others; and this prevented any from attaining such superiority as might have been fatal to all. The nations of Europe in that age, as in the present, were like one great family; there were some features common to all, which fixed a resemblance; there were certain peculiarities conspicuous in each, which marked a distinction. But there was not among them that wide diversity of character and of genius which, in almost every period of history, hath exalted the Europeans above the inhabitants of the other quarters of the globe, and seems to have destined the one to rule, and the other to obey.

A remarkable change in the state of Europe, during the reign of Charles V.

But though the near resemblance and equality in improvement among the different nations of Europe, prevented the reign of Charles V. from being distinguished by such sudden and extensive conquests as occur in some other periods of history, yet, during the course of his administration, all the considerable states in Europe suffered a remarkable change in their political situation, and

and felt the influence of events, which have not hitherto spent their force, but still continue to operate in a greater or in a less degree. It was during his reign, and in consequence of the perpetual efforts to which his enterprizing ambition roused him, that the different kingdoms of Europe acquired internal vigour; that they discerned the resources of which they were possessed; that they came both to feel their own strength, and to know how to render it formidable to others. It was during his reign, too, that the different kingdoms of Europe, which in former times seemed frequently to act as if they had been single and disjoined, became so thoroughly acquainted, and so intimately connected with each other, as to form one great political system, in which each took a station, wherein it has remained since that time with less variation than could have been expected after the events of two active centuries.

THE progress, however, and acquisitions of the house of Austria, were not only greater than those of any other power, but more discernible and conspicuous. I have already enumerated the extensive territories which descended to Charles from his Austrian, Burgundian, and Spanish ancestors*. To these he himself added the Imperial dignity; and, as if all this had been too little, the bounds of the habitable globe seemed to be extended, and a new world was subjected to his command. Upon his resignation, the Burgundian provinces,

The progress of the house of Austria.

* Vol. II. p. 2.

and the Spanish kingdoms with their dependencies, both in the old and new worlds, devolved to Philip. But Charles transmitted his dominions to his son, in a condition very different from that in which he himself had received them. They were augmented by the accession of new provinces; they were habituated to obey an administration which was no less vigorous than steady; they were accustomed to expensive and persevering efforts, which, though necessary in the contests between civilized nations, had been little known in Europe before the sixteenth century. The provinces of Friesland, Utrecht, and Overyssel, which he acquired by purchase from their former proprietors, and the dutchy of Gueldres, of which he made himself master, partly by force of arms, partly by the arts of negociation, were additions of great value to his Burgundian dominions. Ferdinand and Isabella had transmitted to him all the provinces of Spain, from the bottom of the Pyrenees to the frontiers of Portugal; but as he maintained a perpetual peace with that kingdom, amidst the various efforts of his enterprizing ambition, he made no acquisition of territory in that quarter.

Particularly in Spain. Charles had gained, however, a vast accession of power in this part of his dominions. By his success in the war with the commons of Castile, he exalted the regal prerogative upon the ruins of the privileges which formerly belonged to the people. Though he allowed the name of the Cortes

Cortes to remain, and the formality of holding it to be continued; he reduced its authority and jurisdiction almost to nothing, and modelled it in such a manner, that it became rather a junto of the servants of the crown, than an assembly of the representatives of the people. One member of the constitution being thus lopped off, it was impossible but that the other must feel the stroke, and suffer by it. The suppression of the popular power rendered the aristocratical less formidable. The grandees, prompted by the warlike spirit of the age, or allured by the honours which they enjoyed in a court, exhausted their fortunes in military service, or in attending on the person of their Prince. They did not dread, perhaps did not observe, the dangerous progress of the royal authority, which leaving them the vain distinction of being covered in presence of their sovereign, stripped them, by degrees, of that real power which they possessed while they formed one body, and acted in concert with the people. Charles's success in abolishing the privileges of the commons, and in breaking the power of the nobles of Castile, encouraged Philip to invade the liberties of Aragon, which were still more extensive. The Castilians, accustomed to subjection themselves, assisted in imposing the yoke on their more happy and independent neighbours. The will of the sovereign became the supreme law in all the kingdoms of Spain; and princes who were not checked in forming their plans by the jealousy of the people, nor controled in executing them by the power of the nobles, could both aim at great objects, and call forth the whole strength of the monarchy in order to attain them.

Also in other parts of Europe.

As Charles, by extending the royal prerogative, rendered the monarchs of Spain masters at home, he added new dignity and power to their crown by his foreign acquisitions. He secured to Spain the quiet possession of the kingdom of Naples, which Ferdinand had usurped by fraud, and held with difficulty. He united the dutchy of Milan, one of the most fertile and populous Italian provinces, to the Spanish crown; and left his successors, even without taking their other territories into the account, the most considerable Princes in Italy, which had been long the theatre of contention to the great powers of Europe, and in which they had struggled with emulation to obtain the superiority. When the French, in conformity to the treaty of Cateau-Cambresis, withdrew their forces out of Italy, and finally relinquished all their schemes of conquest on that side of the Alps, the Spanish dominions then rose in importance, and enabled their Kings, as long as the monarchy retained any degree of vigour, to preserve the chief sway in all the transactions of that country. But whatever accession, either of interior authority or of foreign dominion, Charles gained for the monarchs of Spain in Europe, was inconsiderable when compared with his acquisitions in the new world. He added there, not provinces, but empires to his crown.

He

He conquered territories of such immense extent; he discovered such inexhaustible veins of wealth, and opened such boundless prospects of every kind, as must have roused his successor, and have called him forth to action, though his ambition had been much less ardent than that of Philip, and must have rendered him not only enterprizing but formidable.

Progress of the German branch of the house of Austria.

WHILE the elder branch of the Austrian family rose to such pre-eminence in Spain, the younger, of which Ferdinand was the head, grew to be considerable in Germany. The ancient hereditary dominions of the house of Austria in Germany, united to the kingdoms of Hungary and Bohemia, which Ferdinand had acquired by marriage, formed a respectable power; and when the Imperial dignity was added to these, Ferdinand possessed territories more extensive than had belonged to any Prince, Charles V. excepted, who had been at the head of the Empire during several ages. Fortunately for Europe, the disgust which Philip conceived on account of Ferdinand's refusing to relinquish the Imperial crown in his favour, not only prevented for some time the separate members of the house of Austria from acting in concert, but occasioned between them a visible alienation and rivalship. By degrees, however, regard to the interest of their family extinguished this impolitical animosity. The confidence which was natural returned; the aggrandizing of the house of Austria became the common object of all

all their schemes; they gave and received assistance alternately towards the execution of them; and each, derived consideration and importance from the other's success. A family so great and so aspiring, became the general object of jealousy and terror. All the power, as well as policy, of Europe were exerted during a century, in order to check and humble it. Nothing can give a more striking idea of the ascendant which it had acquired, and of the terror which it had inspired, than that after its vigour was spent with extraordinary exertions of its strength, after Spain was become only the shadow of a great name, and its monarchs were sunk into debility and dotage, the house of Austria still continued to be formidable. The nations of Europe had so often felt its superior power, and had been so constantly employed in guarding against it, that the dread of it became a kind of political habit, the influence of which remained when the causes, which had formed it, ceased to exist.

Acquisitions of the Kings of France during the reign of Charles V.

WHILE the house of Austria went on with such success in enlarging its dominions, France made no considerable acquisition of new territory. All its schemes of conquest in Italy had proved abortive; it had hitherto obtained no establishment of consequence in the new world; and after the continued and vigorous efforts of four successive reigns, the confines of the kingdom were much the same as Louis XI. had left them. But though France made not such large strides towards

wards dominion as the house of Austria, it continued to advance by steps which were more secure, because they were gradual and less observed. The conquest of Calais put it out of the power of the English to invade France but at their utmost peril, and delivered the French from the dread of their ancient enemies, who, previous to that event, could at any time penetrate into the kingdom by that avenue, and thereby retard or defeat the execution of their best concerted enterprizes against any foreign power. The important acquisition of Metz, covered that part of their frontier which formerly was most feeble, and lay most exposed to insult. France, from the time of its obtaining these additional securities against external invasion, must be deemed the most powerful kingdom in Europe, and is more fortunately situated than any on the Continent either for conquest or defence. From the confines of Artois to the bottom of the Pyrenees, and from the British channel to the frontiers of Savoy and the coast of the Mediterranean, its territories lay compact and unmingled with those of any other power. Several of the considerable provinces, which had contracted a spirit of independence by their having been long subject to the great vassals of the crown, who were often at variance or at war with their master, were now accustomed to recognize and to obey one sovereign. As they became members of the same monarchy, they assumed the sentiments of that body into which they were incorporated, and co-operated

operated with zeal towards promoting its interest and honour. The power and influence wrested from the nobles were seized by the crown. The people were not admitted to share in these spoils; they gained no new privilege; they acquired no additional weight in the legislature. It was not for the sake of the people, but in order to extend their own prerogative, that the monarchs of France had laboured to humble their great vassals. Satisfied with having brought them under entire subjection to the crown, they discovered no solicitude to free the people from their ancient dependence on the nobles of whom they held, and by whom they were often oppressed.

Enables them to assume an higher station among the powers of Europe.

A MONARCH, at the head of a kingdom thus united at home and secure from abroad, was entitled to form great designs, because he felt himself in a condition to execute them. The foreign wars which had continued with little interruption from the accession of Charles VIII. had not only cherished and augmented the martial genius of the nation, but by inuring the troops during the course of long service to the fatigues of war, and accustoming them to obedience, had added the force of discipline to their natural ardour. A gallant and active body of nobles, who considered themselves as idle and useless, unless when they were in the field; who were hardly acquainted with any pastime or exercise but what was military; and who knew no road to power, or fame, or wealth, but war, would not have suffered their sovereign to remain long in inaction.

The people, little acquainted with the arts of peace, and always ready to take arms at the command of their superiors, were accustomed, by the expence of long wars carried on in distant countries, to bear impositions, which, however inconsiderable they may seem if estimated by the exorbitant rate of modern exactions, appear immense when compared with the sums levied in France, or in any other country of Europe, previous to the reign of Louis XI. As all the members of which the state was composed were thus impatient for action, and capable of great efforts, the schemes and operations of France must have been no less formidable to Europe than those of Spain. The superior advantages of its situation, the contiguity and compactness of its territories, together with the peculiar state of its political constitution at that juncture, must have rendered its enterprizes still more alarming and more decisive. The King possessed such a degree of power as gave him the entire command of his subjects; the people were strangers to those occupations and habits of life which render men averse to war, or unfit for it; and the nobles, though reduced to the subordination necessary in a regular government, still retained the high undaunted spirit which was the effect of their ancient independence. The vigour of the feudal times remained, their anarchy was at an end; and the Kings of France could avail themselves of the martial ardour which that singular institution had kindled or kept alive, without being

exposed

exposed to the dangers or inconveniencies which are inseparable from it when in entire force.

Circumstances which prevented the immediate effects of their power.

A KINGDOM in such a state is, perhaps, capable of greater military efforts than at any other period in its progress. But how formidable or how fatal soever to the other nations of Europe the power of such a monarchy might have been, the civil wars which broke out in France saved them at that juncture from feeling its effects. These wars, of which religion was the pretext and ambition the cause, wherein great abilities were displayed by the leaders of the different factions, and little conduct or firmness were manifested by the crown under a succession of weak Princes, kept France occupied and embroiled for half a century. During these commotions the internal strength of the kingdom was much wasted, and such a spirit of anarchy was spread among the nobles, to whom rebellion was familiar, and the restraint of laws unknown, that a considerable interval became requisite not only for recruiting the internal vigour of the nation, but for re-establishing the authority of the Prince; so that it was long before France could turn her whole attention towards foreign transactions, or act with her proper force in foreign wars. It was long before she rose to that ascendant in Europe which she has maintained since the administration of Cardinal Richlieu, and which the situation as well as extent of the kingdom, the nature of her government,

together

together with the character of her people, entitle her to maintain.

Progress of England with respect to its interior state.

WHILE the kingdoms on the continent grew into power and consequence, England likewise made considerable progress towards regular government and interior strength. Henry VIII. probably without intention, and certainly without any consistent plan, of which his nature was incapable, pursued the scheme of depressing the nobility, which the policy of his father Henry VII. had begun. The pride and caprice of his temper led him to employ chiefly new men in the administration of affairs, because he found them most obsequious, or least scrupulous; and he not only conferred on them such plenitude of power, but exalted them to such pre-eminence in dignity, as mortified and degraded the ancient nobility. By the alienation or sale of the church lands, which were dissipated with a profusion not inferior to the rapaciousness with which they had been seized, as well as by the privilege granted to the ancient landholders of selling their estates, or disposing of them by will, an immense property, formerly locked up, was brought into circulation. This put the spirit of industry and commerce in motion, and gave it some considerable degree of vigour. The road to power and to opulence became open to persons of every condition. A sudden and excessive flow of wealth from the West Indies proved fatal to industry in Spain; a moderate accession in England to the sum in circulation

lation gave life to commerce, awakened the ingenuity of the nation, and excited it to useful enterprize. In France, what the nobles lost the crown gained. In England, the commons were gainers as well as the King. Power and influence accompanied of course the property which they acquired. They rose to consideration among their fellow-subjects; they began to feel their own importance; and extending their influence in the legislative body gradually, and often when neither they themselves nor others foresaw all the effects of their claims and pretensions, they at last attained that high authority to which the British constitution is indebted for the existence, and must owe the preservation, of its liberty. At the same time that the English constitution advanced towards perfection, several circumstances brought on a change in the ancient system with respect to foreign powers, and introduced another more beneficial to the nation. As soon as Henry disclaimed the supremacy of the Papal See, and broke off all connexion with the Papal court, considerable sums were saved to the nation, of which it had been annually drained by remittances to Rome for dispensations and indulgences, by the expence of pilgrimages into foreign countries*, or by payment of annates, first fruits, and

---

* The loss which the nation sustained by most of these articles is obvious, and must have been great. Even that by pilgrimages was not inconsiderable. In the year 1428, licence was obtained by no fewer than 916 persons to visit the

and a thousand other taxes which that artful and rapacious court levied on the credulity of mankind. The exercise of a jurisdiction different from that of the civil power, and claiming not only to be independent of it, but superior to it, a wild solecism in government, apt not only to perplex and disquiet weak minds, but tending directly to disturb society, was finally abolished. Government became more simple as well as more respectable, when no rank or character exempted any person from being amenable to the same courts as other subjects, from being tried by the same judges, and from being acquitted or condemned by the same laws.

By the loss of Calais the English were excluded from the continent. All schemes for invading France became of course as chimerical as they had formerly been pernicious. The views of the English were confined, first by necessity, and afterwards from choice, within their own island. That rage for conquest which had possessed the nation during many centuries, and wasted its strength in perpetual and fruitless wars, ceased at length. Those active spirits which had known and followed no profession but war, sought for occupation in the arts of peace, and their country was benefited as much by the one as it had suffered by the other. The nation, which had been exhausted

With respect to the affairs of the continent.

the shrine of St. James of Compostella in Spain. Rymer, vol. x. p. In 1434, the number of pilgrims to the same place was 2460. Ibid. p. In 1445, they were 2100, vol. xi. p.

by

by frequent expeditions to the continent, recruited its numbers, and acquired new strength; and when roused by any extraordinary exigency to take part in foreign operations, the vigour of its efforts was proportionally great, because they were only occasional and of a short continuance.

With respect to Scotland.

THE same principle which had led England to adopt this new system with regard to the powers on the continent, occasioned a change in its plan of conduct with respect to Scotland, the only foreign state, with which, on account of its situation in the same island, the English had such a close connexion as demanded their perpetual attention. Instead of prosecuting the ancient scheme of conquering that kingdom, which the nature of the country, defended by a brave and hardy people, rendered dangerous if not impracticable; it appeared more eligible to endeavour at obtaining such influence in Scotland as might exempt England from any danger or disquiet from that quarter. The national poverty of the Scots, together with the violence and animosity of their factions, rendered the execution of this plan easy to a people far superior to them in wealth. The leading men of greatest power and popularity were gained; the ministers and favourites of the crown were corrupted; and such absolute direction of the Scottish councils was acquired, as rendered the operations of the one kingdom dependent, in a great measure, on the sovereign of the other. Such perfect external security, added to the interior advantages which

which England now possessed, must soon have raised it to new consideration and importance; the long reign of Elizabeth, equally conspicuous for wisdom, for steadiness, and for vigour, accelerated its progress, and carried it with greater rapidity towards that elevated station which it hath since held among the powers of Europe.

During the period in which the political state of the great kingdoms underwent such changes, revolutions of considerable importance happened in that of the secondary or inferior powers. Those in the papal court are most obvious, and of most extensive consequence.

In the Preliminary Book, I have mentioned the rise of that spiritual jurisdiction, which the Popes claim as Vicars of Jesus Christ, and have traced the progress of that authority which they possess as temporal Princes *. Previous to the reign of Charles V. there was nothing that tended to circumscribe or to moderate their authority, but science and philosophy, which began to revive and to be cultivated. The progress of these, however, was still inconsiderable; they always operate slowly; and it is long before their influence reaches the people, or can produce any sensible effect upon them. They may perhaps gradually, and in a long course of years, undermine and shake an established system of false religion,

* Vol. I. p. 149, &c.

legion, but there is no inſtance of their having overturned one. The battery is too feeble to demoliſh thoſe fabricks which ſuperſtition raiſes on deep foundations, and can ſtrengthen with the moſt conſummate art.

<small>The general revolt againſt the doctrines of the church of Rome, and the power of the Popes.</small>

LUTHER had attacked the Papal ſupremacy with other weapons, and with an impetuoſity more formidable. The time and manner of his attack concurred with a multitude of circumſtances, which have been explained, in giving him immediate ſucceſs. The charm which had bound mankind for ſo many ages was broken at once. The human mind, which had continued long as tame and paſſive, as if it had been formed to believe whatever was taught, and to bear whatever was impoſed, rouſed of a ſudden and became inquiſitive, mutinous, and diſdainful of the yoke to which it had hitherto ſubmitted. That wonderful ferment and agitation of mind, which, at this diſtance of time, appears unaccountable, or is condemned as extravagant, was ſo general, that it muſt have been excited by cauſes which were natural and of powerful efficacy. The kingdoms of Denmark, Sweden, England, and Scotland, and almoſt one half of Germany, threw off their allegiance to the Pope, aboliſhed his juriſdiction within their territories, and gave the ſanction of law to modes of diſcipline and ſyſtems of doctrine which were not only independent of his power, but hoſtile to it. Nor was this ſpirit of innovation confined to thoſe countries

countries which openly revolted from the Pope; it spread through all Europe, and broke out in every part of it with various degrees of violence. It penetrated early into France, and made a quick progress there. In that kingdom, the number of converts to the opinions of the Reformers was so great, their zeal so enterprizing, and the abilities of their leaders so distinguished, that they soon ventured to contend for superiority with the established church, and were sometimes on the point of obtaining it. In all the provinces of Germany which continued to acknowledge the Papal supremacy, as well as in the Low Countries, the Protestant doctrines were secretly taught, and had gained so many proselytes, that they were ripe for revolt, and were restrained merely by the dread of their rulers from imitating the example of their neighbours, and asserting their independence. Even in Spain and in Italy, symptoms of the same disposition to shake off the yoke appeared. The pretensions of the Pope to infallible knowledge and supreme power were treated by many persons of eminent learning and abilities with such scorn, or attacked with such vehemence, that the most vigilant attention of the civil magistrate, the highest strains of pontifical authority, and all the rigour of inquisitorial jurisdiction were requisite to check and extinguish it.

THE defection of so many opulent and powerful kingdoms from the Papal See, was a fatal blow

This abridged the extent of the Pope's dominions.

blow to its grandeur and power. It abridged the dominions of the Popes in extent, it diminished their revenues, and left them fewer rewards to bestow on the ecclesiastics of various denominations, attached to them by vows of obedience as well as by ties of interest, and whom they employed as instruments to establish or support their usurpations in every part of Europe. The countries too which now disclaimed their authority, were those which formerly had been most devoted to it. The empire of superstition differs from every other species of dominion; its power is often greatest, and most implicitly obeyed in the provinces most remote from the seat of government; while such as are situated nearer to that, are more apt to discern the artifices by which it is upheld, or the impostures on which it is founded. The personal frailties or vices of the Popes, the errors as well as corruption of their administration, the ambition, venality, and deceit which reigned in their courts, fell immediately under the observation of the Italians, and could not fail of diminishing that respect which begets submission. But in Germany, England, and the more remote parts of Europe, these were either altogether unknown, or being only known by report, made a slighter impression. Veneration for the Papal dignity increased accordingly in these countries in proportion to their distance from Rome; and that veneration, added to their gross ignorance, rendered them equally credulous and passive. In tracing the progress of the Papal domination, the boldest and most successful cefsful inftances of encroachment are to be found in Germany and other countries diftant from Italy. In thefe its impofitions were heavieft, and its exactions the moft rapacious; fo that in eftimating the diminution of power which the court of Rome fuffered in confequence of the Reformation, not only the number but the character of the people who revolted, not only the great extent of territory, but the extraordinary obfequioufnefs of the fubjects which it loft, muft be taken into the account.

Nor was it only by this defection of fo many kingdoms and ftates which the Reformation occafioned, that it contributed to diminifh the power of the Roman Pontiffs. It obliged them to adopt a different fyftem of conduct towards the nations which ftill continued to recognife their jurifdiction, and to govern them by new maxims and with a milder fpirit. The Reformation taught them, by a fatal example, what they feem not before to have apprehended, that the credulity and patience of mankind might be overburdened and exhaufted. They became afraid of venturing upon any fuch exertion of their authority as might alarm or exafperate their fubjects, and excite them to a new revolt. They faw a rival church eftablifhed in many countries of Europe, the members of which were on the watch to obferve any errors in their adminiftration, and eager to expofe them. They were fenfible that the opinions, adverfe to their power and ufurpations, were not adopted by their enemies

and obliged them to change the fpirit of their government.

mies alone, but had spread even among the people who still adhered to them. Upon all these accounts, it was no longer possible to lead or to govern their flock in the same manner as in those dark and quiet ages when faith was implicit, when submission was unreserved, and all tamely followed and obeyed the voice of their pastor. From the æra of the Reformation, the Popes have ruled rather by address and management than by authority. Though the style of their decrees be still the same, the effect of them is very different. Those Bulls and Interdicts which, before the Reformation, made the greatest Princes tremble, have since that period been disregarded or despised by the most inconsiderable. Those bold decisions and acts of jurisdiction which, during many ages, not only passed uncensured, but were revered as the awards of a sacred tribunal, would, since Luther's appearance, be treated by one part of Europe as the effect of folly or arrogance, and be detested by the other as impious and unjust. The Popes, in their administration, have been obliged not only to accommodate themselves to the notions of their adherents, but to pay some regard to the prejudices of their enemies. They seldom venture to claim new powers, or even to insist obstinately on their ancient prerogatives, lest they should irritate the former; they carefully avoid every measure that may either excite the indignation or draw on them the derision of the latter. The policy of the court of Rome has become as cautious, circumspect,

spect, and timid, as it was once adventurous and violent; and though their pretensions to infallibility, on which all their authority is founded, does not allow them to renounce any jurisdiction which they have at any time claimed or exercised, they find it expedient to suffer many of their prerogatives to lie dormant, and not to expose themselves to the risque of losing that remainder of power which they still enjoy, by ill-timed attempts towards reviving obsolete pretensions. Before the sixteenth century, the Popes were the movers and directors in every considerable enterprize; they were at the head of every great alliance; and being considered as arbiters in the affairs of Christendom, the court of Rome was the centre of political negociation and intrigue. Since that time, the greatest operations in Europe have been carried on independent of them; they have sunk almost to a level with the other petty Princes of Italy; they continue to claim, though they dare not exercise, the same spiritual jurisdiction, but hardly retain any shadow of the temporal power which they anciently possessed.

But how fatal soever the Reformation may have been to the power of the Popes, it has contributed to improve the church of Rome both in science and in morals. The desire of equalling the reformers in those talents which had procured them respect; the necessity of acquiring the

The Reformation contributed to improve the church both in science and morals.

the knowledge requisite for defending their own tenets, or refuting the arguments of their opponents, together with the emulation natural between two rival churches, engaged the Roman Catholic clergy to apply themselves to the study of useful science, which they cultivated with such assiduity and success, that they have gradually become as eminent in literature, as they were in some periods infamous for ignorance. The same principle occasioned a change no less considerable in the morals of the Romish clergy. Various causes which have formerly been enumerated, had concurred in introducing great irregularity, and even dissolution of manners among the popish clergy. Luther and his adherents began their attack on the church with such vehement invectives against these, that, in order to remove the scandal, and silence their declamations, greater decency of conduct became necessary. The Reformers themselves were so eminent not only for the purity but even austerity of their manners, and had acquired such reputation among the people on that account, that the Roman Catholic clergy must have soon lost all credit, if they had not endeavoured to conform in some measure to their standard. They knew that all their actions fell under the severe inspection of the Protestants, whom enmity and emulation prompted to observe every vice, or even impropriety in their conduct; to censure them without indulgence, and to expose them without mercy.

This

This rendered them, of courſe, not only cautious to avoid ſuch enormities as might give offence, but ſtudious to acquire the virtues which might merit praiſe. In Spain and Portugal, where the tyrannical juriſdiction of the Inquiſition cruſhed the Proteſtant faith as ſoon as it appeared, the ſpirit of Popery continues invariable; ſcience has made ſmall progreſs, and the character of eccleſiaſtics has undergone little change. But in thoſe countries where the members of the two churches have mingled freely with each other, or have carried on any conſiderable intercourſe, either commercial or literary, an extraordinary alteration in the ideas, as well as in the morals of the Popiſh eccleſiaſtics, is manifeſt. In France, the manners of the dignitaries and ſecular clergy have become decent and exemplary in an high degree. Many of them have been diſtinguiſhed for all the accompliſhments and virtues which can adorn their profeſſion; and differ greatly from their predeceſſors before the Reformation, both in their maxims and in their conduct.

Nor has the influence of the Reformation been felt only by the inferior members of the Roman Catholic Church; it has extended to the See of Rome, to the ſovereign Pontiffs themſelves. Violations of decorum, and even treſpaſſes againſt morality, which paſſed without cenſure in thoſe ages, when neither the power of the Popes, nor the veneration of the people for their character,

The effects of it extend to the character of the Popes themſelves.

had any bounds; when there was no hostile eye to observe the errors in their conduct, and no adversaries zealous to inveigh against them; would be liable now to the severest animadversion, and excite general indignation or horror. Instead of rivalling the courts of temporal Princes in gaiety, and surpassing them in licentiousness, the Popes have studied to assume manners more severe and more suitable to their ecclesiastical character. The chair of St. Peter hath not been polluted during two centuries, by any Pontiff that resembled Alexander VI. or several of his predecessors, who were a disgrace to religion and to human nature. Throughout this long succession of Popes, a wonderful decorum of conduct, compared with that of preceding ages, is observable. Many of them, especially among the Pontiffs of the present century, have been conspicuous for all the virtues becoming their high station; and by their humanity, their love of literature, and their moderation, have made some atonement to mankind for the crimes of their predecessors. Thus the beneficial influences of the Reformation have been more extensive than they appear on a superficial view; and this great division in the Christian church hath contributed, in some measure, to increase purity of manners, to diffuse science, and to inspire humanity. History recites such a number of shocking events, occasioned by religious dissensions, that it must afford peculiar satisfaction to trace any one salutary or beneficial effect

effect to that source from which so many fatal calamities have flowed.

State of the republic of Venice.

THE republic of Venice, which, at the beginning of the sixteenth century, had appeared so formidable, that almost all the potentates of Europe united in a confederacy for its destruction, declined gradually from its ancient power and splendor. The Venetians not only lost a great part of their territory in the war excited by the league of Cambray, but the revenues as well as vigour of the state were exhausted by their extraordinary and long continued efforts in their own defence; and that commerce by which they had acquired their wealth and power began to decay, without any hopes of its reviving. All the fatal consequences to their republic, which the sagacity of the Venetian senate foresaw on the first discovery of a passage to the East-Indies by the Cape of Good Hope, actually took place. Their endeavours to prevent the Portuguese from establishing themselves in the East-Indies, not only by exciting the Soldans of Egypt, and the Ottoman monarchs, to turn their arms against such dangerous intruders, but by affording secret aid to the Infidels in order to insure their success [z], proved ineffectual. The activity and valour of the Portuguese surmounted every obstacle, and obtained such a firm footing in that fertile country, as se-

[z] Freher. Script. Rer. German. vol. ii. 529.

cured to them large possessions, together with an influence still more extensive. Lisbon, instead of Venice, became the staple for the precious commodities of the East. The Venetians, after having possessed for many years the monopoly of that beneficial commerce, had the mortification to be excluded from almost any share in it. The discoveries of the Spaniards in the western world, proved no less fatal to inferior branches of their commerce. The original defects which were formerly pointed out in the constitution of the Venetian republic still continued, and the disadvantages with which it undertook any great enterprize, increased rather than diminished. The sources from which it derived its extraordinary riches and power being dried up, the interior vigour of the state declined, and, of course, its external operations became less formidable. Long before the middle of the sixteenth century, Venice ceased to be one of the principal powers in Europe, and dwindled into a secondary and subaltern state. But as the senate had the address to conceal the diminution of its power, under the veil of moderation and caution; as it made no rash effort that could discover its weakness; as the symptoms of political decay in states are not soon observed, and are seldom so apparent to their neighbours as to occasion any sudden alteration in their conduct towards them, Venice continued long to be considered and respected. She was treated not according to her present condition, but according to to the rank which she had formerly held. Charles V. as well as the Kings of France, his rivals, courted her assistance with emulation and solicitude in all their enterprizes. Even down to the close of the century, Venice remained not only an object of attention, but a considerable seat of political negociation and intrigue.

Of Tuscany.

THAT authority which the first Cosmo di Medici, and Lawrence, his grandson, had acquired in the republic of Florence by their beneficence and abilities, inspired their descendants with the ambition of usurping the sovereignty in their country, and paved their way towards it. Charles V. placed Alexander di Medici at the head of the republic, and to the natural interest and power of the family added the weight as well as credit of the Imperial protection. Of these, his successor Cosmo, sirnamed the Great, availed himself; and establishing his supreme authority on the ruins of the ancient republican constitution, he transmitted that, together with the title of Grand Duke of Tuscany, to his descendants. Their dominions were composed of the territories which had belonged to the three commonwealths of Florence, Pisa, and Siena, and formed one of the most respectable of the Italian states.

A. D. 1550.

Of the Dukes of Savoy.

THE Dukes of Savoy, during the former part of the sixteenth century, possessed territories which were

were not confiderable either for extent or value; and the French, having feized the greater part of them, obliged the reigning Duke to retire for fafety to the ftrong fortrefs of Nice, where he fhut himfelf up for feveral years, while his fon, the Prince of Piedmont, endeavoured to better his fortune, by ferving as an adventurer in the armies of Spain. The peace of Cateau Cambrefis reftored to him his paternal dominions. As thefe are environed on every hand by powerful neighbours, all whofe motions the Dukes of Savoy muft obferve with the greateft attention, in order not only to guard againft the danger of being furprized and overpowered, but that they may chufe their fide with difcernment in thofe quarrels wherein it is impoffible for them to avoid taking part, this peculiarity in their fituation feems to have had no inconfiderable influence on their character. By roufing them to perpetual attention, by keeping their ingenuity always on the ftretch, and engaging them in almoft continual action, it hath formed a race of Princes more fagacious in difcovering their true intereft, more decifive in their refolutions, and more dexterous in availing themfelves of every occurrence which prefented itfelf, than any perhaps that can be fingled out in the hiftory of Europe. By gradual acquifitions the Dukes of Savoy have added to their territories, as well as to their own importance; and afpiring at length to regal dignity, which they obtained about half a century ago, by the

the title of Kings of Sardinia, they hold now no inconfiderable rank among the monarchs of Europe.

The territories which form the republic of the United Netherlands, were loft during the firft part of the fixteenth century, among the numerous provinces fubject to the houfe of Auftria; and were then fo inconfiderable, that hardly one opportunity of mentioning them hath occurred in all the bufy period of this hiftory. But foon after the peace of Cateau Cambrefis, the violent and bigoted maxims of Philip's go- vernment, being carried into execution with unre- lenting rigour by the Duke of Alva, exafperated the free people of the Low-Countries to fuch a degree, that they threw off the Spanifh yoke, and afferted their ancient liberties and laws. Thefe they defended with a perfevering valour, which gave employment to the arms of Spain dur- ing half a century, exhaufted the vigour, ruined the reputation of that monarchy, and at laft con- ftrained their ancient mafters to recognife and to treat with them as a free independent ftate. This ftate, founded on liberty, and reared by induftry and œconomy, grew into great reputation, even while ftruggling for its exiftence. But when peace and fecurity allowed it to enlarge its views, and to extend its commerce, it rofe to be one of the moft refpectable as well as enterprizing powers in Europe.

Of the United Provinces.

The

BOOK XII.

The transactions of the kingdoms in the North of Europe, have been seldom attended to in the course of this history.

Of Russia.

Russia remained buried in that barbarism and obscurity, from which it was called about the beginning of the present century, by the creative genius of Peter the Great, who made his country known and formidable to the rest of Europe.

Of Denmark and Sweden.

In Denmark and Sweden, during the reign of Charles V. great revolutions happened in their constitutions, civil as well as ecclesiastical. In the former kingdom, a tyrant being degraded from the throne, and expelled the country, a new Prince was called by the voice of the people to assume the reins of government. In the latter, a fierce people, roused to arms by injuries and oppression, shook off the Danish yoke, and conferred the regal dignity on its deliverer Gustavus Ericion, who had all the virtues of a hero and of a patriot. Denmark, exhausted by foreign wars, or weakened by the dissensions between the King and the nobles, became incapable of such efforts as were requisite in order to recover the ascendant which it had long possessed in the North of Europe. Sweden, as soon as it was freed from the dominion of strangers, began to recruit its strength, and acquired in a short time such internal vigour, that it became

the

the firſt kingdom in the North. Early in the ſubſequent century, it roſe to ſuch a high rank among the powers of Europe, that it had the chief merit in forming, as well as conducting, that powerful league, which protected not only the Proteſtant religion, but the liberties of Germany againſt the bigotry and ambition of the houſe of Auſtria.

INDEX

TO THE

SECOND, THIRD, and FOURTH VOLUMES.

N. B. The Roman Numerals direct to the Volume, and the Figures to the Page.

A

ABSOLUTION, the form of that used by Father Tetzel in Germany, II. 107.

Adorni, the faction of, assists the Imperial general Colonna in the reduction of Genoa, II. 197.

Adrian of Utrecht, made preceptor to Charles V. under William de Croy, lord of Chievres, II. 27. His character, *ib.* Sent by Charles with power to assume the regency of Castile on the death of his grandfather, 34. His claim admitted by Cardinal Ximenes, and executed in conjunction, *ib.* Authorized by Charles to hold the Cortes of Valencia, which refuses to assemble before him, 82. Made viceroy of Castile on the departure of Charles for Germany, 86. His election remonstrated against by the Castilians, *ib.* Is chosen Pope, 193. Retrospect of his conduct in Spain during the absence of Charles, 206. Sends Ronquillo to reduce the Segovians, who repulse him, *ib.* Sends Fonseca to besiege the city, who is repulsed by the inhabitants of Medina del Campo, 207, 208. Apologizes for Fonseca's conduct to the people, 209. Recals Fonseca,

INDEX.

and dismisses his troops, 209. His authority disclaimed by the Holy Junta, 211. Deprived of power by them, 214. His ill reception on his arrival at Rome on being chosen to the Papacy, 246. Restores the territories acquired by his predecessor, *ib.* Labours to unite the contending powers of Europe, 247. Publishes a bull for a three years truce among them, 248. Accedes to the league against the French King, *ib.* His death, 257. The sentiments and behaviour of the people on that occasion, 258. A retrospect of his conduct towards the Reformers, 270. His brief to the diet at Nuremburg, *ib.* Receives a list of grievances from the diet, 273. His conduct to the Reformers, how esteemed at Rome, 275.

Africa, the Spanish troops sent by Cardinal Ximenes against Barbarossa, defeated there, II. 47.

Aigues Mortes, interview between the Emperor Charles and Francis, there, III. 153.

Aix la Chapelle, the Emperor Charles crowned there, II. 102. Ferdinand his brother crowned King of the Romans there, III. 53.

Alarcon, Don Ferdinand, Francis I. of France, taken prisoner at the battle of Pavia, committed to his custody, II. 298. Conducts Francis to Spain, 309. Delivers up Francis in pursuance of the treaty of Madrid, 329. Is sent ambassador to Francis to require the fulfilment of his treaty, 348. Pope Clement VII. taken prisoner by the Imperialists, is committed to his custody, 372.

Albany, John Stuart, Duke of, commands the French army sent by Francis I. to invade Naples, II. 291.

Albert of Brandenburgh, grand master of the Teutonic Order, becomes a convert to the doctrines of Luther, II. 342. Obtains of Sigismund King of Poland the investiture of Prussia, erected into a dutchy, *ib.* Is put under the ban of the Empire, *ib.* His family fixed in the inheritance of Prussia, *ib.* Commands a body of troops in behalf of Maurice of Saxony, but endeavours to assert an independency, IV. 80. Defeats and takes the Duke d'Aumale prisoner, and joins the Emperor at Metz, 107.

INDEX.

107. Is condemned by the Imperial Chamber for his demands on the Bishops of Bamberg and Wortsburg, 117. A league formed against him, 119. Is defeated by Maurice, 120. Is again defeated by Henry of Brunswick, 122. Is driven out of Germany, and dies in exile, 123. His territories restored to his collateral heirs, *ib.*

Albert, elector of Mentz, the publication of indulgences in Germany committed to him, II. 106.

Alexander VI. Pope, remarks on the pontificate of, II. 136.

Alexander di Medici. See MEDICI.

Algiers, how it was seized by Barbarossa, III. 92. Is seized by the brother of the same name, on the death of the former, 93. Is taken under the protection of the Porte, 94. Is governed by Hascen Aga in the absence of Barbarossa, 222. Is besieged by the Emperor Charles V. 226. Charles forced to re-imbark by bad weather, 230.

Alraschid, brother of Muley Hascen King of Tunis, solicits the protection of Barbarossa against him, III. 95. His treacherous treatment by Barbarossa, 96.

Alva, Duke of, adheres to Ferdinand of Aragon, in his dispute with the Archduke Philip concerning the regency of Castile, II. 11. Forces the Dauphin to abandon the siege of Perpignan, III. 242. Presides at the court-martial which condemns the Elector of Saxony to death, 409. Detains the Landgrave prisoner by the Emperor's order, 421. Commands under the Emperor the army destined against France, IV. 105. Is appointed commander in chief in Piedmont, 165. Enters the ecclesiastical territories and seizes the Campagna Romana, 226. Concludes a truce with the Pope, 227. Negotiates a peace between Philip and the Pope, with Cardinal Caraffa, 256. Goes to Rome to ask pardon of the Pope for his hostilities, 257. Is sent to Paris in the name of Philip to espouse the Princess Elizabeth, 301.

Amerstorff, a nobleman of Holland, associated by Charles V. with Cardinal Ximenes, in the regency of Castile, II. 44.

Z 2 *Anabaptists,*

INDEX.

Anabaptists, the origin of that sect deduced, III. 71. Their principal tenets, 73. Their settlement at Munster, 74. Character of their principal leaders, *ib*. They seize the city of Munster, 75. They establish a new form of government there, *ib*. Chuse Bocold King, 79. Their licentious practices, *ib*. A confederacy of the German Princes formed against them, 81. Are blockaded in Munster by the bishop, 82. The city taken, and great slaughter made of them, 83. Their king put to death, 84. Character of the sect since that period, 85. See *Matthias* and *Bocold*.

Angleria, his authority cited in proof of the extortions of the Flemish ministers of Charles V. II. 58.

Anhalt, Prince of, avows the opinions of Martin Luther, II. 269.

Annats to the court of Rome, what, II. 151.

Aragon, how Ferdinand became possessed of that kingdom, II. 2. The Cortes of, acknowledges the Archduke Philip's title to the crown, 3. Ancient enmity between this kingdom and Castile, 8. Navarre added to this crown by the arts of Ferdinand, 23. Arrival of Charles V. 59. The Cortes not allowed to assemble in his name, *ib*. The refractory behaviour of the Aragonians, 60. They refuse restitution of the kingdom of Navarre, *ib*. Don John Lanuza appointed regent, on the departure of Charles for Germany, 86. Who composes the disturbances there, 242. The moderation of Charles towards the insurgents on his arrival in Spain, 244. See *Spain*.

Ardres, an interview there between Francis I. and Henry VIII. of England, II. 100.

Asturias, Charles son of Philip and Joanna, acknowledged Prince of, by the Cortes of Castile, II. 17.

Augsburg, a diet called there by Charles V. III. 47. His public entry into that city, *ib*. The confession of faith named from this city, drawn up by Melancthon, *ib*. Resolute behaviour of the Protestant Princes at, 49. Its form of government violently altered, and rendered submissive to the Emperor,

INDEX.

454. The diet re-affembled there, IV. 9. The diet takes part with the Emperor againſt the city of Magdeburg, 18. Is ſeized by Maurice of Saxony, 66. Another diet at, opened by Ferdinand, 173. Cardinal Moronè attends the diet as the Pope's nuncio, 175. Moronè departs on the Pope's death, 177. Receſs of the diet on the ſubject of religion, 181. Remarks on this receſs, 187. The diet again aſſembled there, III. 430. Is intimidated by being ſurrounded by the Emperor's Spaniſh troops, 431. The Emperor re-eſtabliſhes the Romiſh worſhip in the churches of, *ib.* The diet, by the Emperor's order, petitions the Pope for the return of the council to Trent, 439. A ſyſtem of theology laid before the diet by the Emperor, 445. The archbiſhop of Mentz declares, without authority, the diet's acceptance of it, *ib.*

Avila, a convention of the malecontents in Spain held there, II. 211. A confederacy termed the Holy Junta, formed there, *ib.* Which diſclaims the authority of Adrian, 212. The Holy Junta removed to Tordeſillas, 213. See *Junta.*

Auſtria, by what means the houſe of, became ſo formidable in Germany, II. 375. The extraordinary acquiſitions of the houſe of, in the perſon of the Emperor Charles V. IV. 305. 309.

B

Barbaroſſa, Horuck, his riſe to the kingdom of Algiers and Tunis, II. 46. Defeats the Spaniſh troops ſent againſt him by Cardinal Ximenes, 47. His parentage, III. 91. Commences pirate with his brother Hayradin, *ib.* How he acquired poſſeſſion of Algiers, 92. Infeſts the coaſt of Spain, 93. Is reduced and killed by Comares the Spaniſh governor of Oran, *ib.*

Barbaroſſa, Hayradin, brother to the former of the ſame name, takes poſſeſſion of Algiers on his brother's death, III. 94. Puts his dominions under the protection of the Grand Signior, *ib.* Obtains the command

INDEX.

command of the Turkish fleet, *ib.* His treacherous treatment of Alrafchid, brother to the king of Tunis, 96. Seizes Tunis, 97. Extends his depredations by sea, *ib.* Prepares to resist the Emperor's armament against him, 99. Goletta and his fleet taken, 101. Is defeated by Charles, 103. Tunis taken, 104. Makes a descent on Italy, 253. Burns Rheggio, *ib.* Besieges Nice in conjunction with the French, but is forced to retire, 254. Is dismissed by Francis, 267.

Barbary, a summary view of the revolutions of, III. 90. Its division into independent kingdoms, *ib.* Rise of the piratical states, 91. See *Barbarossa*.

Barcelona, the public entry of the Emperor Charles V. into that city as its count, III. 36. The treaties of Charles with the Italian States, published there, 41.

Bayard, chevalier, his character, II. 179. His gallant defence of Meziers besieged by the Imperialists, 180. Obliges them to raise the siege, *ib.* His noble behaviour at his death, 265. His respectful funeral, 266.

Bellay, M. his erroneous account of the education of Charles V. corrected, II. 27. *Note*. His account of the disastrous retreat of the Emperor Charles V. from his invasion of Provence, III. 138.

Bible, a translation of, undertaken by Martin Luther, and its effects in opening the eyes of the people, II. 268.

Bicocca, battle of, between Colonna and Mareschal Lautrec, II. 195.

Bocold or Beukles, John, a journeyman-taylor, becomes a leader of the Anabaptists at Munster, III. 74. Succeeds Matthias in the direction of their affairs, 78. His enthusiastic extravagancies, *ib.* Is chosen King, 79. Marries fourteen wives, 80. Beheads one of them, 83. Is put to a cruel death at the taking of Munster, 84. See *Anabaptists*..

Bohemia, the archduke Ferdinand chosen king of, II. 374. Ferdinand encroaches on the liberties of the Bohemians, III. 427. The Reformation introduced by John Huss and Jerome of Prague, 428. Raise an

army

INDEX.

army to no purpose, *ib.* Is closely confined in the citadel of Mechlin, IV. 22.

Bonnivet, admiral of France, appointed to command the invasion of Milan, II. 256. His character, *ib.* Enables Colonna to defend the city of Milan by his imprudent delay, 257. Forced to abandon the Milanese, 264. Is wounded, and his army defeated by the Imperialists, *ib.* Stimulates Francis to an invasion of the Milanese, 285. Advises Francis to besiege Pavia, 287. Advises him to give battle to Bourbon, who advanced to the relief of Pavia, 293. Is killed at the battle of Pavia, 296.

Bologna, an interview between the Emperor Charles V. and Pope Clement VII. there, III. 37. Another meeting between them there, 60.

Bouillon, Robert de la Marck, lord of, declares war against the Emperor Charles, at the instigation of Francis, II. 177. Is ordered by Francis to disband his troops, 178. His territories reduced by the Emperor, 179.

Boulogne, besieged by Henry VIII. of England, III. 274. Taken, 284.

Bourbon, Charles Duke of, his character, II. 250. The causes of his discontent with Francis I. *ib.* His duchess dies, 251. Rejects the advances of Louise the King's mother, 252. His estate sequestered by her intrigues, *ib.* Negociates secretly with the Emperor, 253. Is included in a treaty between the Emperor and Henry VIII. of England, *ib.* Is taxed by the King with betraying him, which he denies, 254. Escapes to Italy, 255. Directs the measures of the Imperial army under Lannoy, 263. Defeats the French on the banks of the Sessia, 265. Instigates Charles to an invasion of France, 280. Advances to the relief of Pavia, 292. Defeats Francis, and takes him prisoner, 296. Hastens to Madrid to secure his own interests in the interview between Charles and Francis, 312. His kind reception by Charles, 320. Obtains a grant of the duchy of Milan, and is made general of the Imperial army, 321. Obliges Sforza to surrender Milan,

INDEX.

352. Is forced to oppress the Milanese to satisfy his troops mutinying for pay, 357. Sets Morone at liberty, and makes him his confident, 357, 358. Appoints Leyva governor of Milan, and advances to invade the Pope's territories, 359, 360. His disappointed troops mutiny, 361. He determines to plunder Rome, 365. Arrives at Rome, and assaults it, 366. Is killed, *ib*.

Brandenburg, Elector of, avows the opinions of Luther, II. 269.

———— Albert of. See *Albert*.

Bruges, a league concluded there between the Emperor and Henry VIII. of England, against France, II. 182.

Brunswick, Duke of, avows the opinions of Luther, II. 269.

———— Henry Duke of, driven from his dominions by the Protestant Princes of the league of Smalkalde, III. 260. Raises men for Francis, but employs them to recover his own dominions, 298. Is taken prisoner, 299.

Buda, siege of, by Ferdinand king of the Romans, III. 218. Is treacherously seized by Sultan Solyman, 219.

C

Cajetan, Cardinal, the Pope's legate in Germany, appointed to examine the doctrines of Martin Luther, II. 117. Requires Luther peremptorily to retract his errors, 118. Requires the Elector of Saxony to surrender or banish Luther, 120. His conduct justified, 122.

Calais, an ineffectual congress there, between the Emperor and Francis, under the mediation of Henry VIII. II. 180. The careless manner in which it was guarded in the reign of Mary Queen of England, IV. 264. Ineffectual remonstrances of Philip, and Lord Wentworth the governor, concerning its defenceless state, *ib*. Is invested and taken by the Duke of Guise, 265. The English inhabitants
turned

INDEX.

turned out, 266. Stipulations concerning, in the treaty of Chateau Cambresis, 297.

Cambray, articles of the peace concluded there, between the Emperor Charles, and Francis of France, III. 31. Remarks on this treaty, *ib.*

Campe, peace of, between Henry VIII. and Francis, III. 334.

Campeggio, Cardinal, made legate from Pope Clement VII. to the second diet at Nuremberg, II. 276, 277. Publishes articles for reforming the inferior clergy, 278. Advises Charles to rigorous measures against the Protestants, III. 50.

Capitulation of the Germanic body, signed by Charles V. and prescribed to all his successors, II. 77.

Caraffa, Cardinal, his precipitate election, IV. 193. Is appointed legate to Bologna, *ib.* Reasons of his disgust with the Emperor, 194. Persuades the Pope to solicit an alliance with France against the Emperor, 195, 196. 201. His insidious commission to the court of France, 219. His public entry into Paris, 220. Exhorts Henry to break his truce with the Emperor, 221. Absolves Henry from his oath, 223. Negociates a peace between the Pope and Philip, with the Duke d'Alva, 256. The fate of him and his brother on the death of Pope Paul, 302.

Carlostadius, imbibes the opinions of Martin Luther, at Wittemberg, II. 130. His intemperate zeal, 267. Awed by the reproofs of Luther, 268.

Carignan, besieged by the Count d'Enguin, and defended by the Marquis de Guasto, III. 267. Guasto defeated in a pitched battle, 270. The town taken, 272.

Castaldo, Marquis of Piadeno. See *Piadeno*.

Castile, how Isabella became possessed of that kingdom, II. 2. The Archduke Philip's title acknowledged by the Cortes of that kingdom, 3. Isabella dies, and leaves her husband Ferdinand of Aragon, regent, 7. Ferdinand resigns the crown of, 8. Ferdinand acknowledged regent by the Cortes, *ib.* Enmity between this kingdom and Aragon, *ib.*

The

INDEX.

The particular dislike of the Castilians to Ferdinand, 8. The regency of, jointly vested in Ferdinand, Philip and Joanna, by the treaty of Salamanca, 14. Declares against Ferdinand, 15. The regency of, resigned by Philip to Ferdinand, 16. Philip and Joanna acknowledged King and Queen by the Cortes, 17. Death of Philip, *ib*. The perplexity of the Castilians on Joanna's incapacity for government, 19. Ferdinand gains the regency and the good will of the Castilians by his prudent administration, 22. Oran and other places in Barbary annexed to this kingdom by Ximenes, 23. Ximenes appointed regent by Ferdinand's will, until the arrival of Charles V. 31. Charles assumes the regal title, 35. Ximenes procures its acknowledgment, 37. The nobility depressed by Ximenes, 38, 39. The grandees mutiny against Ximenes, 40. The mutiny suppressed, *ib*. Ximenes resumes the grants made by Ferdinand to the nobles, 41. The bold reply of Ximenes to the discontented nobles, 43. Other associates in the regency appointed with Ximenes at the instigation of the Flemish courtiers, 44. Ximenes dies, 55. Charles acknowledged King by the Cortes, on his arrival, with a reservation in favour of his mother Joanna, 56. The Castilians receive unfavourable impressions of him, *ib*. Disgusted by his partiality to his Flemish ministers, 57. Sauvage made chancellor, 58. William de Croy appointed archbishop of Toledo, *ib*. The principal cities confederate, and complain of their grievances, 61. The clergy of, refuse to levy the tenth of benefices granted by the Pope to Charles V. 81. Interdicted, but the interdict taken off, by Charles's application, *ib*. An insurrection there, 84. Increase the disaffection, 85. Cardinal Adrian appointed regent, on the departure of Charles for Germany, 86. The views and pretensions of the commons, in their insurrections, 209. The confederacy called the Holy Junta formed, 211. The proceedings of which are carried on in the name of Queen Joanna, 213. Receives circulatory letters from Charles for the insurgents

INDEX.

surgents to lay down their arms, with promises of pardon, 215. The nobles undertake to suppress the insurgents, 221. Raise an army against them under the Condé de Haro, 224. Haro gets possession of Joanna, 225. Expedients by which they raise money for their troops, 227. Unwilling to proceed to extremities with the Junta, 228. The army of the Junta routed and Padilla executed, 232, 233. Dissolution of the Junta, 235. The moderation of Charles toward the insurgents on his arrival in Spain, 244. He acquires the love of the Castilians, 245. See *Spain*.

Catherine of Aragon, is divorced from Henry VIII. of England, III. 69. Dies, 160.

Catherine à Boria, a nun, flies from her cloister, and marries Martin Luther, II. 340.

Catherine di Medici. See MEDICI.

Cavi, peace concluded there between Pope Paul IV. and Philip II. of Spain, IV. 256.

Cercamp, negociations for peace entered into there between Philip II. of Spain. and Henry II. of France, IV. 281. 290. The negociations removed to Chateau Cambresis, 294. See *Chateau Cambresis*.

Characters of men, rules for forming a proper estimate of them, III. 313. Applied to the case of Luther, *ib*.

Charles IV. Emperor of Germany, his observations on the manners of the clergy, in his letter to the archbishop of Metz, II. 139. *Note*.

Charles V. Emperor, his descent and birth, II. 1. How he came to inherit such extensive dominions, 2. Acknowledged Prince of Asturias by the Cortes of Castile, 17. His father Philip dies, *ib*. Jealousy and hatred of his grandfather Ferdinand towards him, 23. Left heir to his dominions, 26. Death of Ferdinand, *ib*. His education committed to William de Croy, Lord of Chievres, *ib*. Adrian of Utrecht appointed to be his preceptor, 27. The first opening of his character, 29. Assumes the government of Flanders, and attends to business, *ib*. Sends Cardinal Adrian to be regent of Castile, who

executes

INDEX.

executes it jointly with Ximenes, 34. Assumes the regal title, 35. His title admitted with difficulty by the Castilian nobility, 37. Persuaded to add associate regents to Ximenes, 44. His Flemish court corrupted by the avarice of Chievres, 47. Persuaded by Ximenes to visit Spain, but how that journey is retarded, 48, 49. The present state of his affairs, 49. Concludes a peace at Noyen with Francis I. of France, and the conditions of the treaty, *ib.* Arrives in Spain, 52. His ungrateful treatment of Ximenes, 54. His public entry into Valladolid, 55. Is acknowledged King by the Cortes, who vote him a free gift, 56. The Castilians receive unfavourable impressions of him, *ib.* Disgusts them by his partiality to his Flemish ministers, 57. Sets out for Aragon, 59. Sends his brother Ferdinand to visit their grandfather Maximilian, *ib.* Cannot assemble the Cortes of Aragon in his own name, *ib.* The opposition made by that assembly to his desires, *ib.* Refuses the application of Francis I. for restitution of the kingdom of Navarre, 60. Neglects the remonstrances of the Castilians, 61. Death of the Emperor Maximilian, 62. View of the present state of Europe, 68. How Maximilian was obstructed in securing the Empire to him, 63. Francis I. aspires to the Imperial crown, 64. Circumstances favourable to the pretensions of Charles, *ib.* 68. The Swifs Cantons espouse his cause, 69. Apprehensions and conduct of Pope Leo X. on the occasion, 70, 71. Assembling the diet at Francfort, 72. Frederic duke of Saxony refuses the offer of the empire, and votes for him, 73, 74. And refuses the presents offered by his ambassadors, 75. Concurring circumstances which favoured his election, 76. His election, 77. Signs and confirms the capitulation of the Germanic body, 77, 78. The election notified to him, 78. Assumes the title of Majesty, 79. Accepts the Imperial dignity offered by the Count Palatine, ambassador from the Electors, 80. The clergy of Castile refuse the tenth of benefices granted him by the Pope, *ib.*

INDEX.

Procures the interdict the kingdom is laid under for refusal, to be taken off, 81. Empowers Cardinal Adrian to hold the Cortes of Valencia, 82. The nobles refuse to assemble without his presence, 82, 83. Authorises the insurgents there to continue in arms, 83. Summons the Cortes of Castile to meet in Galicia, *ib.* Narrowly escapes with his Flemish ministers from an insurrection on that account, 84. Obtains a donative from the Cortes, 86. Prepares to leave Spain, and appoints regents, *ib.* Embarks, 87. Motives of this journey, 89. Rise of the rivalship between him and Francis I. 90. Courts the favour of Henry VIII. of England and his minister Cardinal Wolsey, 96. Visits Henry at Dover, 99. Promises Wolsey his interest for the papacy, 100. Has a second interview with Henry at Gravelines, 101. Offers to submit his differences with Francis to Henry's arbitration, *ib.* His magnificent coronation at Aix-la-Chapelle, 102. Calls a diet at Worms, to check the reformers, 103. Causes which hindered his espousing the party of Martin Luther, 161. Grants Luther a safe-conduct to the diet of Worms, 162. An edict published against him, 164. His embarrassment at this time, 168. Concludes an alliance with the Pope, 172. The conditions of the treaty, 172, 173. Death of his minister Chievres, and its advantages to him, 173, 174. Invasion of Navarre by Francis, 175. The French driven out, and their general L'Esparre taken prisoner, 177. War declared against him by Robert de la Marck, lord of Bouillon, who ravages Luxemburg, 177, 178. Reduces Bouillon, and invades France, 179. His demands at the congress at Calais, 181. Has an interview with Cardinal Wolsey at Bruges, and concludes a league with Henry VIII. against France, 182. Pope Leo declares for him against France, 186, 187. The French driven out of Milan, 190. 195. Visits England in his passage to Spain, 198. Cultivates the good-will of Cardinal Wolsey, and creates the Earl of Surrey his high admiral, 199. Grants the island of Malta

INDEX.

to the Knights of St. John, expelled from Rhodes by Solyman the Magnificent, 202. Arrives in Spain, 203. A retrospect of his proceedings in relation to the insurrections in Spain, 215. Issues circulatory letters for the insurgents to lay down their arms, with promises of pardon, *ib*. His prudent moderation towards the insurgents, on his arrival in Spain, 244. Acquires the love of the Castilians, 245. Enters into a league with Charles Duke of Bourbon, 253. Why he did not endeavour to get Wolsey elected Pope, 259. Invades Guienne and Burgundy, but without success, 262. His troops in Milan mutiny for want of pay, but are pacified by Moronè, 264. Undertakes an invasion of Provence, 280. Orders Pescara to besiege Marseilles, 281. Pescara obliged to retire, 282. Disconcerted by the French over-running the Milanese again, 286. The revenues of Naples mortgaged to raise money, 287. His troops defeat Francis, and take him prisoner at the battle of Pavia, 296. His affected moderation at receiving the news, 298, 299. Avails himself of a treaty concluded between Lannoy and Pope Clement, but refuses to ratify it, 305. His army in Pavia mutiny, and are obliged to be disbanded, 305, 306. His deliberations on the proper improvement of his disadvantages, 306, 307. His propositions to Francis, 308. After many delays grants Sforza the investiture of Milan, 311. Moronè's intrigues betrayed to him by Pescara, 316. Orders Pescara to continue his negotiations with Moronè, *ib*. His rigorous treatment of Francis, 318. Visits Francis, 319. His kind reception of the Duke of Bourbon, 320. Grants Bourbon the dutchy of Milan, and appoints him general in chief of the Imperial army there, 321. Fruitless negotiations for the delivery of Francis, 322. Treaty of Madrid with Francis, 324. Delivers up Francis, 329. Marries Isabella of Portugal, 330. An alliance formed against him at Cognac, 345. Sends ambassadors to Francis to require the fulfilment of the treaty of Madrid, 348. Prepares for war against Francis, 350. The Pope reduced to an accommodation with him, 355. The

exhausted

INDEX.

exhausted state of his finances, 356. His troops under Bourbon distressed and mutinous for want of pay, 357. Bourbon assaults Rome and is slain, but the city taken, 368. The Prince of Orange general on Bourbon's death, takes the castle of St. Angelo, and the Pope prisoner, 371. The Emperor's conduct on that occasion, *ib*. His dissentions with the Pope, how far favourable to the reformation, 375. His instructions to the diet at Spires, *ib*. His manifesto against the Pope, and letter to the Cardinals, 376. France and England league against him, III. 3. Is refused supplies by the Cortes of Castile, 9. Delivers the Pope for a ransom, *ib*. His overtures to Henry and Francis, 11. Their declaration of war against him, 13. Is challenged by Francis to single combat, 14. Andrew Doria revolts from Francis to him, 21. His forces defeat the French in Italy, 23. 26. His motives for desiring an accommodation, 27. Concludes a separate treaty with the Pope, 29. Terms of the peace of Cambray concluded with Francis by the mediation of Margaret of Austria and Louise of France, 30. Remarks on the advantages gained by him in this treaty, and on his conduct of the war, 31. Visits Italy, 36. His policy on his public entry into Barcelona, 37. Has an interview with the Pope at Bologna, *ib*. Motives for his moderation in Italy, 38. His treaties with the states of, 39. Is crowned King of Lombardy and Emperor of the Romans, 41. Summons a diet at Spires to consider the state of religion, 43. His deliberations with the Pope, respecting the expediency of calling a general council, 45. Appoints a diet at Augsburg, 47. Makes a public entry into that city, *ib*. His endeavours to check the reformation, *ib*. Resolute behaviour of the Protestant princes toward him, 49. His severe decree against the Protestants, *ib*. Proposes his brother Ferdinand to be elected King of the Romans, 51. Is opposed by the Protestants, 53. Obtains his election, *ib*. Is desirous of an accommodation with the Protestants, 57. Concludes a treaty with
them

INDEX.

them at Nuremburg, *ib.* Raifes an army to oppofe the Turks under Solyman, and obliges him to retire, 59. Has another interview with the Pope, and preffes him to call a general council, 60. Procures a league of the Italian States to fecure the peace of Italy, 63. Arrives at Barcelona, *ib.* His endeavours to prevent the negotiations and meeting between the Pope and Francis, 67. Undertakes to expel Barbaroffa from Tunis, and reftore Muley Hafcen, 98. Lands in Africa, and befieges Goletta, 100. Takes Goletta, and feizes Barbaroffa's fleet, 102, 103. Defeats Barbaroffa, and takes Tunis, 103, 104. Reftores Muley Hafcen, and the treaty between them, 105. The glory acquired by this enterprife, and the delivery of the Chriftian captives, 106. Seizes the dutchy of Milan on the death of Francis Sforza, 122. His policy with regard to it, *ib.* Prepares for war with Francis, 123. His invective againft Francis at Rome before the Pope in council, 124. Remarks on this tranfaction, 127. Invades France, 130. Enters Provence and finds it defolated, 135. Befieges Marfeilles and Arles, 136. His miferable retreat from Provence, 138. His invafion of Picardy defeated, 139. Is accufed of poifoning the Dauphin, 141. Improbability of its truth, 142. Conjecture concerning the Dauphin's death, *ib.* Flanders invaded by Francis, 144. A fufpenfion of arms in Flanders, how negotiated, 145. A truce in Piedmont, 146. Motives to thefe truces, *ib.* Negotiation for peace with Francis, 149. Concludes a truce for ten years at Nice, 151. Remarks on the war, 152. His interview with Francis, *ib.* Courts the friendfhip of Henry VIII. of England, 160. Indulges the Proteftant Princes, 161. Quiets their apprehenfions of the Catholic league, 166. His troops mutiny, 169. Affembles the Cortes of Caftile, *ib.* Deftroys the ancient conftitution of the Cortes, 171. Inftance of the haughty fpirit of the Spanifh grandees, 172. Defires permiffion of Francis to pafs through France to the Netherlands, 181. His reception in France,

INDEX.

France, 182. His rigorous treatment of Ghent, 186. Refuses to fulfil his engagements to Francis, 188. Appoints a friendly conference between a deputation of Catholic and Protestant divines before the diet at Ratisbon, 211. Result of this conference, 213. Grants a private exemption from oppressions to the Protestants, 214. Undertakes to reduce Algiers, 222. Is near being cast away by a violent storm, 225. Lands near Algiers, *ib*. His soldiers exposed to a violent tempest and rain, 227. His fleet shattered, 228. His fortitude under these disasters, 230. Leaves his enterprize and embarks again, 231. Is distressed with another storm at sea, *ib*. Takes advantage of the French invasion of Spain to obtain subsidies from the Cortes, 242. His treaty with Portugal, 243. Concludes a league with Henry VIII. 244. Particulars of the treaty, 247. Over-runs Cleves, and his barbarous treatment of the town of Duren, 250. His behaviour to the Duke of Cleves, 251. Besieges Landrecy, *ib*. Is joined by an English detachment, *ib*. Is forced to retire, 252. Courts the favour of the Protestants, 259. His negociations with the Protestants, at the diet of Spires, 261. Procures the concurrence of the diet in a war against Francis, 265. Negociates a separate peace with the King of Denmark, 266. Invades Champagne, and invests St. Disiere, 273. Want of concert between his operations and those of Henry, who now invades France, 274. Obtains St. Disiere by artifice, 275. His distresses and happy movements, 277. Concludes a separate peace with Francis, 279. His motives to this peace, 280. His advantages by this treaty, 283. Obliges himself by a private article to exterminate the Protestant heresy, *ib*. Is cruelly afflicted with the gout, 286. Diet at Worms, 288. Arrives at Worms and alters his conduct toward the Protestants, 291. His conduct on the death of the Duke of Orleans, 295. His dissimulation to the Landgrave of Hesse, 315. Concludes a truce with Solyman, 320. Holds a diet at Ratisbon, 321.

INDEX.

His declaration to the Proteftant deputies, 326. His treaty with the Pope, concluded by the Cardinal of Trent, *ib*. His circular letter to the Proteftant members of the Germanic body, 327. The Proteftants levy an army againft him, 336. Is unprepared againft them, 337. Puts them under the ban of the Empire, 339. The Proteftants declare war againft him, 341. Marches to join the troops fent by the Pope, 344. Farnefe, the Pope's legate, returns in difguft, 345. His prudent declenfion of an action with the Proteftants, 348. Is joined by his Flemifh troops, 349. Propofals of peace made by the Proteftants, 360. Their army difperfe, 361. His rigorous treatment of the Proteftant Princes, 364. Difmiffes part of his army, 367. The Pope recalls his troops, 368. His reflection on Fiefco's infurrection at Genoa, 385. Is alarmed at the hoftile preparations of Francis, 391. Death of Francis, 393. A parallel drawn between him and Francis, *ib*. Confequences of Francis's death to him, 397. Marches againft the Elector of Saxony, 398. Paffes the Elbe, 399. Defeats the Saxon army, 404. Takes the Elector prifoner, 405. His harfh reception of him, 406. Invefts Wittemberg, 407. Condemns the Elector to death by a court-martial, 409. The Elector by treaty furrenders the electorate, 411. The harfh terms impofed by him on the Landgrave of Heffe, 416. His haughty reception of the Landgrave, 419. Detains him prifoner, 421. Seizes the warlike ftores of the league, 426. His cruel exactions, 427. Affembles a diet at Augfburg, 430. Intimidates the diet by his Spanifh troops, *ib*. Re-eftablifhes the Romifh worfhip in the churches of Augfburg, 431. Seizes Placentia, 436. Orders the diet to petition the Pope for the return of the council to Trent, 439. Protefts againft the council of Bologna, 441. Caufes a fyftem of faith to be prepared for Germany, 443. Lays it before the diet, 445. The *Interim* oppofed, 451. And rejected by the Imperial cities, 452. Reduces the city of Augfburg to fubmiffion, 453. Repeats the fame violence

INDEX.

violence at Ulm, 454. Carries the Elector and Landgrave with him into the Low Countries, 456. Procures his fon Philip to be recognized by the States of the Netherlands, 457. Eſtabliſhes the *Interim* there, 459. Re-aſſembles the diet at Augſburg, under the influence of his Spaniſh troops, IV. 9. The city of Madgeburg refuſes to admit the *Interim*, and prepares for reſiſtance, 18. Appoints Maurice Elector of Saxony to reduce it, 19. Promiſes to protect the Proteſtants at the council of Trent, 21. Arbitrarily releaſes Maurice and the Elector of Brandenburg from their engagements to the Landgrave for the recovery of his liberty, 22. Endeavours to ſecure the Empire for his ſon Philip, 24. His brother Ferdinand refuſes to reſign his pretenſions, 25. Beſieges Parma, but is repulſed, 32. Proceeds rigorouſly againſt the Proteſtants, 34. Endeavours to ſupport the council of Trent, 35. Puts Magdeburg under the ban of the Empire, 36. Abſolves the city, 42. Is involved in diſputes between the council and the Proteſtant deputies, concerning their ſafe-conduct, 44. Begins to ſuſpect Maurice of Saxony, 59. Circumſtances which contributed to deceive him with regard to Maurice, 61. Maurice takes the field againſt him, 63. Maurice ſeconded by Henry II. of France, 65. His diſtreſs and conſternation, 66. An ineffectual negociation with Maurice, 67. Flies from Inſpruck, 72. Releaſes the Elector of Saxony, 73. Is ſolicited to ſatisfy the demands of Maurice, 81. His preſent difficulties, 83. Refuſes any direct compliance with the demands of Maurice, 88. Is diſpoſed to yield by the progreſs of Maurice's operations, *ib*. Makes a peace with Maurice at Paſſau, 91. Reflections on this treaty, 92. Turns his arms againſt France, 101. Lays ſiege to Metz, 105. Is joined by Albert of Brandenburg, 106. His army diſtreſſed by the vigilance of the Duke of Guiſe, 108. Raiſes the ſiege and retires in a ſhattered condition, 110. Coſmo di Medici aſſerts his independency againſt him, 112. Siena revolts againſt him,

INDEX.

him, 112. Is dejected at his bad success, 116. Takes Terrouane, and demolishes it, 125. Takes Hesden, *ib.* Proposes his son Philip as a husband to Mary Queen of England, 139. The articles of the marriage, 142. Marches to oppose the French operations, 151. Is defeated by Henry, 152. Invades Picardy, 153. Grants Siena, subdued by Cosmo di Medici, to his son Philip, 164. A diet at Augsburg opened by Ferdinand, 173. Leaves the interior administration of Germany to Ferdinand, 177. Applies again to Ferdinand to resign his pretensions of succession to Philip, but is refused, 178. Recess of the diet of Augsburg on the subject of religion, 181. A treaty concluded between Pope Paul IV. and Henry II. of France against him, 202. Resigns his hereditary dominions to his son Philip, *ib.* His motives for retirement, 203. Had long meditated this resignation, 206. The ceremony of this deed, 208. His speech on this occasion, 209. Resigns also the dominions of Spain, 213. His intended retirement into Spain retarded, 215. A truce for five years concluded with France, 216. Endeavours in vain to secure the Imperial crown for Philip, 230. Resigns the Imperial crown to Ferdinand, 231. Sets out for Spain, *ib.* His arrival and reception in Spain, 232. Is distressed by his son's ungrateful neglect in paying his pension, 233. Fixes his retreat in the monastery of St. Justus in Plazencia, 234. The situation of this monastery, and his apartments, described, *ib.* Contrast between the conduct of Charles and the Pope, 235. His manner of life in his retreat, 280. His death precipitated by his monastic severities, 284. Celebrates his own funeral, 285. Dies, *ib.* His character, 286. A review of the state of Europe during his reign, 304. His acquisitions to the crown of Spain, 308.

Chateau Cambresis, the conferences for peace between Philip II. of Spain, and Henry II. of France, removed thither from Cercamp, IV. 294. The peace retarded by the demand of Elizabeth of England for restitution of Calais, 295. Particulars of the treaty signed

INDEX.

signed there between England and France, 297. Terms of the pacification between Philip and Henry, 299.

Cheregato, nuncio from the Pope to the diet at Nuremburgh, his instructions, II. 270. Opposes the assembling a general council, 272.

Chievres, William de Croy, lord of, appointed by Maximilian to superintend the education of his grandson Charles, II. 26. Adrian of Utrecht made preceptor under him, 27. His direction of the studies of Charles, 29. His avarice corrupts the Flemish court of Charles, 47. Negociates a peace with France, 49, 50. Endeavours to prevent an interview between Charles and Ximenes, 51. Attends Charles to Spain, 52. His ascendency over Charles, 56. His extortions, 58. His death and the supposed causes of it, 173.

Christians, primitive, why averse to the principles of toleration, IV. 183.

Clement VII. Pope, his election, II. 258. His character, *ib*. Grants Cardinal Wolsey a legatine commission in England for life, 259. Refuses to accede to the league against Francis, 263. Labours to accommodate the differences between the contending parties, *ib*. His proceedings with regard to the reformers, 276. Concludes a treaty of neutrality with Francis, 290. Enters into a separate treaty with Charles after the battle of Pavia, and the consequences of it, 305. Joins in an alliance with Francis Sforza and the Venetians, against the Emperor, 345. Absolves Francis from his oath to observe the treaty of Madrid, 346. Cardinal Colonna seizes Rome, and invests him in the castle of St. Angelo, 354, 355. Is forced to an accommodation with the Imperialists, 355. His revenge against the Colonna family, 359. Invades Naples, *ib*. His territories invaded by Bourbon, and his perplexity on the occasion, 362. Concludes a treaty with Lannoy viceroy of Naples, *ib*. His consternation on Bourbon's motions towards Rome, 366. Rome taken, and himself besieged in the castle of St. Angelo, 369. Surrenders himself prisoner, 372. The

INDEX.

Florentines revolt againſt him, III. 4. Pays Charles a ranſom for his liberty, with other ſtipulations, 10. Makes his eſcape from confinement, 11. Writes a letter of thanks to Lautrec, *ib.* Is jealous of the intentions of Francis, and negociates with Charles, 18. His motives and ſteps towards an accommodation, 27. Concludes a ſeparate treaty with Charles, 29 His interview with the Emperor at Bologna, 37. Crowns Charles King of Lombardy and Emperor of the Romans, 41. His repreſentations to the Emperor againſt calling a general council, 45. Has another interview with Charles at Bologna, and the difficulties raiſed by him to the calling a general council, 60. Agrees to a league of the Italian States for the peace of Italy, 62. His interview and treaty with Francis, 67. Marries Catherine di Medici to the Duke of Orleans, *ib.* His protraction of the affair of the divorce ſolicited by Henry VIII. 68. Reverſes Cranmer's ſentence of divorce, under penalty of excommunication, 69. Henry renounces his ſupremacy, *ib.* His death, 70. Reflections on his Pontificate, 71.

Clergy, Romiſh, remarks on the immoral lives of, and how they contributed to the progreſs of the Reformation, II. 137. The facility with which they obtained pardons, 139. Their uſurpations in Germany, during the diſputes concerning inveſtitures, 141. Their other opportunities of aggrandizing themſelves there, 142. Their perſonal immunities, 143. Their encroachments on the laity, 144. The dreadful effects of ſpiritual cenſures, 145. Their devices to ſecure their uſurpations, 146. The united effect of all theſe circumſtances, 151. Oppoſe the advancement of learning in Germany, 156.

Cleves, invaded and over-run by the Emperor Charles V. III. 250. Cruel treatment of Duren, *ib.* Humiliating ſubmiſſion of the Duke, 251.

Cnipperdoling, a leader of the Anabaptiſts at Munſter, an account of, III. 75, 76. See *Anabaptiſts*.

Cognac,

INDEX.

Cognac, an alliance formed there against Charles V. by the Pope, the Venetians, the Duke of Milan, and Francis I. II. 345.

Coligny, admiral, governor of Picardy, defends St. Quintin against the Spanish general Emmanuel Phillibert Duke of Savoy, IV. 245. His brother D'Andelot defeated in an endeavour to join the garrison, 246. But D'Andelot enters the town, 247. His character, 252. The town taken by assault, and himself taken prisoner. *ib.*

Cologne, Ferdinand King of Hungary and Bohemia, brother to the Emperor Charles V. elected King of the Romans by the college of Electors there, III. 53.

——— Herman, Count de Wied, Archbishop and Elector of, inclines to the Reformation, and is opposed by his canons, who appeal to the Emperor and Pope, III. 293. Is deprived and excommunicated, 318. Resigns, 365.

Colonna, Cardinal Pompeo, his character, and rivalship with Pope Clement VII. II. 353. Seizes Rome, and invests the Pope in the castle of St. Angelo, 354, 355. Is degraded, and the rest of the family excommunicated by the Pope, 359. Is prevailed on by the Pope, when prisoner with the Imperialists, to solicit his delivery, III. 9.

——— Prosper, the Italian general, his character, II. 187. Appointed to command the troops in the invasion of Milan, *ib.* Drives the French out of Milan, 190. His army how weakened at the death of Pope Leo X. 191. Defeats Marechal de Lautrec, at Bicocca, 195. Reduces Genoa, 197. The bad state of his troops when the French invade Milan, 256. Is enabled to defend the city by the ill conduct of Bonnevet the French commander, 258. Dies, and is succeeded by Lannoy, 263.

Conchillos, an Aragonian gentleman, employed by Ferdinand of Aragon, to obtain Joanna's consent to his regency of Castile, II. 11. Thrown into a dungeon by the Archduke Philip, *ib.*

Confession of Augsburg, drawn up by Melancthon, III. 48.

INDEX.

Constance, the privileges of that city taken away by the Emperor Charles V. for disobedience to the *Interim*, III. 459.

Corsairs of Barbary, an account of the rise of, III. 91. See *Algiers, Barbarossa*.

Cortes of Aragon, acknowledges the Archduke Philip's title to the crown, II. 3. Not allowed to assemble in the name of Charles V. 59. Their opposition to his desires, 60. Is prevailed on by the Emperor to recognize his son Philip as successor to that kingdom, III. 243. See *Spain*.

────── of Castile, acknowledges the Archduke Philip's title to the crown, II. 3. Is prevailed on to acknowledge Ferdinand Regent, according to Isabella's will, 8. Acknowledges Philip and Joanna King and Queen of Castile, and their son Charles, Prince of Asturias, 17. Declares Charles King, and votes him a free gift, 56. Summoned by Charles to meet at Compostella in Galicia, 84. Tumultuary proceedings thereupon, *ib.* A donative voted, 86. Loses all its influence by the dissolution of the Holy Junta, 238, 239. Its backwardness to grant supplies for the Emperor's wars in Italy, 356. Refuses his pressing solicitations for a supply, III. 9. Assembled at Toledo to grant supplies to the Emperor, 169. The remonstrances of, 170. The ancient constitution of, subverted by Charles, 171. See *Spain*.

────── of Valencia, prevailed on by the Emperor Charles V. to acknowledge his son Philip successor to that kingdom, III. 243. See *Spain*.

Cortona, Cardinal di, governor of Florence for the Pope, expelled by the Florentines, on the Pope's captivity, III. 4.

Cosmo di Medici. See *Medici*.

Cranmer, Archbishop of Canterbury, annuls the marriage of Henry VIII. with Catherine of Aragon, which was refused to Henry by the Pope, III. 68. His sentence reversed by the Pope, 69.

Crespy, peace of, between the Emperor and Francis, III. 279.

Croy,

INDEX.

Croy, William de, nephew to Chievres, made Archbishop of Toledo, by Charles V. II. 58. Dies, 237.

D

D'Albert, John, expelled from his kingdom of Navarre by Ferdinand of Aragon, II. 23. Invades Navarre, but is defeated by Cardinal Ximenes, 45.

D'Alembert, M. his observation on the order of Jesuits, III. 203. *Note.*

D'Andelot, brother to Coligni, is defeated by the Duke of Saxony in an endeavour to succour St. Quintin, IV. 247. But enters the town with the fugitives, *ib.* The town taken by assault, 252

Dauphin of France, eldest son of Francis I. is delivered up with the Duke of Orleans to the Emperor Charles V. in exchange for his father, as hostages for the performance of the treaty of Madrid, II. 329. His death imputed to poison, III. 141. The most probable cause of it, 142.

────── late Duke of Orleans, second son of Francis I. commands an army, and invades Spain, III. 240. Is forced to abandon the siege of Perpignan, 241. Is dissatisfied at the peace of Crespy, 285. Makes a secret protestation against it, *ib.*

────── of France, son of Henry II. contracted to Mary the young Queen of Scotland, III. 438. Is married to her, IV. 271.

Denmark, a summary view of the revolutions in, during the sixteenth century, IV. 334.

────── King of, joins the Protestant league at Smalkalde, III. 165.

De Retz, Cardinal, writes a history of Fiesco's conspiracy while a youth, III. 384. *Note.*

Diana of Poitiers, mistress to Henry II. of France, assists the Guises in persuading Henry to an alliance with Pope Paul IV. against the Emperor, IV. 198. Induces Henry to break the treaty of Vaucelles, 223. Marries her grand-daughter to one of Montmorency's sons,

INDEX.

fons, 279. Joins Montmorency againſt the Guiſes, *ib.*

Doria, Andrew, aſſiſts Lautrec in ſubduing Genoa, III. 7. Conquers and kills Moncada in a ſea-engagement before the harbour of Naples, 17. His character, 19. Is diſguſted with the behaviour of the French, 20. Revolts to the Emperor, 21. Opens to Naples a communication by ſea, 22. Reſcues Genoa from the French, 23. Reſtores the government of, to the citizens, 25. The reſpect paid to his memory, 26. Attends the Emperor Charles in his diſaſtrous expedition againſt Algiers, 225. His partial fondneſs for his kinſman Giannetino, 371. His narrow eſcape in Lavagno's inſurrection, 381. Returns on Lavagno's death, and the diſperſion of his party, 384. See *Genoa* and *Lavagno.*

——— Giannetino, his character, III. 371. Is murdered by Lavagno's conſpirators, 381.

Dover, an interview there between Henry VIII. and the Emperor Charles V. II. 99.

Dragut, a corſair, commands the Turkiſh fleet which ravages the coaſt of Naples, IV. 116.

Du Prat, Chancellor of France, his character, II. 252. Commences a law-ſuit againſt Charles Duke of Bourbon, for his eſtate, at the inſtigation of Louiſe the King's mother, *ib.*

Duelling, the cuſtom of, how rendered general, III. 15. Its influence on manners, *ib.*

Duren in Cleves, taken by the Emperor Charles V. the inhabitants put to the ſword, and the town burnt, III. 250.

E

Eccius, an adverſary of Luther's holds a public diſputation with him at Leipſic, on the validity of the papal authority, II. 125.

Eccleſiaſtical cenſures of the Romiſh church, the dreadful effects of, II. 145.

Eccle-

INDEX.

Ecclesiastical Reservation, in the recess of the diet of Augsburg, remarks on, III. 58.

Edinburgh plundered and burnt by the Earl of Hertford, III. 274.

Edward VI. of England, his character, IV. 139.

Egmont, count of, commands the cavalry at the battle of St. Quintin, and puts Montmorency's troops to flight, IV. 248, 249. Engages Marshal de Termes, and defeats him by the casual arrival of an English squadron, 274.

Egypt, how and by whom added to the Ottoman Empire, II. 65.

Ehrenberg, the castle of, taken by Maurice of Saxony, IV. 70.

Eignotz, a faction in Geneva so termed, an account of, III. 118.

Elizabeth, sister of Mary, her accession to the crown of England, IV. 290. Her character, 291. Is addressed by Philip of Spain, and Henry of France, for marriage, *ib*. Her prudent conduct between them, 292. How determined against Henry, 293. Her motives for rejecting Philip, 294. Returns Philip an evasive answer, *ib*. Demands restitution of Calais at the conferences at Chateau Cambresis, 295. Establishes the Protestant religion in England, 296. Treaty between her and Henry signed at Chateau Cambresis, 297.

Emmanuel Phillibert, Duke of Savoy. See *Savoy*.

England, by what means that kingdom was freed from the Papal supremacy, and received the doctrines of the Reformation, III. 69. Mary, Queen of, married to Prince Philip, son of the Emperor Charles V. contrary to the sense of the nation, IV. 141. The marriage ratified by parliament, 145. Is reluctantly engaged by Philip, now King of Spain, in the war against France, 243. Mary levies money by her prerogative, to carry on the war, *ib*. Calais taken by the Duke of Guise, 266. Guisnes and Hames taken, *ib*. Death of Mary, and accession of Elizabeth, 290. The Protestant religion established by Elizabeth, 296. Treaty with France signed at Chateau

INDEX.

Chateau Cambrefis, 297. Its interior ftrength how increafed by the conduct of Henry VIII. 315. Its power no longer fruitlefsly wafted on the continent, 317. Alteration of its conduct towards Scotland, 318.

Enguien, the count de, befieges Carignan, III. 267. Defires of Francis permiffion to engage Guafto, 268. Defeats Guafto in a pitched battle, 270.

Erard de la Mark, ambaffador of Charles V. to the diet of Frankfort, his private motives for thwarting the pretenfions of Francis I. of France to the Imperial crown, II. 76. Signs the capitulation of the Germanic body on behalf of Charles, 77.

Erafmus, fome account of, II. 157. Preceded Luther in his cenfures againft the Romifh church, ib. Concurs with him in his intentions of reformation, 158. Motives which checked him in this, ib.

Efcurial, palace of, built by Philip II. in memory of the battle of St. Quintin, IV. 254.

Europe, a fhort view of the ftate of, at the death of the Emperor Maximilian, II. 62. The contemporary monarchs of all, illuftrious at the time of Charles V. 102, 103. The method of carrying on war in, how improved beyond the practice of earlier ages, 226. The fentiments of, on Charles's treatment of the Pope, III. 1. A review of the ftate of, during the reign of the Emperor Charles V. IV. 303. The remarkable change in, at this period, 304. How affected by the revolt of Luther againft the church of Rome, 320.

Eutemi, King of Algiers, engages Barbaroffa in his fervice, and is murdered by him, II. 90, 91.

Excommunication in the Romifh church, the original inftitution of, and the ufe made of it, II. 145.

F

Farnefe, Alexander, his unanimous election to the Papacy, III. 70. See *Paul* III.

—— Cardinal, accompanies the troops fent by the Pope to the Emperor, againft the army of the Proteftant

INDEX.

testant league, III. 345. Returns disgusted, *ib.* Leads the troops home again by the Pope's order, 368. Contributes to the election of Cardinal di Monte to the Papacy, IV. 6.

Farnese, Octavio, grandson of Pope Paul III. endeavours to surprise Parma, and enters into treaty with the Emperor, IV. 3. Is confirmed in Parma, by Julius, 29. Procures an alliance with France, 31. Is attacked by the Imperialists, but successfully protected by the French, 32. Placentia restored to him by Philip II. of Spain, II. 257.

―――― Peter Lewis, natural son of Pope Paul III. obtains of his father the dutchies of Parma and Placentia, III. 296. His character, 434. Is assassinated, 435.

Ferdinand King of Aragon, how he acquired his kingdoms, II. 2. Invites his daughter Joanna, and her husband, Philip Archduke of Austria, to Spain, 3. Becomes jealous of Philip, 4. Carries on his war with France vigorously, notwithstanding Philip's treaty with Lewis, 6. His Queen Isabella dies, and leaves him regent of Castile, under restrictions, 7. Resigns the kingdom of Castile, and is acknowledged Regent by the Cortes, 8. His character, *ib.* His maxims of government odious to the Castilians, 9. Required by Philip to resign his regency, 10. Joanna's letter of consent procured by him, intercepted by Philip, and herself confined, 11. Is deserted by the Castilian nobility, *ib.* Determines to exclude his daughter from the succession by marrying, 12. Marries Germaine de Foix, niece to Lewis XII. of France, 13. A treaty between him and Philip at Salamanca, by which the regency of Castile is jointly vested in them and Joanna, 14. Prevails on Henry VII. of England to detain Philip for three months, when driven on that coast, 15. The Castilians declare against him, *ib.* Resigns the regency of Castile by treaty, 16. Interview between him and Philip, *ib.* Is absent, at Naples, when Philip died, 21. Returns and gains, with the regency of Castile, the good-will of the natives by his

prudent

INDEX.

prudent administration, 22. Acquires by dishonourable means the kingdom of Navarre, 23. How he destroyed his constitution, 24. Endeavours to diminish his grandson Charles's power, by a will in favour of Ferdinand, 24, 25. Alters his will in favour of Charles, 26. Dies, *ib.* Review of his administration, 31. Ximenes appointed, by his will, regent of Castile until the arrival of Charles V. *ib.*

Ferdinand, second son of Philip Archduke of Austria, born, II. 5. Left regent of Aragon, by his grandfather Ferdinand, 25. This revoked by a subsequent will, by which he obtains only a pension, 26. Discontented with his disappointment, he is taken to Madrid under the eye of Cardinal Ximenes, 35. Sent by Charles V. to visit their grandfather Maximilian, 59. Is elected King of Hungary and Bohemia, 374. Signs a deed called the *Reverse, ib.* The Emperor endeavours to get him elected King of the Romans, III. 52. He is opposed by the Protestants, 53. Is crowned King of the Romans, 54. Forms a confederacy against the Anabaptists at Munster, 81. Opposes the restoration of Ulric Duke of Wurtemberg, 85. Recognizes his title, and concludes a treaty with him, 87. His kingdom of Hungary wrested from him by John Zapol Scaepius, 215. Besieges the young King Stephen and his mother in Buda, but is defeated by the Turks, 218. His mean offers of submission to the Porte, *ib.* Which are rejected, 220. Courts the favour of the Protestants, 260. Opens the diet at Worms, 288. Requires it to submit to the decisions of the council of Trent, 389. Agrees to pay a tribute to Solyman for Hungary, 420. Encroaches on the liberties of Bohemia, 427. His rigorous treatment of Prague, 429. Disarms the Bohemians, 430. Obtains the sovereignty of the city of Constance, 459. Invades Transylvania by invitation of Martinuzzi, IV. 47. Obtains the resignation of Transylvania from Queen Isabella, 48. Orders Martinuzzi to be assassinated, 51. Enters into negociation with Maurice on behalf

INDEX.

of the Emperor, 81. His motives for promoting the Emperor's agreeing with Maurice, 86. Isabella and her son Stephen recover possession of Transylvania, 128. Opens a diet at Augsburg, and excites suspicions in the Protestants, 173. The Emperor leaves the internal administration of German affairs to him, 177. Is again applied to by the Emperor to resign his pretensions of succession to Philip, but refuses, 178. Endeavours therefore to gain the friendship of the diet, 180. Again refuses the Emperor's solicitations, 230. Charles resigns the Imperial crown to him, 231. Assembles the college of Electors at Frankfort, which acknowledges him Emperor of Germany, 267. The Pope refuses to acknowledge him, 268.

Feudal government, a view of, as it existed in Spain, II. 209.

Fiesco, Count of Lavagna. See *Lavagna.*

—— Jerome, engages in his brother's conspiracy, and fails in securing Andrew Doria, III. 380. His imprudent vanity on his brother's death, 382. Shuts himself up in a fort on his estate, 385. Is reduced and put to death, 393.

Flanders. See *Netherlands.*

Florence, the inhabitants of, revolt against Pope Clement VII. on the news of his captivity, and recover their liberty, III. 4. Are reduced to subjection to Alexander di Medici, by the Emperor, 41. Alexander di Medici, Duke of, assassinated by his kinsman Lorenzo, 155. Cosmo di Medici advanced to the sovereignty, 156. Cosmo supported by the Emperor, defeats the partizans of Lorenzo, 157. Cosmo asserts his independency on the Emperor, IV. 112.

Fonseca, Antonio de, commander in chief of the forces in Spain, ordered by Cardinal Adrian to besiege the insurgents in Segovia, II. 207. Is denied liberty of taking military stores, by the inhabitants of Medina del Campo, *ib.* Attacks and almost burns the whole town, 208. Is repulsed, *ib.* His house at Valladolid burnt, *ib.*

France,

INDEX.

France, the acquisitions of that kingdom, during the reign of the Emperor Charles V. IV. 310. The character of the people of, 312. The good consequences of the civil wars in that kingdom to the rest of Europe, 314.

Francis I. King of France, concludes a peace with Charles V. and the conditions of the treaty, II. 49, 50. Sends a fruitless embassy to Charles for the restitution of Navarre to the young king, 60. Aspires to the Imperial crown at the death of Maximilian, 64. Reasons by which he supported his pretensions, 65. Remarks on the equipages of his ambassadors to the German States, 68. His pretensions adopted by the Venetians, 69. Loses the election, 77. Rise of the rivalship between him and Charles, 90. Courts the favour of Cardinal Wolsey, 97. Promises Wolsey his interest for the Papacy, 99. Has an interview with Henry VIII. of England, 100. Wrestles with Henry, and throws him, 101, *Note*. His advantages over Charles, at the commencement of hostilities between them, 168. Concludes an alliance with the Pope, 171. Invades and reduces Navarre, in the name of Henry D'Albret, son of John, the former King, 175. The French driven out by the imprudence of L'Esparre their general, who is taken prisoner by the Spaniards, 176, 177. Retakes Mouson from the Imperialists, 180. Invades the Low Countries, but loses the opportunities of success by imprudence, *ib*. Rejects the demands of Charles at the Congress at Calais, 181. A league concluded between Charles and Henry VIII. against him, 182. His imprudent appointment of the Marechal de Foix to the government of Milan, 185. De Foix attacks Reggio, but is repulsed by the governor Guicciardini the historian, 186. The Pope declares against him, *ib*. His embarrassments on the invasion of Milan, 187. His mother seizes the money appointed for payment of the Milanese troops, 188. Milan taken, and the French driven out, 190. Levies a body of Swiss, 194. Who insist
on

INDEX.

on giving a precipitate battle to the Imperialists, which is lost, 196. War declared against him by Henry VIII. 197. His expedients to supply his treasury, 198. The plan pursued by him to resist the incursions of the English, 200. Picardy invaded by Henry, *ib.* The Venetians league with the Emperor against him, 248. To which Pope Adrian accedes, *ib.* His expeditious movement against the Milanese, 249. Disconcerted by the Duke of Bourbon's conspiracy, *ib.* Taxes him with betraying his cause, which Bourbon denies, 254. Bourbon escapes to Italy, and Francis returns, *ib.* Appoints the Admiral Bonnivet to command against the Milanese, 255. Picardy invaded by the Duke of Suffolk, who is driven back, 261. Repulses the invasion of Guienne and Burgundy by Charles, 262. His successful close of the campaign, *ib.* His prudent care to disappoint the Imperialists in their invasion of Provence, 282. Assembles an army, which causes the Imperialists to retire from Marseilles, *ib.* Determines to invade the Milanese, 284. Appoints his mother Louise regent during his absence, 285. Enters Milan, and takes possession of the city, 285, 286. Advised by Bonnivet to besiege Pavia, 288. His vigorous attacks on Pavia, *ib.* Concludes a treaty of neutrality with Pope Clement, 290. His imprudent invasion of Naples, 291. Resolves, by Bonnivet's advice, to attack Bourbon's army, advanced to the relief of Pavia, 294. Is routed at the battle of Pavia, *ib.* Is taken prisoner, 295. Is sent to the castle of Pizzitchitone under the custody of Don Ferdinand Alarcon, 297, 298. Refuses the propositions made to him by Charles, 308. Is carried to Spain on his desire of a personal interview with Charles, 309. Is rigorously treated in Spain, 318. Falls dangerously ill, *ib.* Is visited by Charles, 319. Resolves to resign his kingdom, 323. Is delivered from this captivity by the treaty of Madrid, 325. His secret protestations against the validity of this treaty, 327. Marries the Queen of Portugal, *ib.* Recovers his liberty, and the Dauphin and the Duke

INDEX.

of Orleans delivered up hostages to Charles for the performance of the treaty of Madrid, 329. Writes a letter of acknowledgment to Henry VIII. of England, 343. His reply to the Imperial ambassadors, *ib.* Enters into a league with the Pope, the Venetians, and Sforza, against Charles, 345. Is absolved from his oath to observe the treaty of Madrid, 346. His behaviour to the Emperor's second embassy, 349. Is dispirited by his former ill success, 350. Enters into a treaty with Henry VIII. of England against the Emperor, III. 3. Successes of his general Lautrec in Italy, 7. His reply to the Emperor's overtures, 12. Declares war against him, and challenges him to single combat, 13, 14. Treats Andrew Doria ill, who revolts from him to the Emperor, 21. His army, under Saluces, driven out of Italy, 23. His troops in Milan routed, 26. His endeavours toward an accommodation, 27. Terms of the peace of Cambray, concluded by the mediation of his mother Louise and Margaret of Austria, 30. Remarks on the sacrifices made by him in this treaty, and on his conduct of the war, 31. Leagues secretly with the Protestant Princes, 55. His measures to elude the treaty of Cambray, 64. His negociations with the Pope, 65. His interview and treaty with the Pope, 66. Gives the Duke of Orleans in marriage to Catherine di Medici, 67. Negociates a treaty with Francis Sforza, Duke of Milan, 109. His envoy Merveille executed at Milan for murder, 110. Is disappointed in his endeavours to negociate alliances against the Emperor, *ib.* Invites Melancthon to Paris, 111. Evidences his zeal for the Romish religion, 112. Causes of his quarrel with the Duke of Savoy, 115. Seizes the Duke's territories, 116. His pretensions to the dutchy of Milan, on the death of Francis Sforza, 122. The Emperor's invective against him before the Pope in council, 124. Is invaded by Charles, 129, His prudent plan of defence, 133. Joins the army under Montmorency, 138. Death of the Dauphin, 141. Obtains a decree of the parliament

INDEX.

liament of Paris against the Emperor, 143. Invades the Low Countries, 144. A suspension of arms in Flanders, and how negotiated, *ib*. A truce in Piedmont, 145. Motives to these truces, 147. Concludes an alliance with Solyman the Magnificent, *ib*. Negotiations for a peace with the Emperor, 149. Concludes a truce for ten years at Nice, 151. Reflections on the war, *ib*. His interview with Charles, 152. Marries Mary of Guise to James V. of Scotland, 159. Refuses the offers of the deputies of Ghent, 179. Informs Charles of the offer made by them, *ib*. Grants the Emperor leave to pass through France to the Netherlands, 181. His reception of the Emperor, 183. Is deceived by the Emperor in respect to Milan, 187. His ambassador to the Porte, Rincon, murdered by the Imperial governor of the Milanese, 236. Prepares to resent the injury, 237. Attacks the Emperor with five armies, 239. His first attempts rendered abortive, by the imprudence of the Duke of Orleans, 241. Renews his negociations with Sultan Solyman, 248. Invades the Low Countries, 250. Forces the Emperor to raise the siege of Landrecy, 252. Dismisses Barbarossa, 267. Gives the Count d'Enguein permission to engage Guasto, 269. Relieves Paris, in danger of being surprised by the Emperor, 278. Agrees to a separate peace with Charles, 279. Henry's haughty return to his overtures of peace, 284. Death of the Duke of Orleans, 295. Peace of Campe, 334. Perceives a necessity of checking the Emperor's ambitious designs, 388. Forms a general league against him, *ib*. Dies, 393. His life and character summarily compared with those of Charles, *ib*. Consequences of his death, 397.

Francis II. his accession to the crown of France, and character, IV. 302.

Francfort, the diet of, assembled for the choice of an Emperor at the death of Maximilian, II. 72. Names and views of the Electors, 72, 73. The Empire offered to Frederick of Saxony, 73. Who rejects

INDEX.

it, with his reasons, 74. Chuses Charles V. Emperor, 77. His confirmation of the Germanic privileges required and agreed to, 78. City of, embraces the reformed religion, 270. The college of Electors assembled there by Ferdinand, who is acknowledged Emperor of Germany, IV. 267.

Frederick Duke of Saxony, assembles with the other Electors at the diet of Francfort, to chuse an Emperor, II. 72. The Empire offered to him, 73. Rejects it, and votes for Charles V. 74. Refuses the presents of the Spanish ambassadors, 75. This disinterested behaviour confirmed by the testimony of historians, *ib. Note.* Chuses Martin Luther philosophical professor at his university of Wittemberg, 110. Encourages Luther in his opposition to indulgences, 113. Protects him against Cajetan, 120. Causes Luther to be seized at his return from the diet of Worms, and conceals him at Wartburg, 164. Dies, 341.

Fregoso, the French ambassador to Venice, murdered by the Marquis del Guasto, the Imperial governor of the Milanese, III. 236.

Fronsperg, George, a German nobleman, some account of, he joins the army of Charles V. II. 356.

G

General of the Jesuits, an enquiry into his office and despotic authority, III. 193.

Geneva, an account of its revolt against the Duke of Savoy, III. 117.

Genoa, reduced by Lautrec, the French general, III. 7. The French endeavour to prejudice its trade in favour of Savona, 20. Is rescued from the French by Andrew Doria, 24. The government of, settled by the disinterestedness of Doria, *ib.* The honour paid to Doria's memory, 26. Is visited by the Emperor, 37. A scheme formed to overturn the constitution of, by Fiesco Count of Lavagno, 373. He assembles his adherents, 376. The conspirators sally forth from Lavagno's palace, 380. Deputies sent to know Lavagno's terms, 381. Lavagno drowned,

INDEX.

drowned, 382. The infurrection ruined by the imprudence of his brother Jerome Fiefco, *ib.* The confpirators difperfe, 383. Jerome reduced and put to death, 393.

Germanada, an affociation in Valencia, fo termed, on what occafion formed, II. 239. Refufe to lay down their arms, *ib.* Their refentment levelled at the nobility, who raife an army againft them, 240. Defeat the nobles in feveral actions, 241. But are routed and difperfed by them, *ib.*

Germany, ftate of, at the death of the Emperor Maximilian, II. 62, 63. Charles V. of Spain, and Francis I. of France, form pretenfions to the Imperial crown, 64. Their refpective reafons offered in favour of their claims, 65, 66. Views and interefts of the other European States in relation to the competitors, 68. Henry VIII. of England advances a claim, 69. But is difcouraged from profecuting it, 70. How the Papacy was likely to be affected in the choice of an Emperor, *ib.* Advice of Pope Leo X. to the German Princes, 71. Opening of the diet at Francfort, 72. In whom the election of an Emperor is vefted, *ib.* Views of the Electors, 73. The Empire offered to Frederick of Saxony, *ib.* Who rejects it, and his reafons, *ib.* Charles V. chofen, 77. The capitulation of the Germanic privileges confirmed by him, 78. Charles fets out for, 87. Charles crowned at Aix-la-Chapelle, 102. Commencement of the Reformation there, by Martin Luther, 104. Treatment of the bull of excommunication publifhed againft Luther, 128. The ufurpations of the clergy there, during the difputes concerning inveftitures, 141. The clergy of, moftly foreigners, 147. The benefices of, nominated by the Pope, 148. The expedient of the Emperors for reftraining this power of the Pope, ineffectual, 149. The great progrefs of Luther's doctrines in, 269. Grievances of the peafants, 331. Infurrection in Suabia, 332, 333. The memorial of their grievances, *ib.* The infurrection quelled, 334. Another infurrection in Thuringia, *ib.* How the Houfe of Auftria became fo formi-

INDEX.

formidable in, 375. Proceedings relating to the Reformation there, *ib.* Great progress of the Reformation there, III. 42. Ferdinand King of Hungary and Bohemia, brother to Charles V. elected King of the Romans, 53. The Protestant religion established in Saxony, 167. The Protestant religion established in the Palatinate, 299. The league of Smalkalde raise an army against the Emperor, 335. Are put under the ban of the Empire, 339. The Protestant army dispersed, 361. The *Interim* enforced by the Emperor, 454. Maurice of Saxony raises an army, and declares in favour of the Protestants, IV. 64. Maurice favoured even by the Catholic princes, and why, 83. Treaty of Passau, between the emperor and Maurice of Saxony, 91. Truce between the Emperor and Henry of France, 217. Charles resigns the Imperial crown to his brother Ferdinand, 231.

Ghent, an insurrection there, III. 173. The pretensions of the citizens, 174. Form a confederacy against the Queen-dowager of Hungary, their governess, 175. Their deputies to the Emperor, how treated by him, *ib.* Offer to submit to France, 176. Is reduced by Charles, 185.

Ghibeline faction in Italy, a view of, II. 353.

Giron, Don Pedro de, appointed to the command of the army of the Holy Junta, II. 223. Resigns his commission, and Padilla replaced, 226.

Goletta in Africa, taken by the Emperor Charles V. III. 99.

Gonzago, the Imperial governor of Milan, procures Cardinal Farnese to be assassinated, and takes possession of Placentia for the Emperor, III. 436. Prepares to seize Parma, IV. 29. Is repulsed by the French, 32.

Gouffer, sent by Francis I. King of France, to negociate a peace with Charles V. II. 49.

Granvelle, Cardinal, his artifice to prevail on the count de Sancerre to surrender St. Disiere to the Emperor, III. 275. Endeavours to lull the Protestants into security with regard to the Emperor's conduct toward them, 308. Is commissioned by Philip to address

INDEX.

dress the assembly at the Emperor's resignation of his hereditary dominions, IV. 212.

Gravelines, an interview there between the Emperor Charles V. and Henry VIII. of England, II. 101.

Grapper, canon of Cologne, is appointed a manager of the Protestant and Catholic conferences before the diet at Ratisbon, III. 211. Writes a treatise to compose the differences between them, *ib*. The sentiments of both parties on this work, 212.

Granada, archbishop of, president of the council of Castile, his imprudent advice to Cardinal Adrian, relating to the insurrection in Segovia, II. 206.

Guasto, the Marquis del, appointed governor of Milan, by the Emperor, III. 140. Procures Rincon the French ambassador to the Porte, to be murdered on his journey thither, 236. Defends Carignan against the French, 268. Defeated by d'Enguien in a pitched battle, 271.

Guicciardini, his account of the publication of Indulgences contradicted, II. 114. *Note*. Defends Reggio against the French, 185. Repulses an attack upon Parma by the French, 192. His sentiments of the Pope's treaty with Lannoy viceroy of Naples, 363.

Guise, Francis of Lorrain, Duke of, is made governor of Metz by Henry II. of France, IV. 103. His character, *ib*. Prepares to defend it against the Emperor, *ib*. His brother d'Aumale taken prisoner by the Imperialists, 107. The Emperor raises the siege, 110. His humane treatment of the distressed and sick Germans left behind, 111. Persuades Henry to an alliance with Pope Paul IV. 198. Marches with troops into Italy, 236. Is unable to effect any thing, 237. Is recalled from Italy after the defeat of St. Quintin, 255. His reception in France, 261. Takes the field against Philip, 262. Invests and takes Calais from the English, 266. Takes also Guisnes and Hames, *ib*. Takes Thionville in Luxembourg, 273.

Guise, Mary of, married to James V. of Scotland, III. 159. Frustrates the intended marriage between her daughter Mary and prince Edward of England, 266.

INDEX.

Gurk, Cardinal de, why he favoured the election of Charles V. to the Imperial crown, II. 76. Signs the capitulation of the Germanic body on behalf of Charles, 78.

Gufman, chancellor to the Emperor Ferdinand, is sent to Pope Paul IV. to notify the election, who refuses to see him, IV. 268.

H

Hamburgh, city of, embraces the reformed religion, II. 269.

Haro, the Conde de, appointed to command the army of the Castilian nobles against the Holy Junta, II. 225. Attacks Tordesillas, and gets possession of Queen Joanna, *ib*. Routs the army of the Junta, and takes Padilla prisoner, who is executed, 233.

Hascen Aga, deputy-governor of Algiers, his piracies against the Christian states, III. 222. Is besieged in Algiers by the Emperor Charles V. 225. Makes a successful sally, 227. The Emperor forced by bad weather to return back again, 230.

Hayradin, a potter's son of Lesbos, commences pirate, III. 91. See *Barbarossa*.

Heathens, ancient, why the principles of mutual toleration were generally admitted among them, IV. 183.

Heldo, vice chancellor to Charles V. attends the Pope's nuncio to Smalkalde, III. 162. Forms a Catholic league in opposition to the Protestant one, 165.

Henry II. King of France, his motives for declining an alliance with Pope Paul III. against the Emperor, III. 438. Procures for Scotland a peace with England, IV. 31. The young Queen Mary contracted to the Dauphin, and sent to France for education, *ib*. Enters into an alliance with Octavia Farnese Duke of Parma, *ib*. Protests against the council of Trent, 33. Makes alliance with Maurice Elector of Saxony, 54. Seconds the operations of Maurice, 65. His army marches and seizes Metz, 68. Attempts to surprise Strasburgh, 77. Is strongly solicited to spare it, 78. Returns, 79. The Emperor

INDEX.

peror prepares for war against him, 101. Instigates the Turks to invade Naples, 115. Terouanne taken and demolished by Charles, 125. Hesdin taken, *ib.* Leads an army into the Low Countries against Charles, 126. Endeavours to obstruct the marriage of Mary of England with Philip of Spain, 148. The progress of his arms against the Emperor, 150. Engages Charles, 152. Retires, *ib.* Cosmo di Medici, Duke of Florence, makes war against him, 155. Appoints Peter Strozzi commander of his army in Italy, 156. Strozzi defeated, 159. Siena taken, 161. Pope Paul IV. makes overtures to an alliance with him against the Emperor, 196. Montmorency's arguments against this alliance, 197. Is persuaded by the Guises to accept it, 198. Sends the Cardinal of Lorrain with powers to conclude it, *ib.* The Pope signs the treaty, 201. A truce for five years concluded with the Emperor, 216. Is exhorted by Cardinal Caraffa to break the truce, 220. Is absolved from his oath, and concludes a new treaty with the Pope, 223. Sends the Duke of Guise into Italy, 239. The Constable Montmorency defeated and taken prisoner at St. Quintin, 248. Henry prepares for the defence of Paris, 250. St. Quintin taken by assault, 252. Collects his troops and negociates for assistance, 253. His kind reception of the Duke of Guise, 261. Calais taken by Guise, 266. Impowers Montmorency to negociate a peace with Philip, 279. Honours him highly on his return to France, 280. Writes to Queen Elizabeth with proposals of marriage, 291. How he failed in his suit, 293. His daughter married to Philip, and his sister to the Duke of Savoy, 298. Terms of the treaty of Chateau Cambresis, 299. The marriage of his sister and daughter celebrated with great pomp, 301. His death, 302.

Henry VII. of England detains the archduke Philip and his duchess when driven on his coast, three months, at the instigation of Ferdinand, II. 15.

Henry VIII. of England sends an ambassador to Germany to propose his claims to the Imperial crown,

INDEX.

II. 69. Is difcouraged from his pretenfions, and takes no part with the other competitors, 70. His perfonal character and political influence in Europe, 94. Entirely guided by Cardinal Wolfey, 95. Receives a vifit from the Emperor Charles V. 99. Goes over to France to vifit Francis, 100. Wreftles with Francis, and is thrown by him, 101, *Note*. Has another interview with Charles at Gravelines, *ib*. Charles offers to fubmit his differences with Francis to his arbitration, *ib*. Publifhes a treatife on the Seven Sacraments, againft Martin Luther, 166. Obtains of the Pope the title of *Defender of the Faith*, 167. Takes part with Charles againft Francis, 169. Sends Wolfey to negociate an accommodation between the Emperor and Francis, 180. Concludes a league with Charles againft Francis, 182. His avowed reafons for this treaty, *ib*. His private motives, 183. Declares war againft Francis, 197. Is vifited by Charles, 198. Makes defcents upon the coaft of France, 199. Advances with an army into Picardy, *ib*. Obliged to retire by the Duke de Vendome, 200. Enters into a treaty with the Emperor and Charles Duke of Bourbon, 252, 253. How he raifed fupplies for his wars beyond the grants of his parliament, 261. Sends the Duke of Suffolk to invade Picardy, who penetrates almoft to Paris, but is driven back, *ib*. Engages to affift Charles in an invafion of Provence, 280. Caufes of his not fupporting the Imperialifts, 282, 283. Effects of the battle of Pavia, and captivity of Francis, on him, 301. Particulars of his embaffy to Charles, 303. Concludes a defenfive alliance with France, 310. Is declared Protector of the league of Cognac againft the Emperor, 345. His motives for affifting the Pope againft the Emperor, III. 2. Enters into a league with Francis, and renounces the Englifh claim to the crown of France, 4. Declares war againft the Emperor, 13. Concludes a truce with the governefs of the Low Countries, 19. Projects his divorce from Catharine of Aragon, 34. Motives which withheld the Pope from granting it, 35. Acquiefces

INDEX.

quiefces in the peace of Cambray, 36. Sends a supply of money to the Proteftant league in Germany, 55. Procures his marriage to be annulled by Cranmer archbifhop of Canterbury, 68. The divorce reverfed by the Pope under penalty of excommunication, 69. Renounces the Papal fupremacy, 70. Refufes to acknowledge any council called by the Pope, 88. Oppofes James V. of Scotland marrying Mary of Guife, 159. His difgufts with Francis and intercourfe with the Emperor, 160. Concludes a league with Charles, 245. Makes war with Scotland, 246. Particulars of his treaty with Charles, *ib.* Invades France, and invefts Boulogne, 274. Refufes the Emperor's plan of operations, 279. Is deferted by the Emperor, 284. Takes Boulogne, *ib.* His haughty propofals to Francis, *ib.* Peace of Campe, 334. Is fucceeded by his fon Edward VI. 390. A review of his policy, IV. 315.

Hertford, earl of, plunders and burns Edinburgh, III. 274. Joins Henry after, in his invafions of France, *ib.*

Heffe, the Landgrave of, procures the reftoration of his kinfman, Ulric Duke of Wurtemberg, III. 85. His views compared with thofe of the Elector of Saxony, 305. The Emperor's deceitful profeffions to him, 315. Quiets the apprehenfions of the Proteftant league with regard to the Emperor, *ib.* Is appointed joint commander of the army of the league with the Elector of Saxony, 343. Their characters compared, *ib.* Urges an attack of the Emperor, but is oppofed by the Elector, 348. His letter to Maurice Duke of Saxony, 357. The army of the league difperfe, 361. Is reduced to accept harfh terms from Charles, 416. His humiliating reception by the Emperor, 419. Is detained in confinement, 421. His offers of fubmiffion flighted by the Emperor, 452. Is carried by the Emperor with him into the Netherlands, 456. Renews his endeavours for liberty, IV. 22. Charles releafes arbitrarily the Elector of Brandenburgh, and Maurice, from their engage-

INDEX.

engagements to him, 23. Obtains his liberty by the treaty of Paſſau, 91. Is arreſted by the Queen of Hungary, but freed by the Emperor, 98. The effects of his confinement on him, 99.

Heuterus, his account of Lewis XII. ſhewn to contradict the relations given by Bellay and other French hiſtorians of the education of Charles V. II. 27, *Note*.

Holy Junta. See *Junta*.

Holy League, againſt the Emperor Charles V. formed at Cognac, under the protection of Henry VIII. of England, II. 345, 346.

Horuc, a potter's ſon of Leſbos, commences pirate, with his brother Hayradin, III. 91. See *Barbaroſſa*.

Hungary, is invaded by Solyman the Magnificent, and its King Lewis II. killed, II. 373. His ſucceſſes, and the number of priſoners carried away, *ib*. The archduke Ferdinand elected King of, together with Bohemia, 374. John Zapol Scæpius wreſts it from Ferdinand, III. 215. Stephen ſucceeds on the death of his father John, 216. Is treacherouſly ſeized by Solyman, 219. See *Iſabella* and *Martinuzzi*.

I

James V. of Scotland levies troops to aſſiſt Francis in Provence, but his intention fruſtrated, III. 158. His negociations for marriage with Francis's daughter, 159. Marries Mary of Guiſe, *ib*. Dies, and leaves Mary his infant-daughter to ſucceed him, 246. See *Mary*.

Jeſuits, the order of, by whom founded, II. 176. Character of that order, *ib*. Character of Ignatio Loyola their founder, III. 190. The order confirmed by the Pope, *ib*. An examination into the conſtitution of the order, 191. Office and power of their general, 193. The rapid progreſs of the order, 197. Engage in trade, and eſtabliſh an empire in South America, 199. Bad tendency of the order, 201. Are reſponſible for moſt of the pernicious effects of Popery ſince their inſtitution, 202. Advantages reſulting from their inſtitution, *ib*. Civilize

the

INDEX.

the natives of Paraguay, 203. Their precautions for the independency of their empire there, 205. How the particulars of their government and institution came to be disclosed, 208. Summary of their character, 209.

Indulgences, in the Romish church, the doctrine of, explained, II. 105. By whom first invented, 106. Martin Luther preaches against them, 111. Writes against them to Albert Elector of Mentz, *ib.* A bull issued in favour of, 123. The sale of, opposed in Switzerland by Zuinglius, 125.

Infantedo, Duke of, his haughty resentment of a casual blow on his horse, III. 179. Is protected by the Constable of Castile, *ib.*

Innocent, a young domestic of Cardinal di Monte, obtains his Cardinal's hat on his election to the Papacy, IV. 7.

Interim, a system of theology so called, prepared by order of the Emperor Charles V. for the use of Germany, III. 445. Is disapproved of, both by Protestants and Papists, 447.

Investitures, usurpations of the Romish clergy in Germany, during the disputes between the Emperors and Popes, concerning, II. 141.

Joanna, daughter of Ferdinand, and mother of Charles V. visits Spain with her husband Philip Archduke of Austria, II. 3. Is slighted by her husband, 4. Her character, *ib.* Is abruptly left in Spain by her husband, 5. Sinks into melancholy on the occasion, and is delivered of her second son Ferdinand, *ib.* Her letter of consent to her father's regency of Castile intercepted, and herself confined, 11. Made joint regent of Castile with Ferdinand and Philip, by the treaty of Salamanca, 14. Sets out for Spain with Philip, are driven on the coast of England, and detained three months by Henry VII. 15. Acknowledged Queen by the Cortes, 17. Her tenderness to her husband in his sickness, and extraordinary attachment to his body when dead, 18. Is incapable of government, 19. Her son Charles assumes the crown, 36. The Cortes acknowledge her son King,

INDEX.

King, with a reservation in her favour, 56. Her reception of Padilla the chief of the Spanish malecontents, 212. The Holy Junta removed to Tordesillas, the place of her residence, 213. Relapses into her former melancholy, *ib*. The proceedings of the Holy Junta carried on in her name, 214. Is seized by the Conde de Haro, 225. Dies, after near fifty years confinement, IV. 207.

John Zapol Scæpius, by the assistance of Sultan Solyman, establishes himself in the kingdom of Hungary, III. 215. Leaves the kingdom to his son Stephen, 216. See *Hungary, Isabella*, and *Martinuzzi*.

Isabella, daughter of John II. of Castile, and wife of Ferdinand King of Aragon, her history, II. 2. Her concern at the Archduke Philip's treatment of her daughter Joanna, 4. Her death and character, 7. Appoints Ferdinand regent of Castile, under restrictions, *ib*.

——— daughter to Sigismund King of Poland, married to John King of Hungary, III. 216. Her character, 217. Is treacherously carried, with her infant son, into Transylvania by Sultan Solyman, 219. The government of this province and the education of her son committed to her jointly with Martinuzzi, IV. 46. Is jealous of Martinuzzi's influence, and courts the Turks, *ib*. Is prevailed on to resign Transylvania to Ferdinand, 48. Retires to Silesia, 49. Recovers possession of Transylvania, 128.

——— of Portugal, married to the Emperor Charles V. II. 330.

Italy, consequences of the league between Pope Leo X. and the Emperor Charles V. to, II. 184. The characters of the Italians, Spaniards, and French, contrasted, *ib*. State of, at the accession of Clement VII. to the Papacy, 263. Views of the Italian States with respect to the Emperor and Francis on the expulsion of the French from Genoa and the Milanese, 279. Their apprehensions on the battle of Pavia and captivity of Francis, 304. The principal States join in the Holy league against the Emperor, 345. Are disgusted at the tardiness of Francis, 352.

A view

INDEX.

A view of the Ghibeline faction, 353. Sentiments of the States of, on the peace of Cambray, III. 33. Is visited by the Emperor Charles, 36. The motives of his moderation toward the States of, 38. A league among the states of, formed by Charles, 63. Placentia granted to Octavio Farnese by Philip II. of Spain, IV. 257. The investiture of Siena given by Philip to Cosmo di Medici, 360. The consequence of these grants, 361.

Junta, Holy, a view of the confederacy in Spain, so termed, II. 211. The authority of Adrian disclaimed by, 212. Removed to Tordesillas, where Queen Joanna resided, 213. Their proceedings carried on in the name of Joanna, *ib*. Receives letters from Charles to lay down their arms, with promises of pardon, 215. Remonstrance of grievances drawn up by, 216. The particulars of this remonstrance, 217. Remarks on the spirit of it, 221. Are intimidated from presenting it to Charles, 222. Propose to deprive Charles of his royalty during the life of Joanna, *ib*. Take the field, 223. Character of their army, *ib*. The Queen seized by the Conde de Haro, 225. How they obtained money to support their army, 227. Lose time in negociating with the nobles, 228. Propose to make their peace with Charles at the expence of the nobles, 230. Their irresolute conduct, 231. Their army defeated by Haro, and Padilla taken prisoner, 232. Padilla executed, 233. His letters to his wife, and the city of Todelo, 234, *Note*. The ruin of the confederacy, 235.

Julius II. Pope, observations on the pontificate of, II. 136.

—— III. Pope, his character, IV. 6. Bestows his Cardinal's hat infamously, 7. Is averse to the calling a council, 8. Summons one at Trent, 9. Asserts his supreme authority peremptorily in the bull for it, 20. Repents confirming Octavio Farnese in Parma, 29. Requires Octavio to relinquish his alliance with France, 31. The manner of his death, 176.

La

INDEX.

L

La Chau, a Flemish gentleman, associated by Charles V. with Cardinal Ximenes in the regency of Castile, II. 44.

Landrecy, siege of, by the Emperor Charles V. III. 251. Is abandoned by him, 252.

Lannoy, mortgages the revenues of Naples, to supply the exigencies of the Emperor, II. 287. Francis surrenders himself prisoner to him at the battle of Pavia, 296. His cautious disposal of him, 297. Delivers him up in pursuance of the treaty of Madrid, and receives the Duke of Orleans and the Dauphin, as hostages in exchange, 330. Is sent ambassador to Francis to require his fulfilment of the treaty of, 348. Concludes a treaty with the Pope, 362. Marches to join the Imperialists at Rome, where the troops refuse to obey him, III. 5.

Lanuza, Don John de, made viceroy of Aragon, on the departure of Charles V. for Germany, II. 86. Composes the disturbances there, 242.

Lavagna, John Lewis Fiesco, count of, his character, III. 372. Meditates subverting the government of Genoa, 373. His preparations, 374. His artful method of assembling his adherents, 376. His exhortation to them, 377. His interview with his wife, 378. Sallies forth, 380. Andrew Doria escapes, 381. Deputies sent to know his terms, *ib*. Is drowned, 382. His brother's vanity ruins their design, *ib*. See *Fiesco*.

Lautrec, Odet de Foix, marechal de, the French governor of Milan, his character, II. 185. Alienates the affections of the Milanese from the French, *ib*. Invests Reggio, but is repulsed by Guicciardini the historian, then governor, 186. Is excommunicated by the Pope, *ib*. The money for paying his troops seized by Louise of Savoy, 188. Is left by his Swiss troops, 189. Is driven out of the Milanese territories, 191. A new body of Swiss under him insist on giving battle to the Imperialists, who defeat him, 195. The Swiss leave him, *ib*.

Retires

INDEX.

Retires into France with the residue of his troops, 196. Delivers up the Dauphin and Duke of Orleans, in exchange for Francis I. as hostages for the performance of the treaty of Madrid, 329. Is appointed generalissimo of the league against the Emperor, III. 6. His successes in Italy, 7. Motives which withheld him from subduing the Milanese, 8. Obliges the Prince of Orange to retire to Naples, 16. Blockades Naples, 17. His army wasted, and himself killed by the pestilence, 23.

Learning, the revival of, favourable to the reformation of religion, II. 154.

Leipsic, a public disputation held there by Martin Luther, and Eccius, on the validity of the Papal authority, II. 125.

Leo X. Pope of Rome, his character, II. 70. His apprehensions on the election of an Emperor of Germany, at the death of Maximilian, 71. His counsel to the German Princes, *ib*. Grants Charles V. a tenth of all ecclesiastical benefices in Castile, 80. Lays Castile under an interdict, but takes it off at the instance of Charles, 81. His conduct on the prospect of war between Charles and Francis, 92. Situation of the Papacy at his accession, and his views of policy, 105. His inattention to Martin Luther's controversy with the Dominicans, concerning Indulgences, 116. Is instigated against him, and summons him to Rome, *ib*. Desires the Elector of Saxony not to protect him, *ib*. Is prevailed on to permit Luther's doctrines to be examined in Germany, 117. Cardinal Cajetan appointed to try him, *ib*. Issues a bull in favour of Indulgences, 123. A suspension of proceedings against Luther, and why, 124. Publishes a bull of excommunication against him, 127. The political views of his conduct between Charles and Francis, 170. Concludes a treaty with Francis, 171. Concludes a treaty also with Charles, 172. The conditions of the treaty with Charles, 173. Its consequences to Italy, 184. Is disappointed in a scheme formed by Moronè, chancellor of Milan, for attacking

Vol. IV.   C c

INDEX.

ing that dutchy, 185. Excommunicates Marechal de Foix for his attack of Reggio, and declares againſt France, 186. Takes a body of Swiſs into pay, *ib.* The French driven out of the Milaneſe, 191. He dies, *ib.* The ſpirit of the confederacy broken by his death, *ib.*

L'Eſparre, Foix de, cammands the French troops in Navarre for Henry D'Albert, II. 175. Reduces that kingdom, *ib.* His imprudent progreſs into Caſtile, 176. Is taken priſoner by the Spaniards, and the French driven out of Navarre, 177.

Leonard, Father, forms a ſcheme of betraying Metz to the Imperialiſts, IV. 167. Introduces ſoldiers clad like friars, 168. Is detected, 170. Is murdered by his monks, 171.

Leveſque, Don, his account of the motives which induced the Emperor Charles V. to reſign his hereditary dominions, IV. 205. *Note.*

Lewis II. King of Hungary and Bohemia, his character, II. 373. Is invaded and killed by Solyman the Magnificent, *ib.*

—— XII. King of France, receives homage of the Archduke Philip, for the earldom of Flanders, II. 3. Concludes a treaty with him, while at war with Ferdinand of Aragon, 6. Beſtows his niece, Germain de Foix, on Ferdinand, and concludes a peace with him, 13. Loſes the confidence of Philip on that occaſion, 27. *Note.* Beſtows his eldeſt daughter, already betrothed to Charles V. on the count of Angoulême, *ib.*

Leyva, Antonio de, defends Pavia for the Emperor againſt Francis, II. 288. His vigorous defence, 289. Sallies out at the battle of Pavia, and contributes to the defeat of Francis, 295. Is left governor of Milan by the Duke of Bourbon, 359. Defeats the forces there, III. 26. Is appointed generaliſſimo of the Italian league, 63. Directs the operations of the invaſion of France, under the Emperor, 129. Dies, 138.

Literature, its obligations to the order of Jeſuits, III. 202.

Lorenzo

INDEX.

Lorenzo di Medici. See *Medici*.

Louise of Savoy, mother of Francis I. of France, her character, II. 187, 188. Her motives for seizing the money appointed for payment of Marechal Lautrec's troops, 188. Cause of her aversion to the house of Bourbon, 250. Her advances toward a marriage with Charles Duke of Bourbon, rejected by him, 251, 252. Determines to ruin him, 252. Instigate a law-suit against him for his estates, *ib.* Goes to dissuade Francis from his intended invasion of the Milanese, who will not wait for her, 284. Is appointed regent during his absence, 285. Her prudent conduct on the defeat of Pavia, and captivity of her son Francis, 300. Concludes a defensive alliance with Henry VIII. 310. Ratifies the treaty of Madrid for the recovery of her son's liberty, 328. Undertakes with Margaret of Savoy to accommodate the differences between the Emperor and Francis, III. 28. Articles of the peace of Cambray, 30.

Loyola, Ignatio, commands the castle of Pampeluna in Navarre, and is wounded in its defence, II. 175. His enthusiastic turn of mind, 176. The founder of the society of Jesuits, *ib.* Prevails on the Pope to establish the order, III. 190. An examination into the constitution of the order, 191. Office and power of the general, 193. The rapid progress of the order, 197. See *Jesuits*.

Lorrain, Cardinal of, persuades Henry II. of France, to accept the offered alliance with Pope Paul IV. and is sent to Rome to negociate it, IV. 199. His imprudent behaviour towards the duchess of Valentinois, 278.

Lunenburgh, Duke of, avows the opinions of Luther, II. 270.

Luther, Martin, the happy consequences of the opinions propagated by him, II. 104. Attacks Indulgences, 109. His birth and education, *ib.* Chosen philosophical professor at the university of Wittemberg, 110. Inveighs against the publishers of Indulgences, 111. Writes to Albert Elector of Mentz against them, *ib.* Composes theses against

INDEX.

Indulgences, 112. Is supported by the Augustinians, and encouraged by Frederick Elector of Saxony, 113. Is summoned to Rome by Pope Leo, 116. Obtains of the Pope leave to have his doctrines examined in Germany, 117. Appears before Cardinal Cajetan at Augsburg, 118. His resolute reply to the peremptory order of Cajetan, to retract his principles, 119. Withdraws from Augsburg, and appeals from the Pope ill-informed, to the Pope when better informed, concerning him, 120. Appeals to a general council, 122. The death of Maximilian, how of service to him, 123. Questions the Papal authority in a public disputation, 125. His opinions condemned by the universities of Cologne and Louvain, 126. A bull of excommunication published against him, 127. Pronounces the Pope to be Antichrist, and burns the bull, 128. Reflections on the conduct of the court of Rome toward him, 130. Reflections on his conduct, 132. Causes which contributed to favour his opposition to the church of Rome, 134. Particularly the art of printing, 153. And the revival of learning, 154. He is summoned to appear at the diet of Worms, 162. A safe-conduct granted him thither, *ib.* His reception there, 163. Refuses to retract his opinions, *ib.* Departs, 164. An edict published against him, *ib.* He is seized and concealed at Wartburg, *ib.* Progress of his doctrines, 165. The university of Paris publishes a decree against him, 166. Wrote against by Henry VIII. of England, *ib.* Answers both, 167. Withdraws from his retreat to check the inconsiderate zeal of Carlostadius, 267, 268. Undertakes a translation of the Bible, 268. His doctrines avowed by several of the German Princes, 269. His moderate and prudent conduct, 340. Marries Catherine a Boria, a nun, *ib.* The great progress of his doctrines among the Germanic States, III. 42. Encourages the Protestants dispirited by the Emperor's decree against him, 50. His concern at the practices of the Anabaptists at Munster, 81. Is invited to Leipsick, by Henry Duke

INDEX.

of Saxony, 167. His opinion of Gropper's treatise to unite the Proteſtants and Catholics, 212. Dies, 309. Summary of his character, 310. Extract from his laſt will, 314. *Note.* See *Proteſtants.* A view of the extraordinary effects of his revolt from the church of Rome, on that court, and on Europe in general, IV. 320.

Luxemburg, invaded by Robert de la Marck, lord of Bouillon, II. 178. Invaded and over-run by the Duke of Orleans, III. 240. Is again invaded by Francis, 250.

M

Madrid, treaty of, between the Emperor Charles V. and his priſoner Francis I. King of France, II. 324, 325. Sentiments of the public with regard to this treaty, 326.

Magdeburg, the city of, refuſes to admit the *Interim* enforced by Charles V. and prepares for defence, IV. 18. Maurice Elector of Saxony appointed to reduce it, 19. Is put under the ban of the Empire, 36. The territories of, invaded by George of Mecklenburg, *ib.* The inhabitants defeated in a ſally, 37. Maurice of Saxony arrives and beſieges the city, 38. Surrenders, 39. The ſenate elects Maurice their burgrave, 40.

Mahmed, King of Tunis, hiſtory of his ſons, III. 94.

Majorca, an inſurrection there, II. 242. Which is quelled with difficulty, *ib.* The moderation of Charles towards the inſurgents, on his arrival in Spain, 243.

Majeſty, the appellation of, aſſumed by Charles V. on his election to the Imperial crown, and taken by all the other monarchs of Europe, II. 79.

Malines, council of, an account of, III. 176.

Malta, the iſland of, granted by the Emperor Charles V. to the knights of St. John, expelled from Rhodes by the Turks, II. 202.

Mamalukes, extirpated by Sultan Selim II. II. 65.

Mammelukes,

INDEX.

Mammelukes, a faction in Geneva, so termed, some account of, III. 118.

Manuel, Don John, Ferdinand's ambassador at the Imperial court, pays his court to the archduke Philip on Queen Isabella's death, II. 10. Intercepts Joanna's letter of consent to Ferdinand's regency of Castile, 11. Negociates a treaty between Ferdinand and Philip, 14. Declares for Maximilian's regency on Philip's death, 20. Is made Imperial ambassador at Rome, and concludes an alliance between Charles V. and Leo X. 172. The conditions of the treaty, 173. Procures Adrian of Utrecht to be elected Pope, 193.

Marcellus II. Pope, his character, IV. 188. Dies, 189.

Marciano, battle of, between Peter Strozzi and the marquis de Marignano, IV. 158.

Margaret of Austria, and Dowager of Savoy, aunt to Charles V. undertakes with Louise, mother of Francis I. of France, to accommodate the differences between those two monarchs, III. 28. Articles of the peace of Cambray, 30.

Marignano, marquis of, appointed commander of the Florentine army, acting against the French, IV. 156. Defeats the French army under Peter Strozzi, 159. Lays siege to Siena, *ib*. Converts the siege into a blockade, 161. Siena surrenders, *ib*. Reduces Porto Ercole, 164. His troops ordered into Piedmont by the Emperor, *ib*.

Marck, Robert de la, Lord of Bouillon, declares war against the Emperor Charles V. II. 177. Ravages Luxemburg with French troops, 178. Is commanded to disband his troops by Francis, *ib*. His territories reduced by the Emperor, 179.

Marseilles, besieged by the Imperialists, II. 281. Rescued by Francis, 282. Interview and treaty there between the Pope and Francis, III. 67.

Martinuzzi, bishop of Waradin, is appointed guardian to Stephen King of Hungary, III. 216. His character, 217. Solicits the assistance of Sultan Solyman against Ferdinand, 218. Solyman seizes

the

INDEX.

the kingdom, 219. Is appointed to the government of Tranſylvania and the education of the young King, jointly with the Queen, IV. 46. Negotiates with Ferdinand, 47. Prevails with the Queen to reſign Tranſylvania to Ferdinand, 48. Is appointed governor of Tranſylvania, and made a Cardinal, 49. Is aſſaſſinated by Ferdinand's order, 51.

Martyr, Peter, his authority cited in proof of the extortions of the Flemiſh miniſters of Charles V, II. 58.

Mary of Burgundy, contracted to Lewis XII. of France, but married to the Emperor Maximilian, II. 2.

Mary of England, her acceſſion, IV. 139. Receives propoſals from the Emperor Charles V. of marrying his ſon Philip, 140. The Engliſh averſe to this union, *ib*. The Houſe of Commons remonſtrates againſt the match, 141. The articles of marriage, 142. The marriage ratified by parliament and completed, 145. Re-eſtabliſhes the Romiſh religion, 146. Perſecutes the Reformers, *ib*. Invites Charles to England on his reſignation and paſſage to Spain, which he declines, 232. Is engaged by Philip to aſſiſt him in his war againſt France, 243. Levies money by her prerogative to carry on the war, *ib*. Her neglect in the ſecurity of Calais, 264. Calais inveſted and taken by the Duke of Guiſe, 265. Dies, 290.

Mary, daughter of James V. of Scotland, ſucceeds to the crown an infant, III. 245. Is contracted to the Dauphin of France, 440. Is educated at the court of France, IV. 31. 271. The marriage completed, *ib*. Aſſumes the title and arms of England on the death of Mary, 293.

Matthias, John, a baker, becomes a leader of the Anabaptiſts at Munſter, III. 74. Seizes the city, and eſtabliſhes a new form of government there, 75. Repulſes the Biſhop of Munſter, 78. Is killed, *ib*. See *Boccold* and *Anabaptiſts*.

Maurice, Duke of Saxony, his motives for not acceding to the Proteſtant league of Smalkalde, III. 255.

INDEX.

Marches to the assistance of Ferdinand in Hungary, 256. His difference with his cousin the Elector, 257. His conduct at the diet of Worms, 292. Joins the Emperor against the Protestants, 337. His motives, 353. His insidious conduct toward the Elector, 354. Seizes the electorate of Saxony, 358. Saxony recovered by the Elector, 366. His ineffectual endeavours to reduce Wittemberg for the Emperor, 408. Obtains possession of the electorate, 414. Is formally invested at the diet of Augsburg, 447. Becomes dissatisfied with the Emperor, IV. 10. His motives to discontent explained, 11. His address and caution in his conduct, 13. Enforces the *Interim* in his territories, 14. Makes, nevertheless, professions of his attachment to the Reformation, 15. Undertakes to reduce Magdeburg to submit to the *Interim*, 16. Protests against the Council of Trent, 17. Is commissioned by the Emperor to reduce Magdeburg, 19. Joins George of Mecklenburg before Magdeburg, 36. The city capitulates, 39. Begins to intrigue with Count Mansfeldt, *ib*. Is elected Burgrave of Magdeburg, 40. Dismisses his troops, 42. His address in amusing the Emperor, 43. Makes an alliance with Henry II. of France, to make war on the Emperor, 53. Makes a formal requisition of the Landgrave's liberty, 56. Joins his troops, and publishes a manifesto, 63. Takes possession of Augsburg and other cities, 66. An ineffectual negotiation with Charles, 67. Defeats a body of the Emperor's troops, 70. Takes the castle of Ehrenburg, *ib*. Is retarded by a mutiny in his troops, 71. Enters Inspruck, and narrowly misses taking Charles, 72. A negotiation between him and Ferdinand, 82. Besieges Francfort on the Main, 89. His inducements to an accommodation, 91. Signs a treaty with the Emperor at Passau, *ib*. Reflections on his conduct in this war, 92. Marches into Hungary to oppose the Turks, 97. Is placed at the head of the league against Albert of Brandenburgh, 119. Defeats Albert, but is killed in the battle, 120. His character, 121. Is succeeded by his brother Auguſtus, 123.

Maximilian, Emperor of Germany, claims the regency of Caſtile on his ſon Philip's death, II. 19. Is ſupported in his claim by Don John Manuel, 20. Loſes it, 22. Obtains the government of the Low Countries by the death of Philip, 26. Appoints William de Croy, Lord of Chievres, to ſuperintend the education of his grandſon Charles, 27. Concludes a peace with France and Venice, 50. Dies, 62. State of Europe at this period, *ib.* His endeavours to ſecure the Imperial crown to his grandſon Charles, 63. How obſtructed, *ib.*

Mecklenburg, George of, invades the territories of Magdeburg for the Emperor, IV. 36. Defeats the Magdeburgers, who ſally out on him, 37. Is joined by Maurice of Saxony, who aſſumes the ſupreme command, *ib.*

Medecino, John James. See *Marignano*.

Medici, Alexander, reſtored to the dominions of Florence, by the Emperor Charles, III. 41. Is aſſaſſinated, 154.

Medici, Cardinal de, elected Pope, and aſſumes the title of Clement VII. II. 258. See *Clement* VII.

Medici, Catherine di, is married to the Duke of Orleans, III. 67. Is conjectured, by the Emperor Charles V. to have poiſoned the Dauphin, 142.

Medici, Coſmo de, made Duke of Florence, III. 156. Is ſupported by the Emperor, and defeats the partizans of Lorenzo, 157. Aſſerts his independency againſt the Emperor, IV. 112. Offers to reduce Siena for the Emperor, 154. Enters into a war with France, 155. See *Marignano*. His addreſs in procuring the inveſtiture of Siena from Phillip II. of Spain, 258. It is granted to him, 260.

Medici, Lorenzo de, aſſaſſinates his kinſman Alexander, III. 155. Flies, *ib.* Attempts to oppoſe Coſmo, but is defeated, 156.

Medina del Campo, the inhabitants of, refuſe to let Fonſeca take the military ſtores there for the ſiege of the inſurgents in Segovia, II. 207. The town almoſt

INDEX.

almoft bernt by Fonseca, 208. The inhabitants repulse him, *ib*. Surrenders after the battle of Villalar, and diffolution of the Holy Junta, 235.

Melancthon, imbibes the opinions of Martin Luther, II. 130. Is employed to draw up a confeffion of faith by the Proteftant Princes at the diet of Augfburg, III. 48. Is dejected by the Emperor's decree againft the Proteftants, but comforted by Luther, 51. Is invited to Paris by Francis, 111. His conference with Eckius, 210. Is prevailed on to favour the *Interim* enforced by the Emperor, IV. 14.

Melito, Conde de, made Viceroy of Valencia, on the departure of Charles V. for Germany, II. 86. Appointed to command the troops of the Nobles againft the Germanada, 241. Defeated by them in feveral actions, *ib*. Deftroys the affociation, *ib*.

Mentz, Archbifhop of, artfully declares before the Emperor, the diet of Augfburg's acceptance of the *Interim*, without being authorifed by it, III. 445.

Merville, a Milanefe gentleman, employed as envoy from Francis I. to Francis Sforza, Duke of Milan, his fate, III. 109.

Metz, feized by Montmorency the French general, IV. 68. The Duke of Guife made Governor of, 103. Is befieged by the Emperor, 105. The Emperor defifts, and retires in a diftreffed condition, 109. A fcheme formed by Father Leonard to betray the city to the Imperialifts, 167. The confpiracy detected by the Governor, 169. Leonard murdered by his monks, and his affociates executed, 171.

Mezieres, in France, befieged by the Imperialifts, II. 179. Gallant defence of, by the Chevalier Bayard, 180. The fiege raifed, *ib*.

Milan, Marechal de Foix, appointed to be the French Governor of, II. 185. His character, *ib*. The Milanefe alienated from the French by his oppreffions, *ib*. Invaded by the Ecclefiaftical troops under Profper Colonna, 187. The French driven out, 189. Oppreffed by the Imperial troops, 248. Invaded by the French, 256. Who are driven out by Colonna,

INDEX.

Colonna, 257. The Imperial troops there mutiny for pay, but are appeased by Morone, 264. Abandoned by the French, *ib.* Over-run again by Francis, who seizes the city, 286. The French retire on news of the battle of Pavia, 297. The investiture of, granted to Sforza, 311. Taken from him and granted to the Duke of Bourbon, 321. Disorders committed by the Imperial troops there, 345. Oppressive measures of Bourbon to supply his mutinous troops, 357. The French forces there defeated by Antonio de Leyva, III. 27. Is again granted by the Emperor to Sforza, 40. Death of Sforza, 121. The pretensions of Francis to that dutchy, *ib.* Is seized by the Emperor, 122. The Marquis del Guasto appointed Governor, 140.

Mohacz, battle of, between Solyman the Magnificent and the Hungarians, II. 373.

Monastic orders, enquiry into the fundamental principles of, III. 191. Peculiar constitution of the order of Jesuits, 193.

Moncado, Don Hugo di, the Imperial Ambassador at Rome, his intrigues with Cardinal Colonna, against Pope Clement II. 354. Reduces the Pope to an accommodation, 355. Is defeated and killed by Andrew Doria in a naval engagement before the harbour of Naples, III. 17.

Monluc, is sent by the Count d'Enguien to Francis for permission to give battle to the Marquis del Guasto, III. 268. Obtains his suit by his spirited arguments, 269. Commands in Siena, when besieged by the Marquis de Marignano, IV. 160. His vigorous defence, *ib.* Is reduced by famine, and capitulates, 161.

Monte Alcino, numbers of the citizens of Siena retire thither after the reduction of that city by the Florentines, and establish a free government there, IV. 162.

Montecuculi, Count of, accused and tortured for poisoning the Dauphin, charges the Emperor with instigating it, III. 141.

Mont-

INDEX.

Montmorency, marechal, his character, III. 133. Francis adopts his plan for resisting the Emperor, and commits the execution to him, 134. His precautions, *ib*. His troops despise his conduct, 137. Observations on his operations, 139. Is disgraced, 239. Conducts the army of Henry II. to join Maurice of Saxony, and seizes Metz, IV. 68. Dissuades Henry from accepting the offered alliance with Pope Paul IV. IV. 197. Commands the French army against the Duke of Savoy, 246. Detaches D'Andelot to relieve St. Quintin, *ib*. Exposes himself imprudently to an action, and is defeated, 247. Is taken prisoner, 248. Negociates a peace between Philip and Henry, 279. Returns to France, and is highly honoured by Henry, 280. His assiduity in forwarding the negociations, 294. His expedient for promoting the treaty of Chateau Cambresis, 398.

Montpelier, a fruitless conference held there for the restitution of the kingdom of Navarre, II. 60.

Morone, Jerome, chancellor of Milan, his character, II. 185. Retires from the French exactions in Milan to Francis Sforza, *ib*. His intrigues, how rendered abortive, 186. Quiets the mutiny of the Imperial troops in Milan, 264. Is disgusted with the behaviour of Charles, 311. Intrigues against the Emperor with Pescara, 313. Is betrayed to the Emperor by Pescara, 315. Is arrested at his visit to Pescara, 317. Is set at liberty by the Duke of Bourbon, and becomes his confident, 357.

Mouson in France, taken by the Imperialists, II. 179. Retaken by Francis, 180.

Mulhausen, battle of, between the Emperor Charles V. and the Elector of Saxony, III. 404.

Muley Hascen, King of Tunis, his inhuman treatment of his father and brothers, III. 95. Is expelled by Barbarossa, 96. Engages the Emperor Charles V. to restore him, 98. Is established again by the surrender of Tunis, 105. His treaty with Charles, *ib*.

Muncer,

INDEX.

Muncer, Thomas, a disciple of Luther, opposes him with fanatical notions, II. 336. Heads the insurrection of the peasants in Thuringia, 337. His extravagant schemes, *ib*. Is defeated and put to death, 339.

Munster, the first settlement of the Anabaptists in that city, III. 74. The city seized by them, 75. They establish a new form of government there, *ib*. Is called Mount Sion, 76. The bishop of, repulsed by them, 77. Is blockaded by the bishop, 82. The city taken, 83. See *Anabaptists*.

Murder, the prices of composition for, by the Romish clergy, II. 140.

Mustapha, the declared heir to Sultan Solyman the Magnificent, is invested with the administration of Diarbequir, IV. 132. His father rendered jealous of his popularity, by the arts of Roxalana, 133. Is strangled by his father's order, 137. His only son murdered, 138.

N

Naples, the revenues of, mortgaged by Lannoy to supply the Emperor in his exigencies, II. 287. Invaded by the French under the Duke of Albany, 291. Invaded by Pope Clement VII. 359. Treaty between the Pope and Lannoy viceroy of, 362. The prince of Orange retreats thither before Lautrec, III. 16. Is blockaded by Lautrec, 17. Sea engagement in the harbour of, between Andrew Doria and Moncada, *ib*. Causes which disappointed the French operations against, 18. Doria revolts, and opens the communication by sea again, 21. Oppressed by the Spanish viceroy Don Pedro de Toledo, becomes disaffected to the Emperor Charles V. IV. 115. Is harassed by a Turkish fleet, 116.

Nassau, Count of, invades Bouillon at the head of the Imperialists, II. 179. Invades France, takes Mouson, and besieges Mezieres, but is repulsed, *ib*.

Navarre, the kingdom of, unjustly acquired by Ferdinand of Aragon, II. 23. D'Albret's invasion of,
defeated

INDEX.

defeated by Cardinal Ximenes, 45. Its castles dismantled, except Pampeluna, which Ximenes strengthens, 46. Invaded by Francis I. in the name of Henry d'Albret, 175. Reduced by L'Esparre, the French general, *ib*. The French driven out by the Spaniards, and L'Esparre taken prisoner, 177.

Netherlands, the government of, first assumed by Charles V. II. 29. The Flemings averse to Charles's going to Spain, 51. Invaded by Francis I. King of France, 180. A truce concluded with, by Henry VIII. of England, III. 19. Invaded by Francis again, 144. A suspension of arms there, *ib*. An insurrection at Ghent, 173. See *Ghent*. Is once more invaded by Francis, 250. Resigned by the Emperor to his son Philip, IV. 208. A review of the alterations in, during the sixteenth century, 333, 334.

Nice, a truce for ten years concluded there between the Emperor and Francis, III. 151. Besieged by the French and Turks, 254.

Noyen, treaty of, between Charles V. and Francis I. of France, II. 50. The terms of, neglected by Charles, 90.

Nuremburgh, the city of, embraces the reformed religion, II. 269. Diet of, particulars of Pope Adrian's brief to, respecting the reformers, 270. The reply to, 271. Proposes a general council, 272. Presents a list of grievances to the Pope, 273. The recess, or edict of, 274. This diet of great advantage to the reformers, *ib*. Proceedings of a second diet there, 277. Recess of the diet, 278. An accommodation agreed to there, between the Emperor Charles V. and the Protestants, III. 57.

O

Oran, and other places in Barbary, annexed to the crown of Castile, by Ximenes, II. 23.

Orange, Phillibert de Chalons, Prince of, general of the Imperial army on the death of the Duke of

INDEX.

Bourbon, takes the castle of St. Angelo, and Pope Clement VII. prisoner, II. 371. Retires to Naples on the approach of Lautrec, III. 16. Takes his successor, the marquis de Saluces, prisoner at Aversa, 23.

Orleans, Duke of, delivered up to the Emperor Charles V. with the Dauphin, as hostages for the performance of the treaty of Madrid, II. 329. Is married to Catherine di Medici, III. 67. Becomes Dauphin by the death of his brother, 142. See *Dauphin*.

—— Duke of, brother to the former, commands the army appointed by Francis I. for the invasion of Luxembourg, III. 240. Is prompted by envy to abandon his conquests, and join his brother the Dauphin in Roussillon, 241. Dies, 296.

P

Pacheco, Donna Maria, wife to Don John de Padilla, her artful scheme to raise money to supply the army of the Holy Junta, II. 227. Her husband taken prisoner and executed, 233. His letter to her, *ib.* Note. Raises forces to revenge his death, 237. Is reduced, and retires to Portugal, 238.

Padilla, Don John de, his family and character, II. 204. Heads the insurrection at Toledo, *ib.* Routs the troops under Ronquillo, 207. Calls a convention of the malcontents at Avila, 211. Forms the confederacy called the Holy Junta, *ib.* Disclaims Adrian's authority, 212. Gets possession of Queen Joanna, *ib.* Removes the Holy Junta to Tordesillas, the place of her residence, 213. Sent with troops to Valladolid, and deprives Adrian of all power of government, 214. Is superseded in the command of the army of the Junta, by Don Pedro de Giron, 223. Is appointed commander at the resignation of Giron, 226. His army supplied with money by an expedient of his wife, 227. Besieges Torrelobaton, 230. Takes and plunders it, *ib.* Concludes a truce with the nobles, 231. Is wounded and taken prisoner

INDEX.

prisoner in an action with the Conde de Haro, 232. Is put to death, 233. His letter to his wife, *ib. Note.* His letter to the city of Toledo, 234. *Note.*

Palatinate, the Reformation established there by the Elector Frederick, III. 299.

Palatine, Count, ambassador from the diet at Francfort, brings Charles V. the offer of the Imperial crown, which he accepts, II. 80.

Pampeluna, castle of, in Navarre, its fortifications strengthened by Cardinal Ximenes, II. 46. Taken by L'Esparre, the French general for Henry D'Albret, 177. Retaken by the French, *ib.*

Papacy, how liable to be affected by the disposal of the Imperial crown, II. 71.

Paraguay, a sovereignty established there by the order of Jesuits, III. 204. The inhabitants of, civilized by them, *ib.* Precautions used by the Jesuits to preserve the independency of their empire there, 205.

Paris, a decree published by the university of, against Martin Luther the Reformer, II. 166. A decree of the parliament of, published against the Emperor Charles V. III. 143.

Parma, the dutchy of, confirmed to Octavio Farnese, by Pope Julius III. IV. 29. Is attacked by the Imperialists, and successfully protected by the French, 32.

Passau, a treaty concluded there between the Emperor Charles V. and Maurice of Saxony, IV. 91. Reflections on this peace, and the conduct of Maurice, 92.

Pavia, besieged by Francis I. of France, II. 288. Vigorously defended by Antonio de Leyva, 289. Battle of, between Francis and the Duke of Bourbon, 294. The Imperial troops in that city mutiny, 305.

Paul III. Pope, elected, III. 71. His character, *ib.* Proposes a general council to be held at Mantua, 88. Negociates personally between the Emperor and Francis, 149. Issues a bull for a council at Mantua, 161. Prorogues and transfers it to Vicenza, 163. A partial reformation of abuses by, 164. Summons

the

INDEX.

the council of Trent, 258. Prorogues it, 259. Summons it again, 287. Grants the dutchies of Parma and Placentia to his illegitimate son, 396. Deprives and excommunicates the electoral bishop of Cologne, 318. Presses the Emperor to declare against the Protestants, 319. Concludes an alliance with him against the Protestants, 325. Indiscreetly publishes this treaty, 326. His troops join the Emperor, 345. Recalls them, 368. Removes the council from Trent to Bologna, 433. Refuses the Emperor's request to carry the council back to Trent, 434. His resentment against the Emperor for the murder of his son Cardinal Farnese, 436. Is petitioned by the diet of Augsburg for the return of the council to Trent, 439. Eludes the complying with this request, 441. His sentiments of the *Interim*, published by Charles, 450. Dismisses the council of Bologna, 456. Annexes Parma and Placentia to the Holy See, IV. 2. Dies, 3. The manner of his death enquired into, 4.

Paul IV. Pope, elected, IV. 189. His character and history, 190. Founds the order of Theatines, 191. Is the principal occasion of establishing the Inquisition in the Papal territories, 192. Lays aside his austerity on his election, 193. His partiality to his nephews, *ib.* Is alienated from the Emperor by his nephews, 196. Makes overtures to an alliance with France, *ib.* Is enraged by the recess of the diet of Augsburg, 199. Signs a treaty with France, 202. Is included in the truce for five years, concluded between the Emperor and Henry, 216. His insidious artifices to defeat this truce, 219 Absolves Henry from his oath, and concludes a new treaty with him, 222. His violent proceedings against Philip, now King of Spain, 223. The Compagna Romana seized by the Duke d'Alva, 226. Concludes a truce with Alva, 227. Contrast between his conduct and that of Charles, 235. Renews his hostilities against Philip, 237. Is unprovided for military operations, 238. Is reduced to make peace with Philip, by the recall of the Duke

INDEX.

of Guife after the defeat of St. Quintin, 256. Receives an ambaſſador from the Emperor Ferdinand to notify his election, but refufes to fee him, or to acknowledge the Emperor, 257. Dies, 302.

Paulin, a French officer, fent ambaſſador from Francis I. to Sultan Solyman, III. 248. His fuccefsful negociations at the Porte, *ib.*

Pembroke, Earl of, fent by Queen Mary of England with a body of men to join the Spaniſh army in the Low Countries, IV. 243.

Perpignan, the capital of Roufillon, befieged by the Dauphin of France, III. 240. The fiege raifed, 241.

Pefcara, Marquis de, takes Milan by affault, II. 190. Drives Bonnivet back to France, 265. His generous care of the Chevalier Bayard, 266. Commands in the invafion of Provence, 281. Befieges Marfeilles, *ib.* His army retires toward Italy, on the appearance of the French troops, 282. Refigns Milan to the French, 286. Prevails on the Spaniſh troops not to murmur at prefent for their pay, 287. Contributes to the defeat of Francis at the battle of Pavia, 295. Is difgufted at Francis being taken to Spain without his concurrence, 312. His refentment inflamed by Moronè, 314. Betrays Moronè's defigns to the Emperor, 316. Arrefts Moronè, 317. Dies, 321.

Philip, Archduke of Auftria, and father of Charles V. vifits Spain, with his wife Joanna, II. 3. Does homage by the way to Lewis XII. of France for the earldom of Flanders, *ib.* His title to the crown acknowledged by the Cortes, *ib.* Is difgufted with the formality of the Spaniſh court, 4. Ferdinand becomes jealous of his power, *ib.* Slights his wife, *ib.* His abrupt departure from Spain, 5. Paſſes through France, and enters into a treaty with Lewis, 6. His fentiments on Ferdinand's obtaining the regency of Caftile, 9. Requires Ferdinand to retire to Aragon, and refign his regency of Caftile, 10. The regency of Caftile vefted jointly in him, Ferdinand, and Joanna, by the treaty of Salamanca, 14. Sets

out

INDEX.

out for Spain, and is driven on the coaſt of England, where he is detained three months by Henry VII. 15. Arrives at Corunna, *ib.* The Caſtilian nobility declare openly for him, *ib.* Ferdinand reſigns the regency of Caſtile to him, 16. Interview between them, *ib.* Acknowledged King of Caſtile by the Cortes, 17. Dies, *ib.* Joanna's extraordinary conduct in regard to his body, 18. See *Joanna*.

Philip, Prince, ſon to the Emperor Charles V. his right of ſucceſſion recogniſed by the Cortes of Aragon and Valencia, III. 243. Is acknowledged by the States of the Netherlands, 458. His deportment diſguſts the Flemings, 459. His character, IV. 26. Is married to Mary Queen of England, 142. 145. The Engliſh parliament jealous of him, 148. His father reſigns his hereditary dominions to him, 202. Is called by his father out of England, 208. The ceremony of inveſting him, *ib.* His father's addreſs to him, 211. Commiſſions Cardinal Granvelle to addreſs the aſſembly in his name, 212. Mary Queen Dowager of Hungary reſigns her regency, 213. The dominions of Spain reſigned to him, *ib.* His unpoliteneſs to the French ambaſſador Coligni, 217, *Note.* The Pope's violent proceedings againſt him, 223. His ſcruples concerning commencing hoſtilities againſt the Pope, 225. His ungrateful neglect in paying his father's penſion, 233. The Pope renews hoſtilities againſt him, 237. Aſſembles an army in the Low Countries againſt France, 241. Goes over to England to engage that kingdom in the war, *ib.* Viſits the camp at St. Quintin, after the victory, 250. Oppoſes the ſcheme of penetrating to Paris, and orders the ſiege of St. Quintin to be proſecuted, 251. St. Quintin taken by aſſault, 252. The ſmall advantages he reaped by theſe ſucceſſes, 254. Builds the Eſcurial in memory of the battle of St. Quintin, *ib.* Concludes a peace with the Pope, 256. Reſtores Placentia to Octavio Farneſe, 257. Grants the inveſtiture of Siena to Coſmo di Medici, 260. Enters into negoci-

INDEX.

negociations for peace with his prisoner Montmo-rency, 279. Death of Queen Mary, 290. Addresses her successor Elizabeth for marriage, 291. Elizabeth's motives for rejecting him, 293. Her evasive answer to him, 294. Supplants his son Don Carlos, and marries Henry's daughter Elizabeth, 298. Articles of the treaty of Chateau Cambresis, 299.

Phillibert, Emanuel, Duke of Savoy. See *Savoy*.

Phillipino, nephew to Andrew Doria, defeats Moncada, in a sea-engagement before the harbour of Naples, III. 17.

Piadena, Marquis de, invades Transylvania for Ferdinand, IV. 47. Misrepresents Cardinal Martinuzzi to Ferdinand, and obtains a commission to assassinate him, 51. Is forced to abandon Transylvania, 128.

Picardy, invaded by Henry VIII. II. 199. Henry forced by the Duke de Vendome to retire, 200. Invaded again under the Duke of Suffolk, 261. Who penetrates almost to Paris, but is driven back, 261, 262. Ineffectual invasion by the Imperialists, III. 140.

Placentia, the dutchy of, granted together with that of Parma by Pope Paul III. to his natural son, Cardinal Farnese, III. 296. Farnese assassinated there, 435. Is taken possession of by the Imperial troops, 436. Restored to Octavio Farnese, by Philip II. of Spain, IV. 257.

Pole, Cardinal, arrives in England with a legatine commission, IV. 146. Endeavours to mediate a peace between the Emperor and the King of France, without success, 172. Is recalled from the court of England by Pope Paul IV. 237.

Printing, its effects on the progress of the Reformation, II. 153.

Prague, its privileges abridged by Ferdinand King of Bohemia, III. 429.

Protestants, the derivation of the name, III. 45. Of whom they originally consisted, *ib*. A severe decree published against them by the Emperor, 49. They enter into a league, 50. See *Smalkalde*. Renew
their

INDEX.

their league, and apply to Francis King of France, and Henry VIII. of England, for protection, 54. Are secretly encouraged by Francis, 55. Receive a supply of money from Henry, 56. Terms of the pacification agreed to between them and the Emperor at Nuremburg, 57. Assist the Emperor against the Turks, 59. Their negociations with the Pope, relative to a general council, 61. Renew the league of Smalkalde for ten years, 89. The motives for refusing to assist the King of France against the Emperor, 113. Refuse to acknowledge the council summoned by the Pope at Mantua, 162. A conference between their principal divines and a deputation of Catholics, at Ratisbon, 210. This conference how rendered fruitless, 212. Obtain a private grant from Charles in their favour, 214. Drive the Duke of Brunswick from his dominions, 260. All rigorous edicts against them suspended by a recess of the diet of Spires, 264. Their remonstrances to Ferdinand at the diet of Worms, 290. Their inflexible adherence to the recess of Spires, *ib.* Disclaim all connection with the council of Trent, 291. Are strengthened by the accession of Frederick Elector Palatine, 299. Are alarmed at the proceedings of the Emperor, 303. 324. The Emperor leagues with the Pope against them, 326. Prepare to resist the Emperor, 331. Levy an army, 335. The operations of the army distracted by the joint commanders, 343. The army dispersed, 361. The Elector of Saxony reduced, 405. The Landgrave deceived by treaty, and confined, 420, 421. The Emperor's cruel treatment of him, 426. The *Interim*, a system of theology recommended by the Emperor to the diet at Augsburg, 445. Are promised protection by the Emperor at the council of Trent, IV. 20. The Emperor proceeds rigorously against them, 34. Their deputies obtain a safe-conduct from the Emperor, but are refused by the council, 44. Maurice of Saxony raises an army in their cause, 63. See *Maurice.* Treaty of Passau, 91. The Protestant Princes again unite to strengthen the

Pro-

INDEX.

Proteſtant intereſt, 179. Receſs of the diet of Augſburg on the ſubject of religion, 181. Why originally
averſe to the principles of toleration, 186.

Provence, is laid waſte by the Mareſchal Montmorency
on the approach of the Emperor Charles V. III. 134.
Is entered by the Emperor, 135. The diſaſtrous
retreat of the Emperor from, 138.

Pruſſia, when conquered by the Teutonic order, II.
341. Is erected into a dutchy, and finally into a
kingdom, and enjoyed by the houſe of Brandenburg, 342.

R

Ratiſbon, a conference between a deputation of Proteſtant and Catholic divines, before the Emperor
and diet there, III. 210. This conference how
rendered fruitleſs, 212. A diet opened there by the
Emperor, 321. The Catholic members of, aſſert
the authority of the council of Trent, 323. The
Proteſtants preſent a memorial againſt it, *ib.* The
Proteſtant deputies retire, 325.

Reformation in religion, the riſe of, explained, II. 104.
The diet at Worms called by Charles V. to check
the progreſs of, *ib.* Account of Martin Luther, the
Reformer, 109. Beginning of, in Switzerland by
Zuinglius, 125. State of, in Germany, at the arrival of Charles V. 129. Reflections on the conduct
of the court of Rome toward Luther, 130. And on
Luther's conduct, 132. Inquiry into the cauſes
which contributed to the progreſs of, 134. Obſer-
vations on the pontificate of Alexander VI. and
Julius II. 136. The immoral lives of the Romiſh
clergy, 137. The progreſs of, favoured by the invention of printing, 153. And the revival of learning, 154. The great progreſs of, in Germany,
269. Advantages derived to, from the diet at Nuremburgh, 274. Its tendency in favour of civil
liberty, 335. The diſſenſions between the Emperor
and the Pope, favourable to, 375. The great ſpread
of, among the German Princes, III. 42. The

INDEX.

confession of Augsburg drawn up by Melancthon, 48. Causes which led to that of England, 67. The excesses it gave rise to, 71. See *Protestants*, *Maurice*, and *Smalkalde*. Is established in Saxony, 167. The great alteration occasioned by, in the court of Rome, IV. 320. Contributed to improve both the morals and learning of the Romish church, 325.

Reggio, invested by the French, who are repulsed by the governor Guicciardini the historian, II. 186.

Remonstrance of grievances drawn up by the Holy Junta, the particulars of, II. 216, 217. Remarks on, 221.

Reverse, a deed so called, signed by the Archduke Ferdinand on being elected King of Bohemia, II. 374.

Rheggio, plundered and burnt by Barbarossa, III. 253.

Rhodes, the island of, besieged by Solyman the Magnificent, II. 201. Taken by him, 202. The island of Malta granted to the knights of, by the Emperor Charles V. *ib.*

Richlieu, Cardinal, his remarks on De Retz's history of Fiesco's conspiracy, III. 384. *Note.*

Rincon, the French ambassador at the Porte, the motives of his return to France, III. 235. Is murdered in his journey back to Constantinople, by order of the Imperial governor of the Milanese. 236.

Rome, reflections on the conduct of the court of, respecting the proceedings against Martin Luther, II. 131. The exorbitant wealth of the church of, previous to the reformation, 141. Venality of, 150. How it drained other countries of their wealth, 151. The city seized by Cardinal Colonna, and Pope Clement VII. besieged in the castle of St. Angelo, 354. The city taken by the Imperialists, and Bourbon killed, 355. Is plundered, *ib.* The great revolution in the court of, during the sixteenth century, III. 328. How affected by the revolt of Luther, 329. The spirit of its government changed by, 332.

Ronquillo, sent by Cardinal Adrian with troops to suppress the insurrection in Segovia, II. 207. Is routed by the insurgents, *ib.*

Roveré,

INDEX.

Roverè, Francesco Maria de, restored to his dutchy of Urbino by Pope Adrian, II. 246.

Roxalana, a Russian captive, becomes the favourite mistress of Sultan Solyman the Magnificent, IV. 129. Her only daughter married to Rustan the Grand Vizier, 130. Procures herself to be declared a free woman by the Sultan, 131. Is formally married to him, *ib*. Renders Solyman jealous of the virtues of his son Mustapha, 132. Mustapha strangled, 137.

Rustan, Grand Vizier to Solyman the Magnificent, is married to his daughter by Roxalana, IV. 130. Enters into Roxalana's scheme to ruin Solyman's son Mustapha, *ib*. Is sent with an army to destroy him, 135. Draws Solyman to the army by false reports, *ib*.

S

Salamanca, treaty of, between Ferdinand of Aragon, and his son-in-law Philip, II. 14.

Salerno, Prince of, heads the disaffected Neapolitans, against the oppressions of the viceroy Don Pedro de Toledo, IV. 115. Solicits aid from Henry II. of France, who instigates the Turks to invade Naples, *ib*.

Saluces, Marquis de, succeeds Lautrec in the command of the French army before Naples, III. 23. Retires to Aversa, where he is taken prisoner by the Prince of Orange, *ib*. Betrays his charge in Piedmont, 132.

Sancerre, Count de, defends St. Disiere against the Emperor Charles, III. 273. Is deceived into a surrender by the Cardinal Granvelle, 275.

Sauvage, a Fleming, made chancellor of Castile by Charles, on the death of Ximenes, II. 58. His extortions, *ib*.

Savona, is fortified, and its harbour cleared by the French, to favour its rivalship with Genoa, III. 20.

INDEX.

Savoy, Charles Duke of, marries Beatrix of Portugal, sister to the Emperor Charles V. III. 115. The cause of Francis's displeasure against him, *ib.* His territories over-run by the French troops, 116. Geneva recovers its liberty, 117. His situation by the truce at Nice, between the Emperor and Francis, 152. Is besieged at Nice, by the French and Turks, 253.

—— Emanuel Phillibert, Duke of, appointed by Philip of Spain to command his army in the Low Countries, IV. 243. Invests St. Quintin, 244. Defeats D'Andelot in an endeavour to join the garrison, 246. But does not hinder him from entering the town, 247. Defeats the Constable Montmorency, and takes him prisoner, 248. Is graciously visited in the camp by Philip, 250. Takes St. Quintin by assault, 252. Assists Montmorency in negotiating peace between Philip and Henry, 280. Marries Henry's sister Elizabeth, 299. 301.

Saxony, Elector of, appointed joint commander of the army of the Protestant league, with the Landgrave of Hesse, III. 343. Their characters compared, *ib.* Opposes the Landgrave's intention of giving battle to the Emperor, 348. His electorate seized by Maurice, 358. The army of the league disperse, 361. Recovers Saxony, 366. Is amused by Maurice with a negociation, *ib.* Raises an army to defend himself against the Emperor, 399. Is irresolute in his measures, 400. Charles passes the Elbe, *ib.* Is attacked by the Imperialists, 404. Is taken prisoner and harshly received by the Emperor, 405. Is condemned to death by a court-martial, 409. His resolution on the occasion, 411. Is induced by regard to his family to surrender his electorate, 413. Refuses the Emperor's desire of his approving the *Interim*, 450. The rigour of his confinement increased, 451. Is carried by the Emperor with him into the Netherlands, 456. Is released by the Emperor on Maurice's taking arms against him, but chooses to continue with the Emperor, IV. 73. Obtains his liberty after the treaty of Passau, 99.

Saxony,

INDEX.

Saxony, George Duke of, an enemy to the Reformation, III. 167. His death an advantage to the Reformation, *ib*. The Proteſtant religion eſtabliſhed by Henry Duke of, *ib*. Henry is ſucceeded by his ſon Maurice, 255. His motives for not acceding to the league of Smalkalde, *ib*. Marches to the aſſiſtance of Ferdinand in Hungary, 256. Joins the Emperor againſt the Proteſtants, 336. 354. See *Maurice*.

Schertel, Sebaſtian, a commander in the army of the Proteſtant league, his vigorous commencement of hoſtilities, III. 341. Is injudiciouſly recalled, 343. Is expelled from Augſburg on the diſperſion of the Proteſtant army, 363.

Scotland, James V. of, married to Mary of Guiſe, ducheſs-dowager of Longueville, III. 159. Death of James and acceſſion of his infant daughter Mary, 246. Mary contracted to the Dauphin of France, 438. The marriage celebrated, IV. 271. Mary aſſumes the title and arms of England on the death of Mary of England, 293. Included in the treaty of Chateau Cambreſis, 298. Alteration in the conduct of England toward, 318.

Sects in religion, reflections on the origin of, III. 71.

Segovia, an inſurrection there, on account of their repreſentative Tordeſillas voting for the donative to Charles V. II. 204. Is killed by the populace, 205. The inſurgents there defeat Ronquillo, ſent to ſuppreſs them by Cardinal Adrian, 206. Surrenders after the battle of Villalar, 235.

Selim II. Sultan, extirpates the Mamalukes, and adds Egypt and Syria to his empire, II. 65. Conſidered as formidable to the European powers, *ib*.

Sforza, obtains of Charles V. the inveſtiture of Milan, II. 312. Forfeits the dutchy, by his intrigues with Morone, 317. Joins in a league againſt Charles for the recovery of Milan, 345. Is forced to ſurrender Milan to the Imperialiſts, 352. Obtains again of the Emperor the inveſtiture of Milan, III. 40. Enters into a private treaty with Francis, 109. Merveille,

INDEX.

veille, Francis's envoy, executed for murder, 110. Dies, 121.

Siena, the inhabitants of, implore the affiftance of the Emperor Charles V. to defend them againft their nobles, IV. 113. The Imperial troops endeavour to enflave them, *ib.* Regain poffeffion of their city, 114. Repulfe an attack of the Germans, 127. Are befieged by the Marquis de Marignano, 159. The commander Monluc repulfes the affaults vigoroufly, 160. The town reduced by famine, 161. Numbers of the citizens retire, and eftablifh a free government at Monte Alcino, 162. The remaining citizens oppreffed, 163. And flock to Monte Alcino, *ib.* Is granted by the Emperor to his fon Philip, 164. The inveftiture given by Philip to Cofmo di Medici, 260.

Sieverhaufen, battle of, between Maurice of Saxony and Albert of Brandenburg, IV. 120.

Sion, Cardinal of, his fcheme for weakening the French army in the Milanefe, II. 189. Leaves the Imperial army to attend the conclave on the death of Leo X. 191.

Smalkalde, the Proteftants enter into a league there for their mutual fupport, III. 51. The league renewed at a fecond meeting there, 54. The league of, renewed for ten years, 89. A manifefto, refufing to acknowledge a council called by the Pope, 162. The King of Denmark joins the league, 165. The Princes of, proteft againft the authority of the Imperial chamber, and the recefs of the diet at Nuremburg, 261. Publifh a manifefto againft the proceedings of the council at Trent, 303. Are alarmed at the proceedings of the Emperor, *ib.* A want of unity among the members, 305. The views of the Elector of Saxony, and the Landgrave, explained, *ib.* Appear at the diet of Ratifbon by deputies, 322. Their deputies proteft againft the council of Trent, 324. Their deputies, alarmed at the Emperor's proceedings and declarations, leave the diet, 326. The Emperor leagues with the Pope againft them, 327. Prepare to refift the Emperor, 328. Are

difap-

INDEX.

disappointed in their application to the Venetians and Swifs, 332. As also with Henry VIII. and Francis, 334. Assemble a large army, 335. Are put under the ban of the Empire, 339. Declare war against the Emperor, 341. Hostilities begun by Schertel, *ib.* They recall him, 342. The Elector of Saxony and Landgrave of Hesse appointed joint commanders of their army, 343. The characters of the two commanders compared, *ib.* Their operations distracted by this joint command, 344. Cannonade the Emperor's camp, 348. Make overtures of peace to the Emperor, 360. Their army disperse, 361. The Elector of Saxony reduced, 405. The Landgrave deceived and confined, 420. Their warlike stores seized by the Emperor, 426. See *Maurice.*

Solyman the Magnificent ascends the Ottoman throne, II. 102. Invades Hungary and takes Belgrade, 201. Takes the island of Rhodes, *ib.* Defeats the Hungarians at Mohacz, 373. His successes, and the number of prisoners he carried away, *ib.* Besieges Vienna, III. 38. Enters Hungary again with a vast army, but is forced to retire by the Emperor Charles, 58. Takes Barbarossa the pirate under his protection, 94. Concludes an alliance with Francis King of France, 147. Prepares to invade Naples, 148. Protects Stephen King of Hungary, and defeats Ferdinand, 218. Seizes Hungary for himself, 219. Over-runs Hungary again, in fulfilment of his treaty with Francis, 252. Concludes a truce with the Emperor, 320. Loses Transylvania, IV. 49. Ravages the coasts of Italy, 86, 116. Carries a mighty army into Hungary, 88. Re-establishes Isabella and her son in Transylvania, 128. His violent attachment to his concubine Roxalana, 129. Is prevailed on to declare her a free woman, 131. Formally marries her, *ib.* Is rendered jealous of the virtues of his son Mustapha, by the arts of Roxalana, 133. Orders him to be strangled, 137. Orders the murder of Mustapha's son, 138.

Spain,

INDEX.

Spain, the ſtate of, at the death of Ferdinand of Aragon, II. 30. Charles king of, aſpires to the Imperial crown on the death of Maximilian, 64. Is elected Emperor, 77. Reflections of the Spaniards on that event, 79. Charles appoints viceroys, and departs for Germany, 87. Inſurrections there, 204. A view of the feudal ſyſtem in, 209. An account of the confederacy termed the Holy Junta, 211. Cauſes which prevented an union of the malcontents in the reſpective provinces, 244. The moderation of Charles toward them on his arrival, *ib.* Inſtance of the haughty ſpirit of the grandees, III. 172. Is invaded by the Dauphin, 240. The dominions of, reſigned by Charles to his ſon Philip, IV. 208. The arrival of Charles, and his reception there, 232. The place of his retreat deſcribed, 234. The regal power in, how enlarged by Charles, 307. The foreign acquiſitions added to, 308. See *Aragon, Caſtile, Galicia, Valencia, Cortes, Germanada*, and *Holy Junta*.

Spires, diet of, its proceedings relative to the Reformation, II. 375. Another diet called there by the Emperor, III. 43. Another diet at, 261. Receſs of, in favour of the Proteſtants, 264.

Spiritual cenſures of the Romiſh church, the dreadful effects of, II. 145.

St. Diſier, in Champagne, inveſted by the Emperor, III. 273. Is obtained by the artifice of Cardinal Granvelle, 275.

St. Juſtus, monaſtery of, in Plazencia, is choſen by the Emperor Charles V. for his retreat after his reſignation, IV. 234. His ſituation deſcribed, *ib.* His apartments, 235.

St. Quintin, inveſted by the Spaniſh troops, and defended by Admiral Coligni, IV. 244. D'Andelot defeated in an endeavour to join the garriſon, 246. But enters the town, 247. Montmorency defeated by the Duke of Savoy, *ib.* The town taken by aſſault, 248.

Strozzi, Peter, ſome account of, IV. 156. Is intruſted with the command of the French army in Italy, 157.

INDEX.

157. Is defeated by the Marquis de Marignano, 159.

Suabia, an infurrection of the peafants againft the nobles there, II. 333. They publifh a memorial of their grievances, *ib.* The infurgents difperfed, 334. The Proteftant religion fuppreffed there by the Emperor Charles V. IV. 34.

Suffolk, Duke of, invades Picardy, penetrates almoft to Paris, but is driven back, II. 261.

Surrey, Earl of, created high admiral to the Emperor Charles V. II. 199. Obliged to retire out of Picardy by the Duke de Vendome, 200.

Sweden, a fummary view of the revolutions in, during the fixteenth cetury, IV. 334.

Switzerland, the Cantons of, efpoufe the pretenfions of Charles V. to the Imperial crown, II. 69. Commencement of the Reformation there by Zuinglius, 125. The regulation under which they hire out their troops, 189. The precipitate battle, infifted on by their troops under Lautrec, loft, 195.

Syria, how and by whom added to the Ottoman empire, II. 65.

T

Termes, marefchal de, governor of Calais, takes Dunkirk by ftorm, IV. 273. Engages the count of Egmont, and is defeated by the accidental arrival of an Englifh fquadron on the coaft, *ib.* Is taken prifoner, 275.

Terauane, taken and demolifhed by the Emperor Charles V. IV. 125.

Tetzel, a Dominican friar, his fhameful conduct in the fale of Indulgences in Germany, II. 106. His form of abfolution, and recommendation of the virtues of Indulgences, 107, *Note.* His debauched courfe of life, 108. Publifhes thefes againft Luther, 113.

Teutonic order, a character of, II. 341. Conquer the province of Pruffia, *ib.* Their grand mafter Albert made Duke of Pruffia, 342.

Theatines, the order of, by whom founded, IV. 191.

Thionville,

INDEX.

Thionville, in Luxembourg, taken by the Duke of Guise, IV. 273.
Thuringia, an insurrection of the peasants there, against the nobility, II. 335. The fanatical notions inspired into them by Thomas Muncer, 337. Their disorderly army defeated, 339.
Toledo, insurrection in, at the departure of Charles V. for Germany, II. 87. 204. The cathedral of, stripped of its riches to support the army of the Holy Junta, 227. Padilla's letter to, at his execution, 234, *Note*. Is instigated to continue in arms by Padilla's wife, 236. Is reduced, 238.
Toledo, Ludovico de, nephew to Cosmo di Medici, sent by his uncle to negociate with Philip II. of Spain, for the investiture of Siena, IV. 259.
Toledo, Don Pedro de, viceroy of Naples, oppresses the Neapolitans, IV. 115. And occasions the Turks to ravage the coasts of Naples, *ib.*
Toleration, reflections on the progress of, in Germany, IV. 182. Why mutually allowed among the ancient Heathens, 183. How the primitive Christians became averse to, *ib.*
Tomorri, Paul, a Franciscan monk, archbishop of Golocza, is made general of the Hungarian army against Solyman the Magnificent, and is defeated by him, II. 373.
Tordesillas, the residence of Queen Joanna, the confederacy of malcontents called the Holy Junta, removed thither, II. 213. The Queen taken there by the Conde de Haro, 225.
―――― one of the representatives of Segovia, killed by the populace for voting the donative to Charles V. at the Cortes assembled in Galicia, II. 205.
Transylvania, is surrendered to Ferdinand King of the Romans, by Queen Isabella, IV. 49.
Tremouille, La, drives the English under the Duke of Suffolk out of Picardy, II. 262.
Trent, the council of, summoned, III. 258. Prorogued, *ib.* Again summoned, 287. Is opened, 300. Declares the apocryphal scriptures canonical, 307. Establishes the authority of the church-traditions, *ib.* The

INDEX.

council, on rumours of an infection in the city, is translated to Bologna, 433. Henry II. of France protests against the council, IV. 33. The council breaks up on the approach of Maurice of Saxony, 74. Historical remarks on this council, 75. Characters of its historians, 76.

Trent, Cardinal of, sent by the Emperor Charles V. to conclude an alliance with the Pope, III. 324. The nature of this treaty, 325.

Tunis, the means of its coming under the power of Barbarossa, traced, III. 94. The Emperor and other Christian powers unite to expel Barbarossa, and restore Muley Hascen, 98. Is taken by the Emperor, 104. Muley Hascen restored, and his treaty with Charles, 105.

Tuscany, a review of the state of, during the sixteenth century, IV. 331.

V

Valencia, an insurrection in, II. 81. The people there greatly oppressed by the nobles, *ib*. The nobles refuse to assemble the Cortes except the King is present, 82. Charles authorises the people to continue in arms, 83. They expel the nobles, *ib*. Associate under the *Germanada*, and appoint their own magistrates, *ib*. Don Diego de Mendora, Conde de Melito, appointed regent, on the departure of Charles for Germany, 86. The Germanada refuse to lay down their arms, 239. Defeat the nobles in several actions, 241. Are at length routed by the Conde de Melito, *ib*. The moderation of Charles toward the insurgents on his arrival, 244.

Valentinois, Duchess of. See *Diana* of *Poitiers*.

Valladolid, the first public entry of Charles V. to that city, II. 55. The inhabitants rise, burn Fonseca's house, and fortify the town, II. 208. Surrenders after the battle of Villalar, and dissolution of the Holy Junta, 235.

Vaucelles, treaty of, between Charles V. and Henry II. of France, IV. 216.

Vendome,

INDEX.

Vendome, duke of, his plan of operations in oppofing the progrefs of the invafion of Picardy by Henry VIII. II. 200. Obliges him to retire, *ib*.

Venice, the republic of, incline in favour of the pretenfions of Francis I. of France, to the Imperial crown, II. 69. Their views and apprehenfions on the approaching rupture between the Emperor Charles V. and Francis, 92. Leagues with the Emperor againft Francis, 248. A final accommodation between, and the Emperor, III. 39. Refufes to enter into the league of the Italian ftates, formed by the Emperor, 63. A review of the ftate of that republic during the fixteenth century, IV. 329.

Verrina, the confident of the Count of Lavagno, encourages him in his fcheme of overturning the government of Genoa, III. 373. Is protected by Francis on the ruin of that confpiracy, 392.

Vielleville, the French governor of Metz, detects Father Leonard's confpiracy to betray the city to the Imperialifts, IV. 170. Executes the confpirators, 171.

Vienna is befieged by Sultan Solyman the Magnificent, III. 38.

Villalar, battle of, between Padilla and the Conde de Haro, II. 231.

Villena, marquis de, his fpirited reply to the requeft of the Emperor to lodge Bourbon in his palace, II. 320.

Ulm, the government of that city violently altered, and its reformed minifters carried away in chains, by the Emperor Charles V. III. 454.

United Provinces of the Netherlands, a brief view of their revolt againft the dominion of Spain, IV. 333.

Urbino, reftored by Pope Adrian to Francefco Maria de Roverè, II. 246.

W

Wallop, Sir John, joins the Emperor Charles V. at the fiege of Landrecy, with a body of Englifh troops, III. 252.

War,

INDEX.

War, the method of carrying on, in Europe, how improved at this period from the practice of earlier ages, II. 260. General reflections on the vicissitudes of, IV. 302.

Wartburg, Martin Luther concealed there by the Elector of Saxony, II. 164.

Wentworth, Lord, governor of Calais, remonstrates in vain with the English Privy Council to provide for its security, IV. 264. Is attacked by the Duke of Guise, and forced to capitulate, 266.

Wittemberg, invested by the Emperor Charles V. and defended by Sybilla of Cleves, wife to the Elector of Saxony, III. 407.

Wolsey, Cardinal, his rise, character, and influence over Henry VIII. of England, II. 95. Receives a pension from Francis I. of France, 97. And from the Emperor Charles V. 98. Detached from the French interest by the latter, 99. Inclines Henry to join the Emperor against Francis, 169. Sent by Henry to Calais, to negociate an accommodation between the Emperor and Francis, 180. Has an interview with Charles at Bruges, and concludes a league with him on the part of Henry, against France, 182. Meditates revenge against Charles on his second disappointment of the Papacy by the election of Clement VII. 259. Obtains of Clement a legantine commission in England for life, *ib.* Negotiates a league with Francis against the Emperor, III. 3.

Worms, a diet called there by Charles V. to check the progress of the Reformers, II. 103. Proceedings of, 161. Martin Luther cited before it, 162. Refuses to retract his opinions, *ib.* An edict published against him, 164. Diet at, opened, III. 288.

Wurtemburg, Ulric Duke of, why expelled his dominions, III. 85. Recovers his dominions by the assistance of Francis King of France, and receives the Protestant religion, 86.

Wyat,

INDEX.

Wyat, Sir Thomas, raises an insurrection in Kent against Queen Mary of England, on account of the Spanish match, IV. 144. Is subdued and punished, 145.

X

Ximenes, archbishop of Toledo, adheres to Ferdinand of Aragon, in his dispute with the archduke Philip concerning the regency of Castile, II. 11. Espouses Ferdinand's claim to the regency of Castile on Philip's death, 21. Conquers Oran, and other places in Barbary, for the crown of Castile, 23. Appointed regent of Castile, by Ferdinand's will, until the arrival of Charles V. in Spain. 31. His rise and character, 32. Admits the claim to the regency of Cardinal Adrian, sent with that commission by Charles, and executes it jointly with him, 34. Takes the Infant Don Ferdinand to Madrid under his own eye, 35. Procures Charles, who assumed the regal title, to be acknowledged by the Castilian nobility, 37. Schemes to extend the regal prerogative, *ib.* Depresses the nobility, 38. Frees the king from the feudal limitations, and establishes a regal army to check the Barons, 39. Suppresses a mutiny headed by the grandees, 40. Resumes the grants of Ferdinand to his nobles, 41. His prudent application of the revenue, 42. His bold assertion of his authority to the discontented nobles, 43. Other associates in the regency appointed at the instigation of the Flemish courtiers, 44. Retains the superior management, 45. Defeats John D'Albret's invasion of Navarre, *ib.* Dismantles all the castles there, except Pampeluna, which he strengthens, 46. The troops sent by him against Barbarossa defeated, and his equanimity on that occasion, 47. Alarmed at the corruption of the Flemish court, he persuades Charles to visit Spain, 48. Falls sick on his journey to meet Charles at his arrival, 53. His letter of counsel to Charles,

INDEX.

54. Requests an interview, *ib.* The ingratitude of Charles to him, *ib.* His death, 55. His character, *ib.* Reverence paid to his memory by the Spaniards, *ib.*

Z

Zamora, bishop of, raises a regiment of priests to defend Tordesillas, for the Holy Junta, which is forced by the Conde de Haro, II. 225.

Zuinglius attacks the sale of Indulgences at Zurich in Switzerland, II. 125.

FINIS.